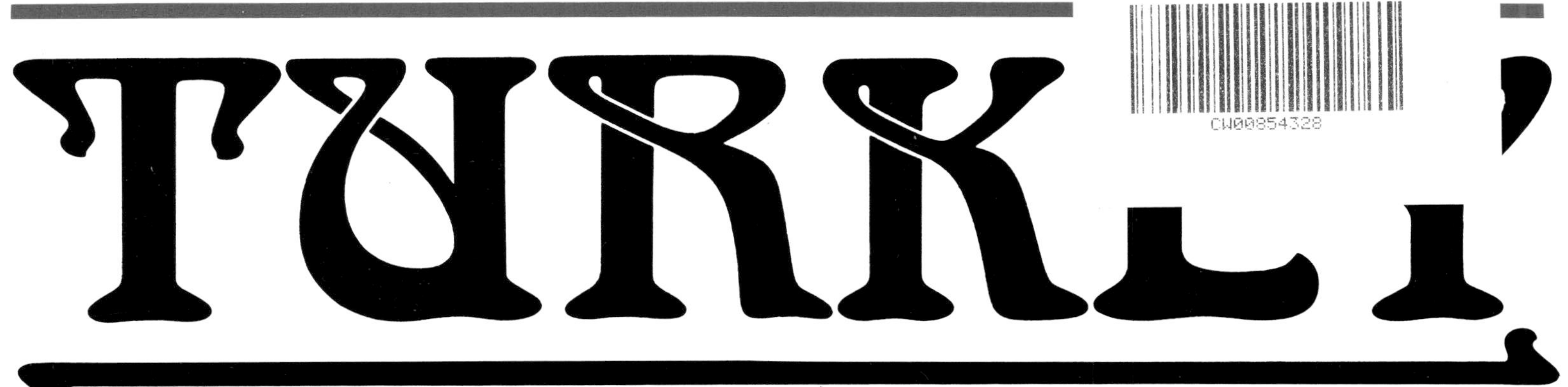

hoş geldiniz!

Translation from the Dutch by drs. Jacky ter Horst-Meijer
Photo editing Peter Homan
Overall final editing drs. Christine Waslander

welcome
to the cultures of Asia Minor

COLOPHON

Design: CINEMASTER,
Bergen, The Netherlands
Translated from Dutch by
Drs. Jacky ter Horst-Meijer
First published in English in 1992
by Edu'Actief Publishing
Company, The Netherlands
Publisher: Izaäk Buwalda
This edition is first published in
1992 by Kegan Paul
International Ltd
PO Box 256, London WC1B
3SW, England

Distributed by
John Wiley & Sons Ltd
Southern Cross Trading Estate
1 Oldlands Way, Bognor Regis
West Sussex PO22 9SA,
England

Routledge, Chapman & Hall Inc.
29 West 35th Street
New York, NY 10001, USA

Printed in The Netherlands by
Ten Brink Meppel bv

British Library Cataloguing
in Publication Data

Turkey hoş geldiniz!
I. Homan, Peter II. Waslander,
Christine, 1957-III. [Turkey hoş
geldiniz]. English 915.610438

ISBN 0-7103-0441-2

Library of Congress Cataloging-
in-Publication Data

Turkey hoş geldiniz! English
edited by Peter Homan and
Christine Waslander.
162 p. 295 cm.
Translation of: Turkije hoş
geldiniz!
Includes index.
ISBN 0-7103-0441-2
1. Turkey-Civilization.
2. Turkey-Antiquities. 3. Art
Turkish. 4. Art-Turkey. I.
Homan, Peter. II. Waslander,
Christine, DR432.T85 1992
949.61--dc20
91-23409
CIP

TURKEY

hoş geldiniz!

CONTENTS

1 Journey through Time

In İstanbul the Bosporus Bridge and the Mehmed II Bridge form the arterial roads which connect Europe and Asia both in a literal and in a symbolic sense. The age-old interaction between these two so very different cultural areas has shaped Turkey into a colourful and vivid museum. Wherever one goes impressive monuments bear witness to the rich and stirring history of the country.

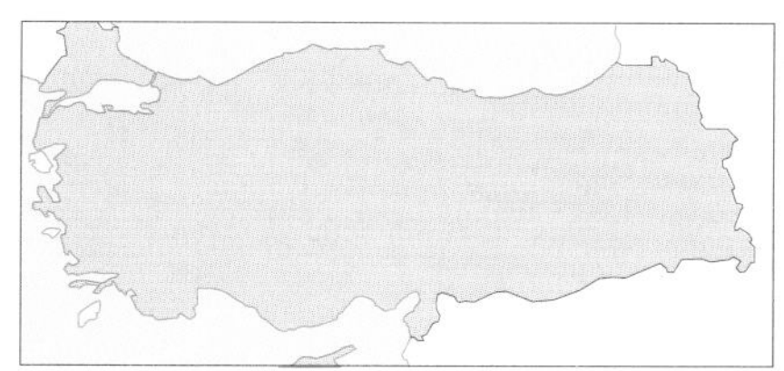

The surface area of Turkey amounts to 780,576 square kilometres.
The Black Sea, the Aegean Sea and the Mediterranean surround this vast territory. The Central Anatolian Plateau is hemmed in by the Pontic Mountains in the north and the Taurus Mountains in the south. To the west, the mountain ridges run up to the sea, providing easy access from the coast to the inland. The east, where the northern and southern mountain ranges meet, is less accessible. This is also the site where the Euphrates and the Tigris rise.
Many civilizations attained their full development in this geographically favourable and at the same time isolated area. Primitive farmers, followed by several Mesopotamian cultures, Greeks, Romans, Byzantines, Seljuks, and Ottomans have left their traces in Anatolia. In this book these civilizations and their cultural-historical significance will be further examined. Seven 'tours' through different regions and periods will serve as guidelines. A general map on page 154 and many detailed maps indicate the location of the places described. Both in the cartography and in the text the Turkish spelling is used.
This first chapter presents a journey through time and discusses the historical development of Asia Minor from the Old Stone Age up to and including the modern Turkish Republic.

Nomads still inhabit the fertile valleys of East Anatolia. ▾

◂ *The ruins of the Urartic double-castle Çavustepe in East Turkey dominate the landscape. This very elongated fortress dating from the eight century B.C. was comfortably equipped. The inhabitants had a bathroom, a toilet, 'guest rooms', kitchens and water-reservoirs at their disposal.*

▲ *A fragment of a Urartic text in cuneiform script (eighth century B.C.).*

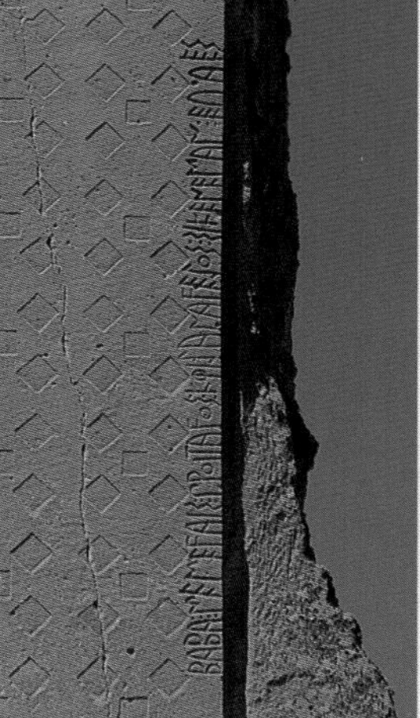

▲ *An inscription on the side of the Midas Monument in Phrygia. The word 'Baba' (father) does not belong to the original text.*

Language and writing

The complicated language history of Western Asia has been subject to many influences and comprises numerous kinds of writing. In the course of the millennia many variations of pictography, cuneiform script and the Greek, Latin and Arabic alphabets were used. Prohattic is a non-Indo-European language dating from before 2000 B.C. This language was later used by the Hittites for worship only.
Hittite itself belongs, just like the related Lycian, to the extinct Anatolian language group which, however, is counted among the Indo-European languages. In Boğazkale the state archives of the Hittite kings have been disclosed, documented in cuneiform script on thousands of clay tablets. Their decyphering has led to an enormous increase in the knowledge about the Hittite period.
Lycian has mainly been preserved in epitaphs. By comparing these texts with analogous Greek inscriptions the contents of Lycian can now be interpreted to a large extent.
The decyphering of Lydian, often also handed down in the form of epitaphs, has not been a complete success as yet. This language might also belong to the Indo-European group or might be related to the Etruscan language.
Together with the Greeks and Romans, Greek and Latin made their entry into Asia Minor. In the Byzantine period Greek ousted almost all other languages from the area. After the fall of Byzantium in 1453 Arabic, already an extensively used language by then, became the most common written language for a considerable span of time. The roots of the Anatolian language group already originated in the east (India), and now for the second time round, words from the east (Persia) came to enrich the language via Islamic culture. In 1928 Atatürk abolished Arabic script and introduced the Latin alphabet. For a number of specific sounds linguists then introduced new letters, like ş and ğ. Modern Turkish belongs to the so-called Altaic language family and is an agglutinating language. Elements which in most Indo-European languages are expressed by separate words are conveyed in Turkish by a series of juxtaposed suffixes. For example: 'bilmiyorum': 'I don't know'. Another characteristic of contemporary Turkish is vocal harmony or vowel harmony. This means that as far as the 'tone colour' is considered, the suffixes adapt themselves to the preceding syllable. Agglutination, vocal harmony, a complex grammar and numerous dialects make Turkish a 'complicated' language. Easily recognizable are the loanwords from English and French such as berber, kuaför, şoför and pansyon. Just like Turkish itself these words are written phonetically. Minor differences in the pronounciation of certain letters sometimes lead to typical Turkish solutions as in the word 'Wolksvagen'.

The first inhabitants

Turkey has a great variety of landscapes. Plateaus and plains, fertile valleys and steppes alternate with swamps and mountain ranges. Through the ages many cultures have felt at home here. The earliest traces of human presence, found in the south and the south-east of the country, are about 600,000 years old. In that Old Stone Age (Palaeolithicum) the population lived from hunting and from collecting wild crops. People lived in caves and used stone tools. These celts, scrapers, and spearheads are about the only implements the investigators have discovered. Other possessions were of perishable material like wood and in most cases could not bear the test of time.
During the New Stone Age (Neolithicum, 8000-5000 B.C.) man started to cultivate the land, to breed cattle and to produce earthenware. Houses were built of unbaked clay. An important settlement from this period is Çatal Höyük, where the inhabitants made remarkable paintings on the walls of their houses.

The Bronze Age

From 5000 years B.C. man started to use metal. Initially only copper was used but about 3000 years B.C. bronze was discovered, an alloy of copper and tin which is more solid than pure copper.
In the Early Bronze Age – between 3000 and 2000 B.C. – pottery was for the first time produced with the help of a potter's wheel. The sides of pots became thinner, the forms more regular and the finishing more beautiful. The settlements from this period were larger than before and protected by thick walls.
Around 1650 the first great Anatolian Empire arose, that of the Hittites. At its height it extended from Central Asia well into Syria. The capital of the empire was Hattuşa, located east of Ankara near the present village of Boğazkale. Hattuşa was a large, heavily fortified city with a citadel, walls, gates, temples and official archives. During excavations many clay tablets were found with administrative data in a cuneiform script copied from Mesopotamia. The Hittite Empire lasted till about 1200 B.C.

Pageant of the gods on the west face of the gallery in the ▼ *Hittite sanctuary at Yazılıkaya (around 1250 B.C.).*

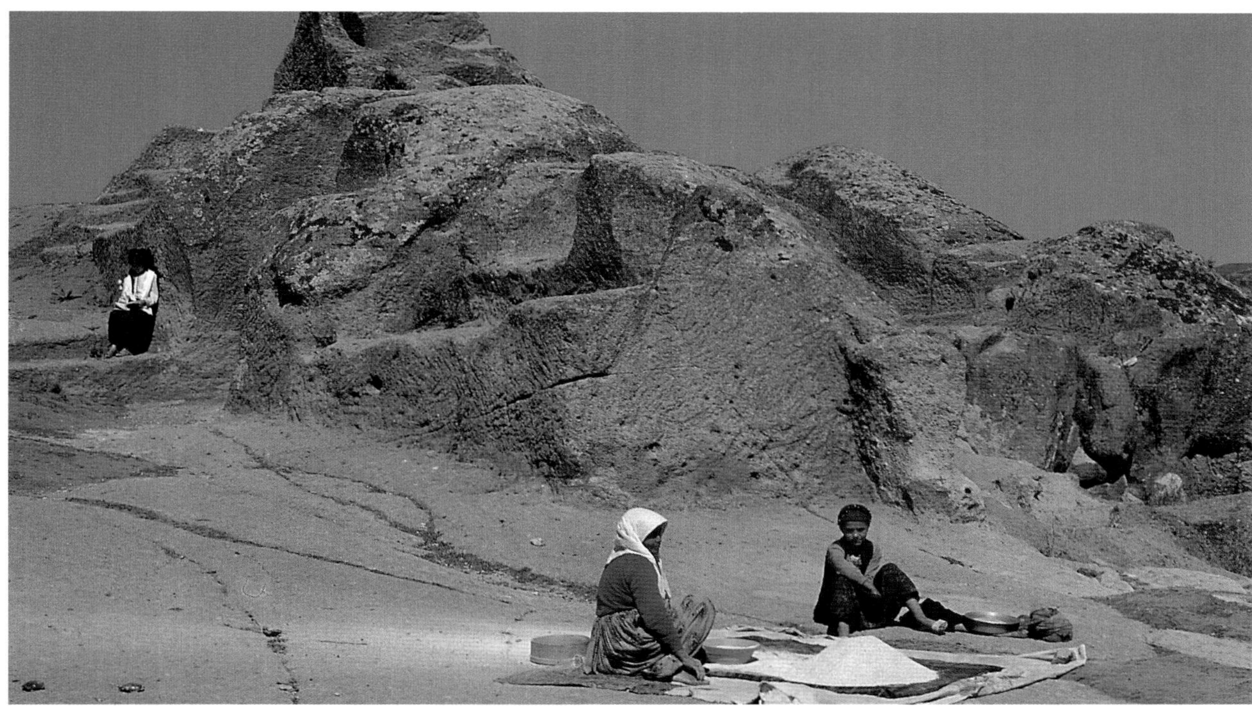

◂ *In Kümbet time seems to have come to a standstill. In the foreground women bake cheese biscuits. Phrygian monuments shape an idyllic background to simple village life.*

The city walls of Assus from the fourth century B.C. have been remarkably well preserved, in places even to a height of fourteen metres. At some spots the walls have been fortified with round or square towers. ▾

Greeks and Persians in Anatolia

From the chaotic situation which arose after the fall of the Hittite Empire several empires emerged around the year 1000 B.C., such as that of Urartu in the east, Phrygia in Central Anatolia and Lydia in the west. Spurred on by overpopulation and lack of land Greek colonists founded cities on the west and south coast of the country in this period. These cities are still often inhabited, like Smyrna (the present İzmir) and Byzantium (İstanbul). This marked the beginning of the Greek presence in Anatolia which was to last until into the twentieth century. The Greek settlements were, just like the cities in the motherland, independent city-states with a dynamic cultural life. In their turn they also founded colonies, among others on the Black Sea coast.

From around 550 B.C. the Greek cities in Ionia, as the Turkish west coast was called, formed part of the Persian Empire which had extended more and more to the west. The Ionians lost their independence and were ruled by Persian governors, the *satraps*. Despite a number of revolts, the Greeks of Asia Minor would live under Persian oppression for about 200 years. Yet, the Greek character of their culture was preserved. This can be clearly deduced from major excavations in some of the Ionian cities.

The region fell into Greek hands again when Alexander the Great crossed the Bosporus in the spring of 334 B.C. During his campaigns of conquest Alexander founded an empire that extended from Greece to Egypt and the Indus. This was the beginning of what in history is referred to as the period of Hellenism. After Alexander's death in 323 B.C. his empire was divided among the generals of his army. After years of battle the western part of Anatolia fell under the regime of the dynasty of the Attalids, who ruled their empire from Pergamum. Hellenistic culture reached its culmination in this period with Art and Science thriving.

▲ In the sheltered surroundings of excavation-sites numerous plant and flower species can be found. In the background the Celsus library in the city-centre of Ephesus.

Flora

Turkey has several climate zones. The coastal areas have a Mediterranean climate and the south coast is even subtropical. On the fertile coastal plains citrus fruits, bananas, figs, dates, tabacco and cotton are cultivated on a large scale.

The non-cultivated land has a luscious vegetation too. Mimosa, oleanders, wild orchids and numerous other trees, shrubs and plants create an overwhelming floral splendour in spring.

The Anatolian Plateau has a continental climate. The average yearly precipitation amounts to only 305 millimetres. The area is largely deforested and, with the exception of the extremely dry middle region, consists of an endless grassy plain. In the neighbourhood of villages, where the land is irrigated, wheat and barley are the main agricultural products. On the steppes, which are closely-cropped due to grazing, there is only room for poplars and tenacious thistle species among the agricultural crops and the olive orchards.

The mountainous eastern part of Turkey is considerably more humid than the central plateau. In winter this region is covered with snow for four months. Only coniferous trees can survive in this extreme mountain climate. In the sheltered valleys lie pasturelands and on the higher mountain slopes there is steppe-vegetation.

Along the Black Sea coast a mild and humid climate prevails. Tea plantations, fruit trees and hazelnut shrubs provide the main (export) products.

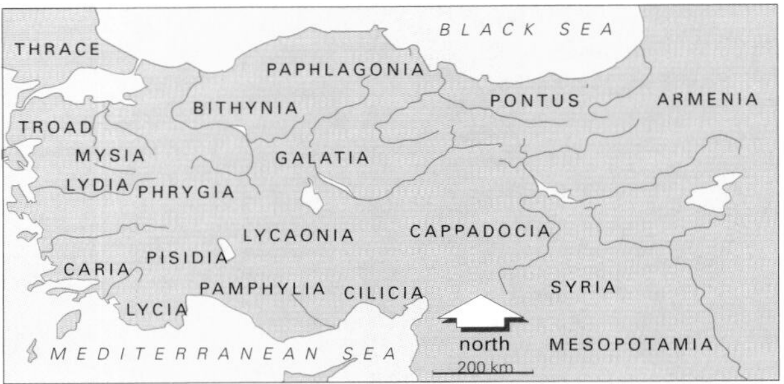

▲ *The classical provinces of Anatolia.*

The Roman province of Asia

In 133 B.C. the last king of Pergamum, Attalos III, left his entire empire to the Roman Republic in his will. From that province of Asia Minor Rome gradually captured more territory in Anatolia. The Empire of the Seleucids, which encompassed East Turkey and the Middle East, was conquered in 66 B.C. Under emperor Trajan (98-117 A.D.) this area was split up into three parts and annexed as province of the Roman Empire respectively called Armenia, Assyria and Mesopotamia. In the eastern region of the empire the situation remained unstable. The borders in that desolate district were very difficult to defend and quite often invaders from across the border had to be driven away.

The wealthy citizens of Ephesus lived in a town quarter built against the mountain slope. That is how the houses derive their German name: Hanghäuser. Almost all houses were equipped ▼ *with running water and heated by hot air.*

◄ *A fresco in the side chapel of the Chora Church in İstanbul. From left to right the saints Basil, Gregory 'the Evangelist' and Cyril of Alexandria.*

Rise and Fall of the Byzantine Empire

During the reign of emperor Diocletian (284-305) major governmental reforms were instituted in the Roman Empire. The government was decentralised and the territory divided into four autonomous provinces. The emperor remained seated in Rome. Capital of the East became Byzantium (the present İstanbul), at that time a rather insignificant provincial town.
Constantine the Great (324-337) enforced a large-scale building programme in this 'second Rome' and named the city after himself: Constantinople.
After the death of emperor Theodosius in 395 the division of the Roman Empire, already started by Diocletian, became permanent. The empire fell apart into an East and a West Roman Empire. The West Roman Empire was shortlived; in 476 Rome was conquered by Germanic invaders. The East Roman Empire, at the height of its bloom comprising the whole eastern part of the Mediterranean, would last for another 1000 years. This era is referred to as the Byzantine period.
The East Roman Empire was governed according to Roman law. The official language was Greek and the state religion was Christianity; the emperor headed the church as 'God's substitute on earth'.
The Byzantine Empire experienced its first 'Golden Age' during the reign of emperor Justinian (527-565). He tried to restore the glory of the Roman Empire and partly succeeded. Italy, Sicily, North Africa and Southern Spain were conquered. Constantinople was embellished with magnificent palaces, public buildings and above all churches. Some of them still exist, such as the imposing Hagia Sophia, the Hagia Irene and the church of the Saints Sergius and Bacchus.
Despite a number of successes, including the christianization of Russia and the Balkans, the Byzantine Empire gradually fell apart. Slavs, Persians and Arabs formed a constant threat and the territories in Italy and Spain were lost again.
In particular the invasion of the Seljuks, an Islamic nomad tribe from Central Asia, was to have a great influence on the history of Turkey.
There were problems in the interior too. One of these was the iconoclastic controversy disrupting the empire between 726 and 843. Under the influence of numerous eastern sects a powerful movement came into being, which denounced the adoration of images.
Because of the effect of this stream of thought (*iconoclasm*) examples of sculpture, painting and mosaic dating from before that period are very rare.
When the orthodox church broke away from the church of Rome in 1054, the separation between East and West was not merely political but also religious. For a long time the relationship between the two remained problematic, because Rome considered the orthodox believers to be heretics. A sad all-time low was the Fourth Crusade (1202-1204). Crusaders from Western Europe, particularly those from Venice, occupied Constantinople in their incessant zeal to combat the 'disbelievers' by fire and sword and ruthlessly looted the city. Innumerable art treasures were destroyed or taken away. That is how a considerable part of the present relics of the Roman Catholic church ended up in Western Europe. Until 1261 the Byzantine emperor was forced to rule the remnants of his empire from his place of exile, Nicea (İznik). Although in that year the capital was recaptured, the once so mighty empire would never regain its former glory. The decline of the Byzantine Empire was spurred on by the effects of conflicts about the succession to the throne, which were often fought out with the help of Turkish and Slavonic mercenaries. Even when emperor John VIII (1425-1448) in a final attempt to save his empire was converted to the catholic faith, help from the west failed to arrive. On 29 May 1453 the inevitable fall of Constantinople followed.

The Small Fruit Asphodel (Asphodelus microcárpus) is poisonous for cattle and is therefore considered a dangerous weed. Still the harmlesss tuberiform roots of this member of the Liliaceae used to be eaten and were used for making starch. ▼

The significance of the Byzantines for Western Europe has been tremendous. As the Byzantine Empire in the east had functioned as a shield against invasions from the Slavs, Arabs and Turks, Western Europe had the opportunity to restore itself from the chaos of its many migrations and could develop a flourishing mediaeval culture. Moreover, Byzantine society played an important role in handing down the classical Greek culture and traditions which had been more or less completely lost after the fall of the Roman Empire in Western Europe. The many eminent scholars who had fled to Italy after the conquest of Constantinople – bringing with them precious manuscripts – were of invaluable importance to the development of Renaissance and Humanism in Europe. The monastic orders in Western Europe also came into being under the influence of ideals from orthodox oriental monks.

Seljuk nomads and Ottoman sultans

As early as the eleventh century, Turkish speaking islamic nomads, the Seljuks, had invaded the rich and fertile regions of Anatolia from Central Asia. After their victory against the Byzantines at Mantzikert in 1071, the Seljuks settled in West Turkey and here they founded the 'Sultanate of Rum'. With 'Rumi' those Byzantines were denoted who had continued calling themselves 'Romans'. Until the Greek war of independence (1821-1829), when the term 'Hellenes' became fashionable, the Greeks called themselves 'Romaioi'. 'Rum' mostly signified the Byzantine Empire, but at a later date, also those parts of Anatolia captured from the Byzantines.
In the second half of the thirteenth century another mass migration started to take effect. Well-organised troops of horsemen penetrated even further into West Anatolia. Their leader Osman proclaimed himself sultan and became the founder of the Ottoman Empire. The

Near the old city of Vastan lies a Seljuk cemetery with beautifully decorated tombstones.
▾ The motives applied have been derived from architecture.

north-western part of Anatolia was captured and the capital was established at Bursa. In 1354 the Ottoman army crossed the Bosporus and occupied part of the Balkans. After the capture of Adrianopolis (the present Edirne) the Byzantine Empire amounted to hardly anything more than the city of Constantinople and a small area on the European side of the Bosporus. In 1453 Constantinople was captured by Mohammed the Conqueror and proclaimed capital of the Ottoman Empire. The name of the city was altered into İstanbul. In the next century the Ottoman sultans enlarged their empire spectacularly. The Balkans, Persia, Mesopotamia, Arabia and North Africa were conquered. These successes can be partly explained by the efficient and, for those days, very progressive organization of the Ottoman state. The sultan had a highly educated body of civil servants at his disposal and the army consisted of a group of well-trained professional soldiers. Newly captured areas were lent to soldiers who had been of extraordinary service to their country. In order to avoid the rise of a feudal class, whose growing power could prove a threat to central government, the areas lent out were not inheritable. The sultan's pillar was the corps of Janissaries formed in 1360, deriving its name from the Turkish yeni tseri = new army. They were recruited from among the sons of oppressed Christians. They received a strict Islamic education, were more or less brainwashed into Turks and were trained to become a very effective professional army. As far as weapons or training goes, there were not many armed forces in Europe who could compete with the Janissaries. As long as the conquered peoples duly paid their taxes, they were left in peace and their religion was respected. Trade and shipping were mostly left to minorities such as the Greeks, Armenians and Jews. Yet it was not uncommon that from among these groups senior civil servants or even grand viziers (prime ministers) were appointed.

The empire reached its full bloom, both culturally and politically, during the reign of Suleyman the Great (1520-1566). One of the most important representatives of Ottoman architecture was the architect Mimar Sinan (1491-1588). This military engineer held the post of royal architect from 1538 till his death. According to the chronicles he has 323 buildings to his name, varying from elegant mosques to ingenious aquaducts. A number of them are still in excellent condition today.

In spite of measures built into the governmental system to avoid the rise of new power centres beyond the sultan's control, such new powerful areas did arise after some time due to the weakening of the central government. The direct result was arbitrariness and corruption, which in turn stimulated the pursuit of independence on the part of the oppressed peoples. Gradually, the inhabitants of the Balkans managed to obtain an autonomous status within the empire or even independence. The armed force lost its superiority over the West-European armies, although West-European officers were often appointed as military advisors.

From the seventeenth till the nineteenth century the Ottoman culture increasingly felt the influence of Western Europe, yet never lost its inherent Turkish character. Fine examples are the many buildings in Baroque, Rococo and classicistic style that adorn the city of İstanbul. Western ideas also made their entry in the political field. The liberal ideas of the French Revolution gradually gained a firmer footing in the course of the nineteenth century.

▲ *Mohammed the Conqueror's fifteenth century fortress Rumeli Hisar. In the background the suspension bridge over the Bosporus bearing his name and connecting Europe and Asia.*

The entrance to the Green Mosque at Bursa.
▼ *The stalactite vault of this Ottoman porch has been carefully executed.*

Turkish carpets

During a period of 2000 years the nomads of Anatolia developed the tradition of knotting carpets to a milestone in artistic handicraft. In the twelfth century the Seljuks introduced the method of the 'double knot' up to the Mediterranean coast. Marco Polo in his days mentioned the splendour of carpets in mosques and palaces.

◄ *Important carpet production centres.*

Each region has its own techniques and patterns handed down from generation to generation. Families, villages and even entire tribes join forces in co-operatives combining all their skill, knowledge and craftsmanship. In the course of the centuries new patterns were developed continuously: geometrical and floral motives, Kufic script, stylized dragons, birds and mammals, medallions and Chinese cloud motives.

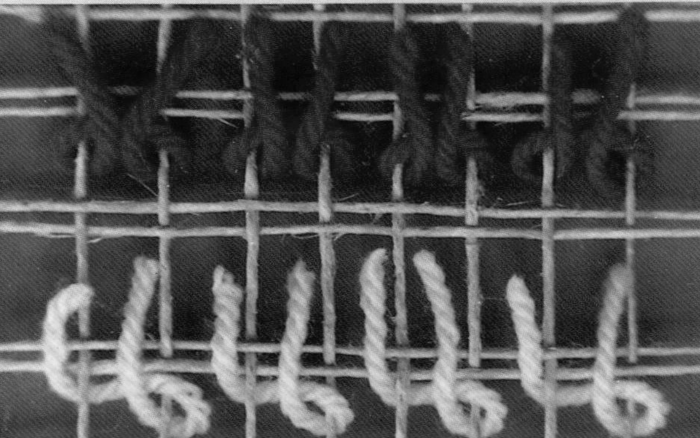

The wool is coloured with dyes compiled of vegetable pigments from walnuts, sumak, gal nuts, buckthorn, onion skins, pomegranate peelings and tobacco.

◄ *Top: the Turkish double-knot. Bottom: the asymmetrical Persian knot.*

Most Turkish carpets are made with the 'Ghiordes-knot', a symmetrical double-knot, in which the thread is wrapped around the adjacent warps and pulled through the surface. Thereafter the thread is knotted together with the weft thread, beaten downwards with a comb and shortened with a knife or a pair of scissors to the correct length. With the traditional carpets both warp, weft and knotted threads are of pure natural wool. Nowadays a cotton base is also often used.
The hand-knotted carpets are used for numerous purposes by the local population. The floor-carpets, carpet strips, tent screens, tapestries, prayer rugs, and cushions are often given as a dowry. The value of these durable carpets increases in the course of time, because the knots tighten and the wool acquires a soft lustre (patina).

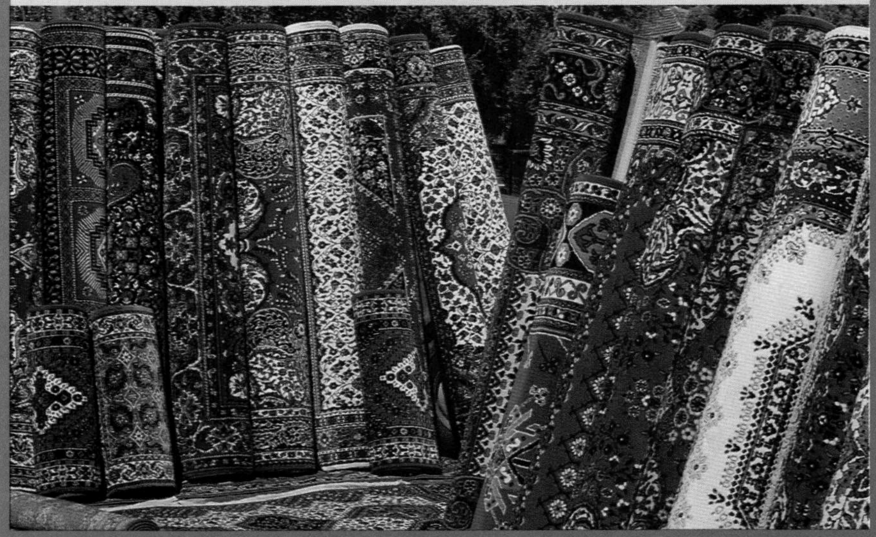

The interference of the superpowers England, France and Russia in Turkish politics increased, especially during the Greek war of independence between 1821 and 1829. As the national debts grew, Turkish dependence on the west increased too. These debts were a direct result of the investments made in infrastructure which had been financed with borrowed money. When the country went bankrupt in 1875 the superpowers demanded radical reforms. A constitution based on a western liberal model was introduced. Through their embassies the powers of the west held a firm grip on Turkish politics. From the middle of the nineteenth century this started to cause opposition in circles of students and soldiers. They criticized both the autocratic character of the regime and the foreign interference. The main representative of this 'Young Turkish Movement' was Mustafa Kemal (1880-1938), who would at a later date become famous under the honorary name 'Atatürk' (Father of the Turks). Through military revolts in the years 1909-1918 the Young Turks exacted more and more power, and consequently the sultan's authority was gradually undermined.
In 1914 Germany and the Ottoman Empire entered into a defence treaty, causing Turkey to be involved in the Great War on the side of the Central Powers. After the end of the war the Ottoman Empire was immersed in chaos. On the Russian border the independent Republic of Armenia was proclaimed. In the east of the country Kurdish rebels were active. The Turkish army went into the offensive. Armenia was recaptured and divided between the Soviet Union and Turkey.
In 1919 İstanbul was occupied by the Allies and a part of the south coast by Italy. A vast area around Smyrna (İzmir) and European Turkey were occupied by Greece. With Mustafa Kemal in the lead a large-scale attack was launched against the Greek troups. The army recaptured Smyrna, causing many Greek casualties. This is how, after a period of two thousand years, Greek presence in Anatolia came to an end.
In the year 1923 the Peace Treaty of Lausanne was concluded, in which the new borders of the Turkish state were determined. The League of Nations assigned the territories which had been lost in the war in the Middle East as a mandatory area to England and France. All foreign troups, in this case those of Italy and Greece, had to leave Anatolia just like all Greeks living in Turkey. The only exception was İstanbul. Vice versa the Muslims, excluding those who inhabited the Turkish border region, were forced to leave Greece.

The Republic of Turkey

On 29 October 1923 the last sultan, Mehmed VI, was dethroned and the Republic of Turkey was proclaimed with as its president Mustafa Kemal. As İstanbul brought all sorts of associations to mind of the former sultan regime, Ankara was made the new capital of the country.
The foundations of the Republic were: nationalism, social stability and the separation of religion and state. In order to realize these aims radical measures were taken in the first few years. The religious courts were abolished, the separation between religion and state was constitutionalized and Arabic script was replaced by Latin script. Nationalism was aimed at forging the population of Turkey into one people, despite its considerable ethnical differences. This resulted in a sometimes bloody repression of separatistic

More than 2000 years ago pupils scratched their names
▼ in the walls of the gymnasium in Priene.

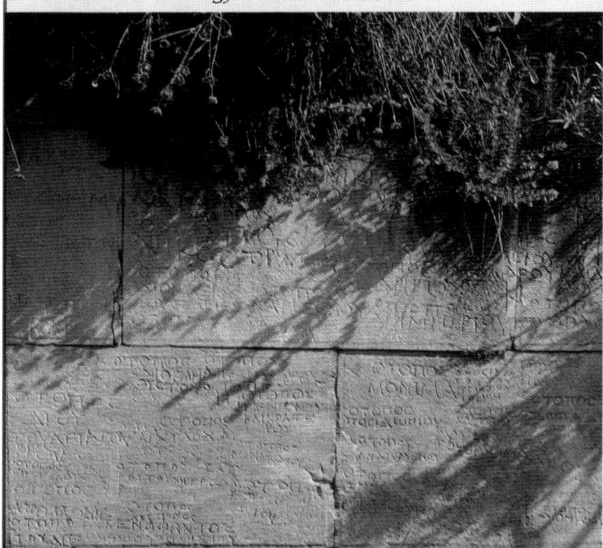

School-life in Turkey

In ancient times education mainly consisted of training sportsmen in a *gymnasium*. That name is derived from the Greek 'gymnos' (= nude), because physical exercise took place in the nude. As well as education in fighting sports and athletics, intellectual development acquired more and more importance: the *gymnasium* became a school.
During the reign of the Seljuks and the Ottomans the majority of education was Islamic. Lessons were given at *medresses*, Koran schools. Besides lessons from the Koran, Islamic law, music, mathematics and language were subjects on the curriculum.
After the foundation of the Turkish Republic education was profoundly changed under the inspired leadership of Atatürk. The separation of religion and state from now on caused the government to be responsible for the contents of public education. From 1924 there has been compulsory education for boys ánd girls up to the age of fourteen. In 1928 Latin script became obligatory. At the same time a major literacy project was started. Although the situation has improved considerably since then, checking compulsory education remains difficult and illegal school absence is great. Moreover many educational institutes are facing a serious lack of facilities and instructional equipment. Teachers are scarce too. In the big cities pupils attend school in morning and afternoon shifts, each with a teaching team of their own. The school director is present the whole day for the benefit of both shifts. His tasks are mainly organizational and administrative. Despite the two-shift system there are on average fifty pupils in one class. In the countryside classes are usually smaller; sometimes there are no schools at all if there are not enough pupils. In that case the children go to a neighbouring village, often on foot. Because of the shift-system and the distances they have to walk, pupils are a common sight along the Turkish roads.
Striking are the black uniforms with a white collar worn by primary school pupils. Secondary schools often have the same strict clothing regulations, both for pupils and teachers. Girls are forbidden to wear their shawls in class.
Education in Turkey is divided into three school types: primary school (five years), middle school (three years) and grammar school (three years). Compulsory education starts at the age of seven. Only primary schools are free of charge. In schoolbooks a lot of attention is paid to the achievements and sayings of Atatürk. From the fourth form onwards one or two hours of education is given in the subjects of religion, moral philosophy and knowledge of the modern world.
Secondary education is split up into technical and general (middle and higher) education. Higher general education provides access to university. Private schools have been founded both in the field of primary and secondary education. These institutions are run by English, French, German and American organizations. School fees are high and educational tools are expensive. Two-thirds of the lessons are given in the foreign language. The advantages are obvious: classes are smaller, the level is higher and a foreign language is part of basic education.

Chronological Table according to the Christian era

Turkish Republic
△ *1923* △

Ottomans
1300-1923

Seljuks
1071-1243

Byzantine Empire
330-1453

Roman Period
133 B.C.-295 A.D.

Hellenism
334-133 B.C.

Persian Empire
546- 334 B.C.

Phrygia, Lycia, Caria
800-546 B.C.

Urartu
900-600 B.C.

Hittites
1650-1200 B.C.

(Bronze Age)

3000 B.C.

(Chalcolithicum)

5000 B.C.

(Neolithicum)

8000 B.C.

(Mesolithicum and Palaeolithicum)

▽ *600,000 B.C.* ▽

GÜLLÜK
HALKININ
YURDU
KURTARAN
CUMHURİYETİ
KURAN
ATATÜRK'E
MİNNET
VE
SAYGI
ANITIDIR
29_10_1935

From soldier to statesman

Mustafa Kemal was born in 1881 in Saloniki. From 1893 till 1905 he received a strict military education. As a military officer he fought in Libya and in the Balkan Wars. Having risen to *pasja* (general), he was involved in the defence of the Dardanelles in the Great War. After that war he organized the resistence against the Greeks who had landed at Smyrna and had occupied the whole of West Anatolia. In 1921 the Greeks were driven back at Inönü in a gigantic battle and in September 1922, after a second offensive, Smyrna fell. At the Treaty of Lausanne, drawn up after laborious negotiations on 24 July 1923, the humiliating Treaty of Sèvres from 1920 was revised and the independence of Turkey restored. Sultan Mehmed VI was dethroned and on 29 October 1923 the Republic was proclaimed, with the charismatic Mustafa Kemal as its president. Turkey became a one-party state presided over by the Kemalistic Republican Party of Atatürk. This honorary name (Father of Turks) was given to Kemal at the institution of official surnames. The constitution provided Atatürk with almost unlimited powers which he used to reshape the feudal Turkey into a modern nation according to West-European models. He abolished the Religious Law, the mystical brotherhoods, the caliphate and the sultanate. That caused the political and social supremacy of Islam to disappear. An adapted version of Latin script, the western calendar and female suffrage were introduced.
The ideals of Atatürk have had their effects on education. They emphasize patriotism, collectivity, respect for one's seniors and consideration for one's inferiors, sense of duty, diligence and cleanliness.
On 10 November 1938 Atatürk died in his residence, the Dolmabahçe palace in İstanbul. Almost all clocks in that palace were stopped at the time of his death, five past nine in the morning. In 1953 Atatürk was interred in the enormous mausoleum built to his honour in Ankara.
Atatürk still symbolizes the feeling of independence and the national identity of the Turkish people. His portrait is found everywhere, at schools, council houses, public squares and on stamps.

movements among the ethnic minorities. The economy was rigorously organized by the government through Five-Year Plans and the foundation of state companies. During the Second World War Turkey remained neutral. After the war democratic reforms were enforced, such as the authorization of unions and political parties. Overtures to the west appeared from the membership of the OECD (1948) and NATO (1952). The economy was liberalised and state influence diminished. In the second half of the fifties political and social unrest cropped up due to the enormous rise in the cost of living resulting from large loans; money that was used to realize a rapid economic growth. When the unrest reached its climax in 1960 the army seized power. After eighteen months the army withdrew to make way again for a civil government. The state influence in the economy, which had been reinforced by the army, was reversed and the liberalization was continued.
In the sixties a large left-wing organization arose within the boundaries of the law. An organization mainly aiming at diminishing the great influence of the United States. As a reaction to this, extreme right-wing organizations came into being not shunning the use of violence. Political repression increased, stirred up by the decreasing standard of living.
Finally the army seized power again in 1970. In 1973 elections were held again, in which however no party obtained a majority. Coalitions formed with great difficulty and many cabinet crises were the consequence.
The economy deteriorated; national debt, inflation and the cost of living continued to increase. Riots occurred more and more often and the country was facing the threat of becoming entangled in a bloody civil war. In order to end this and to enforce an unpopular economic stabilization programme, the army again asserted control on 12 September 1980. This time the Kemalistic principles of a planned economy were not restored, as in 1960, but the liberalization of the economy was unyieldingly pursued. Renewed overtures to Western Europe and the United States were also made. In 1983 power was again handed over to a civil government, presided over by the Motherland Party of Turgut Özal. He has not been able to suppress the infamous spectre of inflation either. The government continues the realization of liberal economic principles at high speed. The development of industry and tourism is given all possible opportunities. After a period of decline caused by the Gulf War tourism is rapidly increasing again. Alliance with Europe is sought, for example by applying for the E.E.C. membership. As a result of the radical reorganizations of the past few years the country is continuously changing.

All over Turkey tourism is developing. The growing crowds of tourists receive a warm welcome. ►

PAMUKKALE
TURİZM
FETHİYE'YE
HOŞ GELDİNİZ
Welcome
TO FETHİYE

In Turkey numerous newspapers and magazines are available. Besides daily news female beauty gets a lot of attention. ►

AKBANK
AKBANK
TIME
The World's Newsmagazine
GÜNAYDIN
KADIN
Kapital
REKLAMCILIK
ATAKTA
SABAH
Sonntags hier

2 Cradle of many Civilizations

Present and past meet in the vast territory of the Anatolian Plateau. This is the birthplace of the earliest civilizations of Turkey. The visitor is acquainted with the varied cultural treasures of Ankara and the surrounding area. Across endless plains, interspersed with bizarre rock formations, the roads lead to various places of interest.

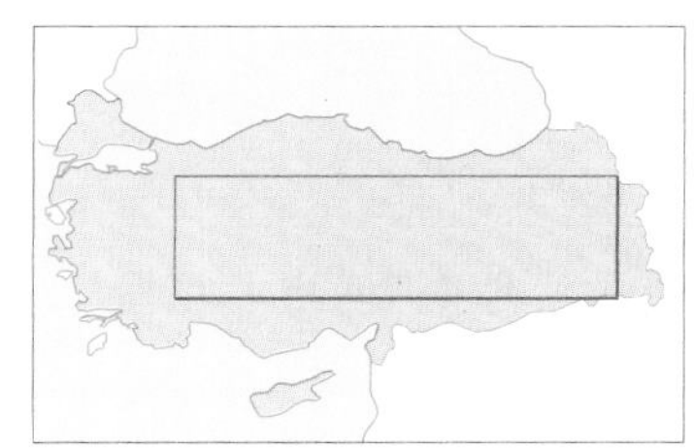

At the very edge of the plateau lie the remains of the Stone Age settlement Çatal Höyük, a town without streets and with doorless houses. Hacılar was an important pottery centre, of which many findings in the Museum of Anatolian Civilizations in Ankara give evidence. In the neighbourhood of Ankara Hittite monuments can be found in Boğazkale and Yazılıkaya as well as the remnants of the Assyrian trading colony Kültepe. Further to the east are the impressive sculpture groups of Nemrut Dağ and around Lake Van lie the remnants of the Urartian Bronze Age civilization.

Alternating rulers

The capital of Turkey, Ankara, has developed from a small provincial town counting 30,000 inhabitants in 1923, into a modern city with over a million inhabitants. The cause of this explosive growth was Atatürk's decision to move the central government from İstanbul to Ankara. The old citadel and the market centre have remained almost untouched. Around the district of Ulus Meydanı, west of the citadel, a luxurious shopping-centre arose. South of the old city-centre the institutes of the Hacetepe University were built. A big north-south arterial road was constructed: the Atatürk Bulvarı. On both sides of this axis the town grew into its present shape. On the east side Yenişehir arose, a modern district with an even more expensive shopping-centre than in Ulus Meydanı. The government buildings lie south of Yenişehir. The ministries, parliament buildings and embassies are enclosed by large parks. Kavaklıdere and Çankaya are the favourite upper class residential areas.
The Hittite name 'Ankuwash' is the first mention of

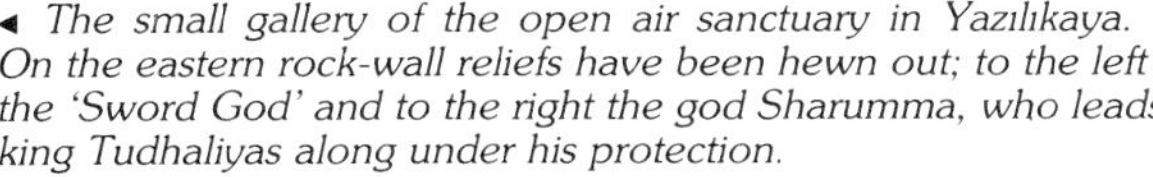

◂ *The small gallery of the open air sanctuary in Yazılıkaya. On the eastern rock-wall reliefs have been hewn out; to the left the 'Sword God' and to the right the god Sharumma, who leads king Tudhaliyas along under his protection.*

◂ *The horseman-statue of Atatürk in the Ulus Square, the dynamic heart of the old city of Ankara.*

The Atatürk Mausoleum

A monument of recent date is the Atatürk Mausoleum (Anıt Kabir) in Ankara which was built in two phases in 1944 and 1953. On both sides of the stairs to the main entrance of the museum are sculpture groups symbolizing the Turkish population. In the space to the right are a scale-model of the grave and photographs made during the construction of the Mausoleum. The monumental avenue leading up to the forecourt, is flanked by stone lions in Hittite style. Under the right colonnade in the forecourt lies the sarcophagus in which Ismet Inönü (1884-1973) has been interred. This Ottoman *pasja* and republican general was Atatürk's closest friend. In 1921 he defeated the Greek occupational army at Inönü, the place that provided him with a name when in 1934 surnames were introduced in Turkey. Inönü was a diplomat and Prime Minister for many years. In 1938 he succeeded Atatürk as president of Turkey.
On the left side of the forecourt is the museum dedicated to Atatürk, containing all sorts of memorabilia. The collection even comprises the Lincoln limousines in which Atatürk loved to travel best. In front of the grave are inscriptions with parts from the speeches Atatürk delivered on the occasion of the tenth anniversary of the republic (1933). Heavy bronze doors give access to the room with the marble tomb. The burial chamber is lined in red marble and frugally decorated with age-old Turkish motives. The Mausoleum was built to reflect the wealth of Anatolian civilization and to honour the founder of modern Turkey.

Ankara in history. The settlement was situated on a cross-roads of east-west and north-south trading routes. After the Hittites the Phrygians inhabited the place and called it Ankyra. Lydians and Persians threatened and attacked Ankyra several times. In 334 B.C. Alexander the Great conquered the city. Around 250 B.C. Ankara became the most important city of the province of Galatia under the name Galatia. Emperor Augustus annexed the area as part of the Roman Empire and officially proclaimed the city capital of the province of Galatia in 25 B.C. Twice a council was convened in Galatia in the third century A.D.
Byzantine power was weakened in the ninth century A.D. by Arab forces pushing on. Finally, the Seljuks ended Byzantine supremacy. During one of the crusades Engüriye, by then the name of Galatia, was recaptured from the Seljuks. The crusaders returned the city to the Byzantines, who would rule it for another hundred years (1101-1213). From 1304 the Mongolians held sway over Engüriye, followed by the Ottomans after 1360. In Europe the city was known as Angora; the fine, soft hair (tiftik) of the angora-goats has become a well-known quality product. To modern Turks Ankara is the capital they have built shedding a lot of blood, sweat and tears. İstanbul however is the city of the glorious past.
As a result of the alternating rulers, the number of historical places of interest in Ankara is limited, especially if compared with İstanbul. During a walk through the picturesque streets of the citadel it is easy to recognize building elements from former eras which have been re-used. The ruin at the top of the citadel dates from the Byzantine period; the Seljuks, Mongolians and Ottomans renovated and extended various parts. Across the citadel, in Ulus Meydanı, remnants of the Roman period can be found such as the fourteen metres high column of Julian. This column was erected in honour of the Roman emperor Julian Apostata during his visit to Galatia in 362. Turkish inhabitants of Ankara later renamed the column Belkız Minaresi, 'Minaret of the queen of Sheba'.
The Hacı Bayram Camii, Ankara's most renowned mosque is built on the ruins of the temple of Augustus and Roma. Emperor Augustus had this temple built on the occasion of the annexation of Galatia as part of the Roman Empire (25-20 B.C.). The walls of the temple depict the most complete version of the 'Res gestae divi Augusti': a kind of report on Augustus' feats. In several cities in Asia Minor copies of this 'will' have been preserved and they constitute an important source of information on the earliest history of our era.
The location of this temple strikingly illustrates the saying: 'the gods change, but the holy site remains the same'. The Phrygians already worshipped the god *Men* here. The kings of Pergamum founded a sanctuary for *Kybele* on the same spot. The next step was the temple dedicated to Augustus and Roma. The Byzantines turned the temple into a church. Later muslims built a mosque on the temple remnants and a sacred tomb for Hacı Bayram Veli, an Islamic saint who founded the Bayramiye order of the *Dervishes* in 1400.
Close to the former temple are the Roman baths (third century A.D.). The changing rooms and the baths for cold, luke-warm and hot water are still clearly

◄ *The ancient Roman baths form a striking contrast with the smog-polluted modern city of Ankara.*

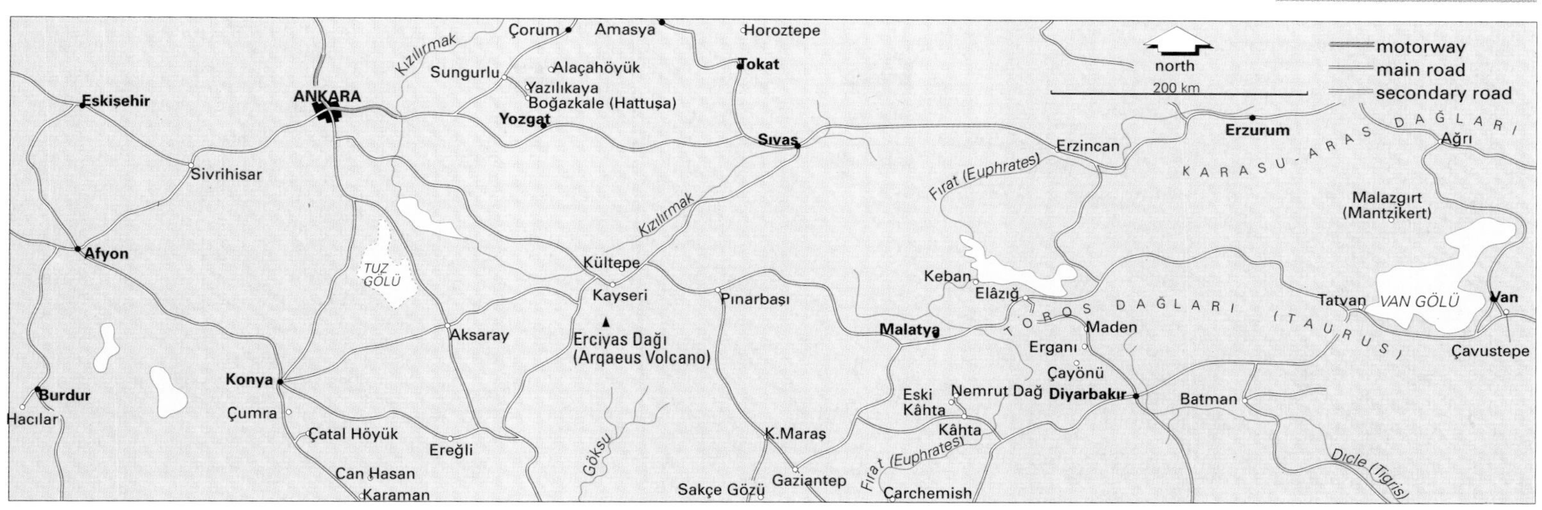

recognizable. The tunnels used for heating the baths have also been well-preserved.

The Arslan Hane Camii in the old market centre dates from the thirteenth century. This mosque owes its name to an antique lion-sculpture in the court (arslan = lion). The ceiling of the prayer room with its five aisles rests on 24 wooden pillars. The *mihrab*, a prayer alcove built in the direction of Mecca, is provided with stucco and a mosaic of *faience* (glazed pottery).

The Ethnographical Museum at the foot of the citadel contains a collection providing a splendid picture of Turkish handicrafts from the recent past. The traditional clothing, carpets and metal objects give a good picture of colourful everyday life in Turkey.

The old citadel is actually a ruin-hill with numerous re-used remnants, *spolia*, from the Byzantine and the Ottoman period. The Museum of Anatolian Civilizations on the citadel is housed in a renovated *bedesten*, a market hall, which was built in 1471 under the authority of the grand vizier Mahmut Paşa. The adjoining Kurşunlu Han, an Ottoman warehouse, is also part of the museum block. The idea to exhibit the national archaeological treasures of Turkey here came from Atatürk himself. The magnificent collection is displayed in two large rooms. The central room contains the impressive Alacahöyük, Carchemish, Malatya and Sakçe Gözü reliefs, as they have been found on the sites. In the U-shaped room the objects are arranged chronologically. As is often the case with excavations, the original architectural remains at the site itself have mostly disappeared after years of snow, rain and wind. In the museum a successful attempt has been made to present a picture of the history of Anatolia with the help of photographs, reconstructions and, of course, the finds themselves.

Central hall of the Museum for Anatolian Civilizations in Ankara: a procession of officers. These finely stylized figures originally decorated the bases of walls at ▼ Carchemish.

Art and cultus

RECONSTRUCTION DRAWING OF THE 'TERRACE-HOUSES' OF ÇATAL HÖYÜK.

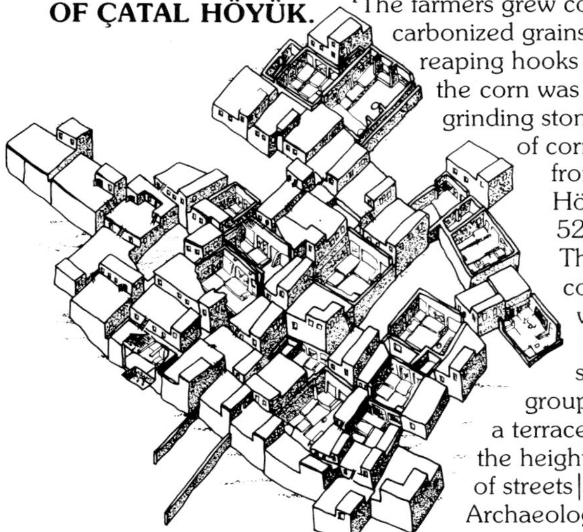

Climatological and geographical circumstances 11,000 years ago provided the conditions for the hunter-collectors to settle on a more permanent base in Anatolia. Developments in the field of food production, such as the selective exploitation of crops and animals, lie at the root of the 'Stone Age Revolution'. One of the settlements of that period is Çayönü (7250-6750 B.C.), seven kilometres south-west of Ergani. 'The farmers grew corn, which can be deduced from the carbonized grains of corn found in Çayönü. With reaping hooks made of flint and set in deer antlers the corn was harvested. The presence of grinding stones indicates the further processing of corn into flour. The largest settlement from the Stone Age is Çatal Höyük (6500-5750). This town lies 52 kilometers south-east of Konya. The excavated part of the settlement consists of a blind outer wall, behind which lie a large number of rectangular houses. The rooms, strongly varying in height, are grouped around courts. Çatal Höyük has a terrace-like character due to differences in the height of the houses. Striking is the lack of streets and of door-openings. Archaeologists presume that the house-entries were situated on the roofs: with the help of ladders people descended into the rooms. Communication between the houses must have taken place via the roofs as well.

The rooms had platforms which could be used for sitting or sleeping. In the seven habitation phases of Çatal Höyük more than 40 sanctuaries could be distinguished through the analysis of numerous decorations. The walls of these spaces were decorated with geometrical motives and/or vivid hunting scenes. Bull-hunts and deer-hunts have been frequently depicted. Very special are a few paintings revealing vultures eating the meat of decapitated human beings. In addition to paintings there are also a lot of plastered reliefs on the walls: two felines facing each other, bulls' heads, rams' heads and goddesses giving birth to bulls. These scenes have contributed to the reconstruction of the religious life of the people of Çatal Höyük. The reliefs of animal heads (ram and bull) consisted of the frontal part of the skull and the horns. Some platforms in the rooms had a horizontal row of horns and sometimes pillars with a vertical row of horns next to them. The symbolism in the murals and reliefs show numerous predecessors of characteristic Anatolian motives: hands, crosses and horns. Yet a lot of the significance and the function of the symbols still remains a mystery.

A gigantic volcanic outburst is likely to have made a deep impression. For, in one of the sanctuaries a volcanic eruption is depicted on a wall. This is the oldest known landscape picture (circa 6200 B.C.).

Many murals have burial rites as their subject. It appeared possible to reconstruct these rites from the examination of excavated graves. After the flesh had

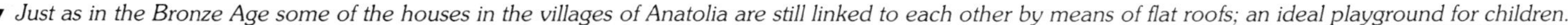

▾ *Just as in the Bronze Age some of the houses in the villages of Anatolia are still linked to each other by means of flat roofs; an ideal playground for children.*

been stripped off them, the dead were interred under elevations in the rooms. The flesh was probably removed with the help of vultures, as is depicted in some places. The remains were then wrapped in cloth, rush-mats or hides and buried within the rooms. Often the remains were painted with ochre, vermillion, blue or green paint.
The burial gifts for women and children consisted of jewels (bracelets, necklaces and anklets), stone hoes, bone spatulas and spoons. Men were accompanied by clubheads, flint daggers, obsidian spearheads, stamps of clay and bone belt-clasps. Prominent persons (both men and women) were sometimes given obsidian mirrors and baskets with toiletries. Pottery and clay statuettes have not been found as burial gifts. In daily life the inhabitants of Çatal Höyük used containers made of wood or baked clay, baskets and hides. Stamps bearing geometrical patterns were probably used to print cloth. It is not unlikely that the human bodies were also adorned with similar stamps.
An object of worship was a fertility goddess with extremely pronounced sexual characteristics. Stone and clay statuettes show this mother-goddess in all sorts of poses and situations: standing behind a feline, giving birth on a throne flanked by two felines, embracing another person or accompanied by a child. Male gods are often depicted riding an animal (bull or feline). This reflects a very old Anatolian tradition, which would be raised to a high artistic standard in Hittite art.

◄ Mother goddess from Çatal Höyük in the museum of Ankara.

Pottery as a means of expression

Hacılar, 25 kilometres south-west of Burdur, is a settlement with remnants from the sixth millennium B.C. Once more the somewhat stylized statuettes of the mother-goddess catch the eye. Just as in Çatal Höyük (layer I, 5400 B.C.) Hacılar lacks pictures of male gods. Murals have not been found in Hacılar. The early pottery from Hacılar is polished and sometimes decorated. Striking are the use of projecting parts in the shape of human heads and animals. A beaker found in Hacılar in the shape of a woman's head is the predecessor of a well-known Hittite tradition. Hittite texts mention drinking from such beakers as a means to bring about unification with the gods. The Hacılar pottery from layer V-VII (5400-5000 B.C.) belongs to the finest from the Old Near East. Oval jars and beakers are decorated with geometrical motives on a red-on-cream-coloured base.
Carbonized grain remains from Hacılar show progressive development in the cultivation of crops at the end of the Stone Age. Various natural products such as emmer, einkorn, wheat, barley, peas, bitter vetch, acorns and berries have been frequently found in soil samples.

The traditional ▲ lifestyle of the nomads, who inhabit the eastern mountain region with their enormous flocks, recalls images of a bygone age when the first hunter-collectors settled in Anatolia.

Characteristic ▲ Hacılar pottery in the Archaeological Museum of Antalya (top) and in the Museum of Anatolian Civilizations in Ankara (below). ▼

▲ *This beautiful native plant (Scutellaria orientalis) can be found on rocks, rubble hills and in mountain regions.*

Local cultures in the Copper Stone Age

In the Stone Age and the following Copper Stone Age (Chalcolithicum) the Anatolian Plateau became the centre of a number of local cultures. This is evident from the results of archaeological fieldwork at Suberde (south-west of Konya) and from excavations near Gözlükule (in the Tarsus area) and in the Amuq-plain (near Antakya). One of the habitation layers in Hacılar reveals the most advanced material expressions of culture dating from the Copper Stone Age. The settlement Hacılar II is surrounded by an outer wall, at some places with a diameter of at least three metres. The houses are concentrated in the western part of the settlement. In the eastern part were the workshops, a well and a small temple. In the centre was a pottery workshop with three courts. Hacılar II appears to have been destroyed around 5000 B.C.

In Can Hasan, near Karaman, layers of a somewhat later date than those in Hacılar have been exposed. The houses in Can Hasan were rectangular or square and built without courts or streets between them. A building method falling back on the old one known from Çatal Höyük with houses also only accessible via the roofs. Thick buttresses in some rooms give the impression that the houses had a second floor. A large housing unit had been preserved up to a height of three metres and the roof-entry proved to be in perfect condition. The superstructure of mud bricks revealed parts of the window-opening, in some places even still provided with its original painted plaster application. In this building the remains of a man of about 50 years old were discovered. It is more than likely that he perished in a great fire. Next to the man lay a clubhead of massive copper and he wore a copper bracelet. The copper findings in all layers of Can Hasan resemble those of Hacılar.

The pottery from Can Hasan is also an obvious continuation of the tradition from Hacılar. The patterns however are more complex and mostly consist of zigzag lines and shadings. The red-on-cream pottery was gradually replaced by pottery with dark motives painted on a lighter base.

The next periods in Anatolia are characterized by a growing influence from adjoining areas like the Balkans and Mesopotamia. From the Early Bronze Age on, urbanization increased due to developments in the economy which relied more and more on trade. Regional dynasties found ways to exploit the existing sources and to supplement shortages with products from neighbouring areas. Indications for this were found in the archaeological rescue-operations implemented at the construction of the Keban and Atatürk dams in the Euphrates. The architecture in the cities mainly consisted of large-scale and monumental buildings for religion and government. The houses appear to have been inhabited by civil servants who held functions in the bureaucratic city councils. Metallurgical industry was the main factor at the root of the prominent position of Anatolia in the third millennium B.C. The presence of many raw materials (copper, gold, silver and wood) and the tooling of them was very conducive to the development of specializations. Copper has been discovered dating back to the earliest periods of human inhabitation in Anatolia. Yet the richest copper findings come from the cemeteries of the Early Bronze Age settlements.

Cotton plant

The cotton plant (Gossypium herbaceum) is still found in the wild in some places in Turkey, but has also been cultivated on a large scale on behalf of cotton production. The plant is presumably native in West-Asia. The flowering time is in September and after the buds have popped open, a large tuft of soft white hair emerges covering the seeds. These seeds are full of cotton seed oil which is used in pharmacy and in cosmetics. Cotton is the most important textile fibre in the world and is mainly cultivated in Turkey for the country's own use.

The 'Royal Graves' of Alaçahöyük

The ruin-hill of Alaçahöyük lies 50 kilometres south-west of Çorum. On Atatürk's instigation the archaeologists Arık and Koşay started the excavations in 1935. In the seventies the reconstruction and conservation were set up.

In the Early Bronze Age Alaçahöyük was one of the main cultural centres. The 'Royal Graves' of the city have a strong appeal to the imagination. These graves are sometimes described as 'shaft-graves' but in reality a shallow hole was dug. At the bottom of the hole a low burial chamber was built. The burial chambers have stone walls, in the corners wooden posts carry a ceiling made of wood as well. The sizes vary from three to eight metres lengthwise and from two to five metres widthwise. In general these graves were only 75 centimetres high. The dead were buried in the fetal position. The burial gifts were exceptionally rich and from a cultural-historical point of view unique for the Near East. Clay was cast across the joisted ceiling; on top of that clay remnants have been found of materials which were used during all sorts of burial rites such as heads and legs of sacrificial animals. Thereafter the hole, or shallow shaft, was filled up with earth. Grave-markings are missing, which is not strange, because the graves were situated in a part of the settlement especially used as a cemetery.

One would expect that these 'Royal Graves' could be related to the monumental architecture in Alaçahöyük. Building remnants, however, clearly indicate that Alaçahöyük, compared to other settlements from the same period, had a rural character. In the west of Anatolia (e.g. Troy, see Chapter 5), the east (Korucu

Tepe and Norşun Tepe) and the south-east (Malatya, Lidar Höyük) the settlements had a much more urban kind of architecture.
The great wealth of the buried persons leads to suspect that the cemetery in Alaçahöyük is that of a semi-nomadic tribe. A part of this tribe must have been living in settlements like Alaçahöyük, while another part replenished the agricultural products of the settlement with dairy products of cattle which they brought from summer to winter grazing fields. The great wealth of the tribe might have been owed to their specialization in metallurgical industry. The museum at Ankara has an impressive selection: precious diadems, necklaces, brooches and objects of gold, silver, cornelian and rock-crystal. The beautifully arranged display cases exhibit among other things statuettes of goddesses, deer and bulls. The ceremonial standards probably belonged to tribal chiefs.

◄ *Ritual bronze standard from Alaçahöyük with a deer and two does.*

Findings from Horoztepe and Mahmatlar in the area of Amasya and from Ayakpınar near Adana strongly resemble those from Alaçahöyük and prove that Anatolia thrived enormously in the third millennium B.C. because of the excessive development of metallurgical industry. Findings in Mesopotamia confirm the idea that the inhabitants from the alluvial low lands showed great interest in the highly developed art from Anatolia at a very early date.

Assyrian trading posts

In the second millennium B.C. the developments had already led to intensive trade between the various regions in the Near East. Particularly merchants from Assur had found their way to Anatolia and its rich metal sources. A network of trade routes and trading posts (*karum*, a large trading centre and *wabartum*, a smaller stopping place) was set up in order to trade gold, silver and copper from Anatolia for luxury goods, high-quality textile and tin from Assyria. The flourishing bronze industry caused an increase in the need for tin, which was practically unavailable in Anatolia.
The excavations in Kültepe revealed the administration of these trade activities. Information was noted down in cuneiform script on clay tablets, which in a number of cases were wrapped in an envelope with writing on it. On these envelopes the contents of the 'letter' were briefly mentioned and cylinder sealings were applied as a signature. Although the texts mainly deal about contracts, debts (and loans), and trade correspondence as seen from the Assyrian perspective, they also touch upon information about Anatolian society. Assyrian merchants introduced the cylinder seal and cuneiform script.
The Anatolian-Mesopotamian synthesis can be clearly observed in Hittite art; many old themes as discovered in Çatal Höyük and Hacılar continued to exist but were combined with Mesopotamian motives.

This sphinx has been guarding the entry to Alaçahöyük
▼ *for 3000 years.*

Boğazkale and Yazılıkaya

At the beginning of the second millennium B.C. there was also an Assyrian *karum* in Boğazkale (200 kilometres east of Ankara). From findings in Boğazkale it appears that not long after the decline of Assyrian trade with Anatolia local monarchs succeeded in establishing a new culture which would soon be vital to the image of the whole of Anatolia. Excavations in Boğazkale/Hattuşa, the capital of the Hittite empire, have provided a wealth of information since the middle of the previous century. The discovery of the Hittite civilization took place in three phases and started at the time of the great exploratory expeditions in the Near East. Spurred on by a longing for adventure and out of scientific interest the French traveller Charles Texier constructed the first drawings and maps of Boğazkale in 1834. In the second phase of the investigation it was assumed on the basis of texts from the Old Testament and Assyrian documents that the centre of the Hittite empire had to be located in Syria. Remnants which had been discovered and publicized before, appeared to have been wrongly interpreted as Hittite. The third phase of the investigation started in 1906. In that year during excavations in Boğazkale the archaeologist Winckler discovered clay tablets with a cuneiform script that could not be decyphered immediately. In 1915 the Tsjech Bedřich Hrozný concluded that it concerned a new language: Hittite, an Indo-European language. The investigations of Hugo Winckler, Theodor Makridi and Otto Puchstein have been continued up to this very day under the auspices of the 'Deutsche Orient-Gesellschaft' and the German Archaeological Institute in Turkey. Meanwhile, excavations in Alaçahöyük, Masat Höyük and other places have demonstrated the vast distribution of Hittite culture.

A spectacular view across the foundations of the Great Temple in Hattuşa with, in the background, the present ▾ village of Boğazkale.

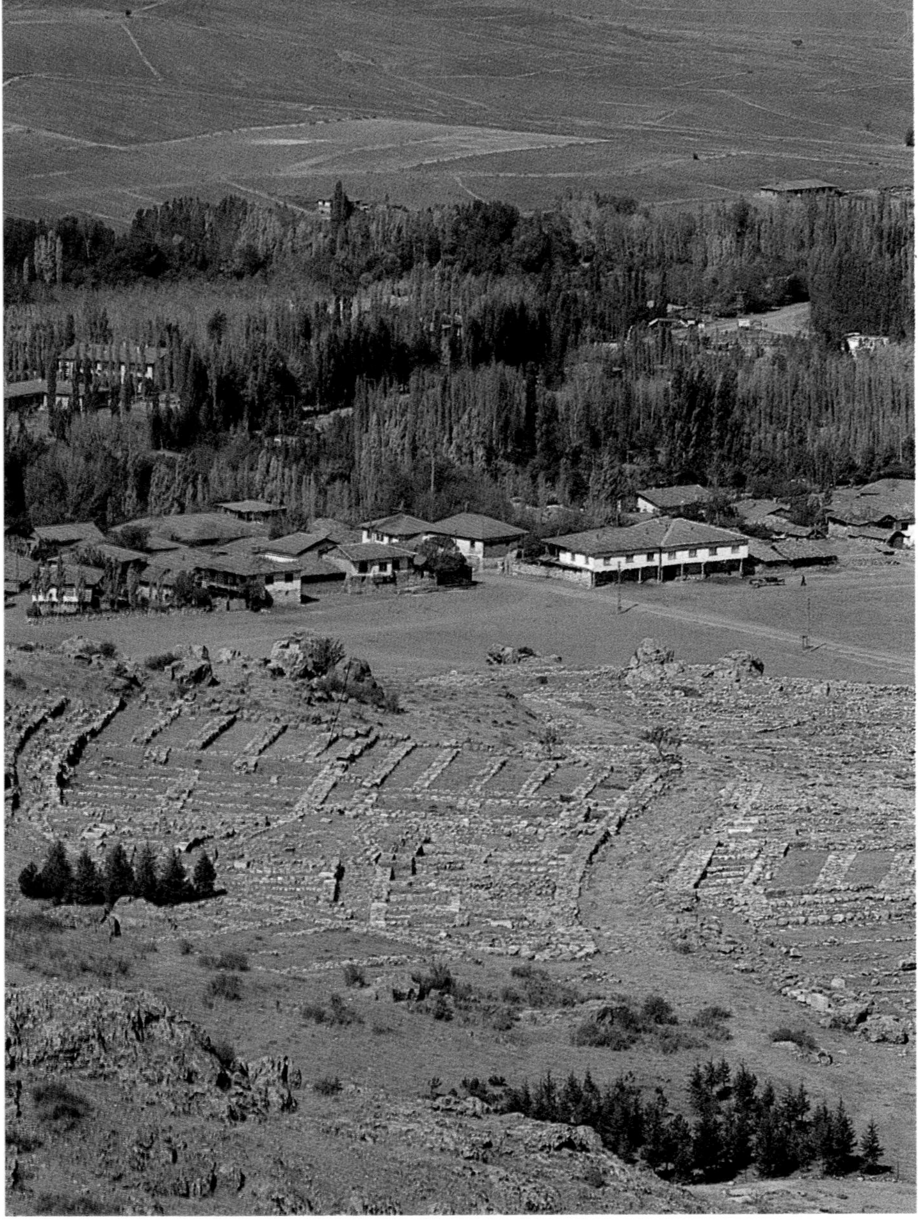

The capital Hattuşa lies in a rugged mountain area and is surrounded by a seven kilometres long wall. Although most tourists visit the excavation by car or bus, it is worthwhile to explore the places of interest on foot and meanwhile enjoy the beneficent peace and beauty of the area. The townscape is dominated by the religious centre in the north. The Great Temple of the weather-god of *Hatti* and the sun-goddess of *Arinna* (Temple I) is one of the many temples uncovered in Hattuşa. The map immediately gives an impression of the massiveness of Hittite architecture. The temple itself is situated in a court and is enclosed by large storage rooms. In the adjoining rooms the temple administration was executed and the votive gifts and ritual objects were stored. North of the inner court lie two *cellae* (holy of holies), dedicated to the chief god and goddess. South of the temple block are houses of persons who held functions in the temple.
In the long city wall city gates have been constructed at regular distances. The most bulky gates can be found in the upper city. This quarter was built in a later stadium of the Hittite period. The eastern passageway is called the King's Gate. This name is based on an inaccurate interpretation of the relief on the inside of the gate. It is the god *Shulinkatte* and not, as was originally assumed, one of the Hittite kings.
The Sphinxes' Gate (Yerkapı), the most monumental of all, is built on an artificial hill which was erected to allow for the construction of a 72 metres long tunnel or *poterne*. This tunnel was used to make an undetected and, above all, unexpected sortie in the event of sieges. A walk through this *poterne* of enormous dimensions shows that the Hittites took the defence of their capital very seriously. The Yerkapı was decorated with four *sphinxes*, two in the inner portal and two on the outside of the gate. The western passageway in the city wall is called the Lions' Gate after the two lion *protomas* on the outside.
The governmental centre of the city was situated on Büyükkale and was completely walled-in. The entry consisted of a monumental staircase which led to a series of three courts. Around these courts lay the monumental buildings of the royal archives, the royal palace (in the north-west) and the royal reception room. In the lower court the envoys from other parts of Anatolia and the Near East were received. Guests and royal household were housed in the surrounding buildings. The central and upper courts were reserved for the royal family and their royal household. Unfortunately only a few remnants of the upper court are left.

▲ *Detail from the Lions' Gate; the fierce manes and wide-opened muzzle are a warning intended for unwanted visitors. It is assumed that the eye sockets were originally set with coloured stones.*

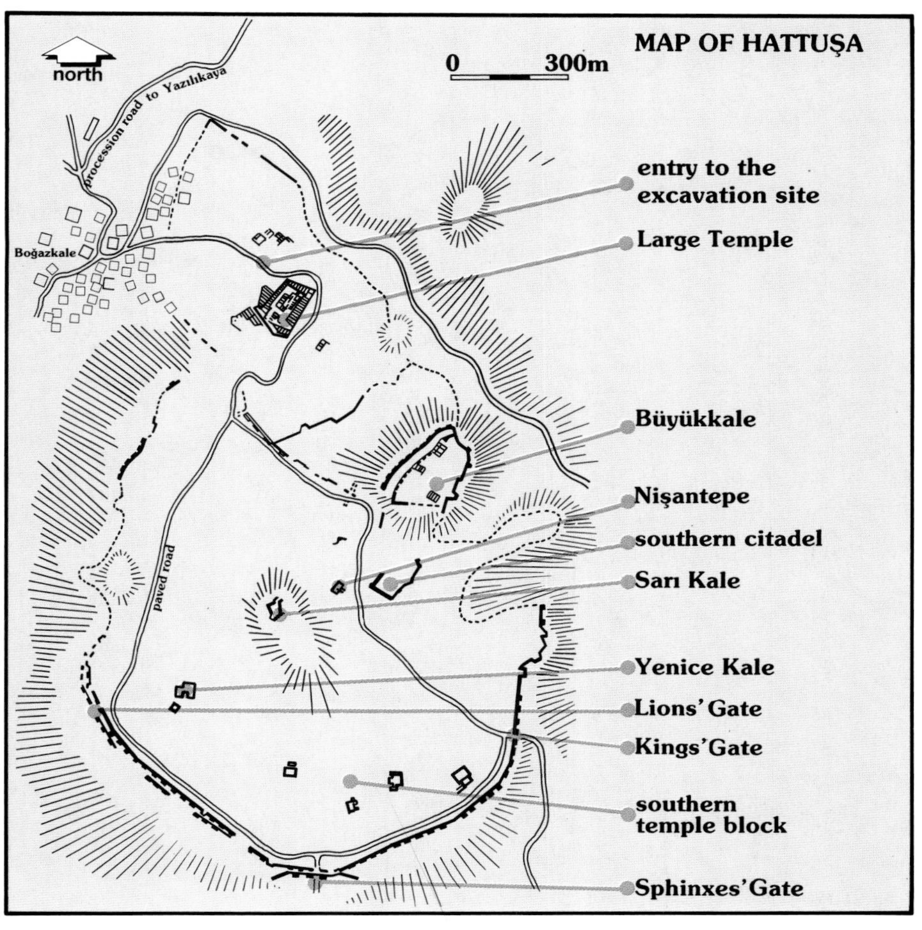

The outer side of the Lions' Gate in Hattuşa. From their high post the lions overlook the vast landscape. ▼

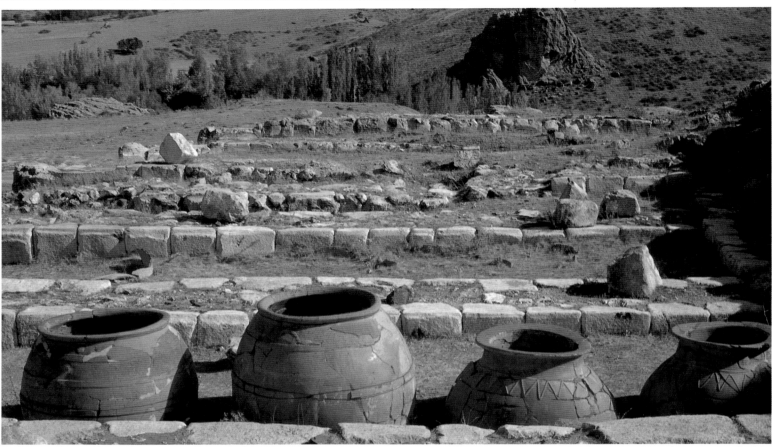

▲ Giant pitchers in the north-western stock rooms of the Great Temple. From the temple administration it appears that these pitchers served to store liquids like oil and wine.

Panel with the twelve 'running gods' on the western wall of the small gallery. The gods wear tiaras on their heads and croziers over their right shoulders. ▼

Originally the Hittites were an Anatolian mountain tribe which can be deduced from the rock sanctuary Yazılıkaya. A two-kilometres long processional road connects Hattuşa with this sacred place. In front of this rock sanctuary a temple was built at a later date. Yazılıkaya consists of two rock chasms with walls decorated with a series of fascinating reliefs. In the great 'gallery' a long procession of Hittite gods is depicted, ending on the northern side of the gallery in a relief portraying the principal gods. The west procession is formed by male gods who march behind the storm-god *Teshub*, in the east procession female gods stand behind the sun-goddess *Hepat* and the god *Sharumma*, the son of *Teshub* and *Hepat*. At the head of the east procession the Hittite grand king Tudhaliyas IV (circa 1250 B.C.) is depicted. The reliefs of the great gallery represent a meeting of the gods on the occasion of a feast that took place every year in spring.
In the small gallery twelve gods in a row are hewn out in relief. Opposite this rock wall are the *cartouche* of Tudhaliyas IV in Hittite hieroglyphics, the 'Sword god', and next to that again a relief of Tudhaliyas IV tightly embraced by the god *Sharumma*. The significance of this small west gallery is unclear. The emphasis laid on King Tudhaliyas could be an indication that this site was the original burial chamber of this king or that a burial ritual in his honour took place there.
The temple archives from Hattuşa have provided a great deal of information about the religion of the Hittites, as have the royal archives about the government of the empire. The Hittite writers recorded all details of the rituals and government very precisely. The royal annals make detailed mention of the military campaigns of the respective grand kings. The treaties with conquered enemies meticulously describe the rights and duties of both parties. The Treaty of Kadesh from the thirteenth century B.C. is the oldest preserved example of an international peace treaty. This treaty was signed after the war with Egypt which had been fought out in western Syria. The document has been drawn up in the diplomatic language of that time, Akkadian. In a number of documents Hittite laws were disclosed. In combination with accurate reports on criminal trials they offer the possibility to reconstruct the Hittite legal system.
Land-donation charters, descriptions of rituals in the temple, prayers and instructions for temple staff present a clear picture of the Hittite world. Outside Boğazkale, e.g. in Masat Höyük, written documents were found too, supplementing the picture.

The inhabitants of Boğazkale cordially greet the increasing flow of tourists. The bull horns are symbols of a longstanding ▾ Anatolian tradition.

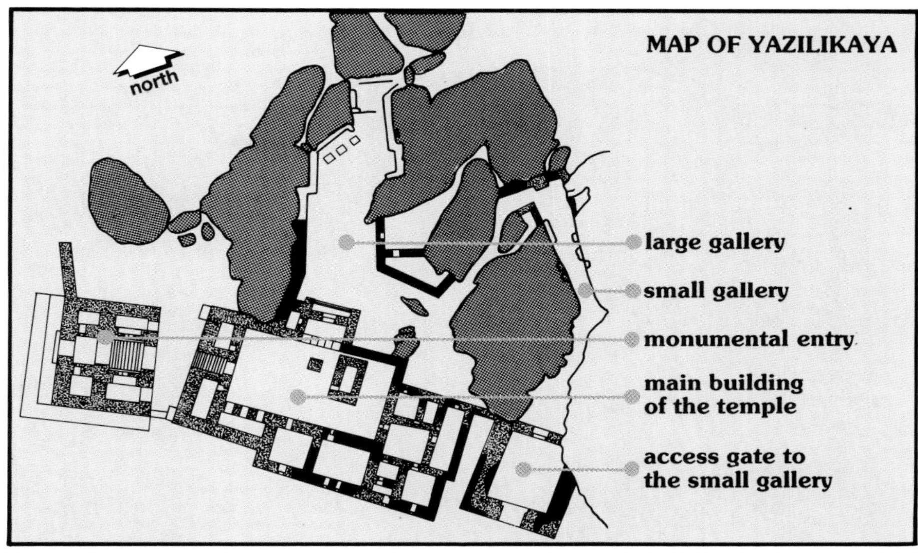

◂ Yazılıkaya, the small gallery. The god Sharumma and king Tudhaliyas IV. The god could be indentified on the basis of Hittite hieroglyphics near the image. The king's name appears in the cartouche next to the deity's head.

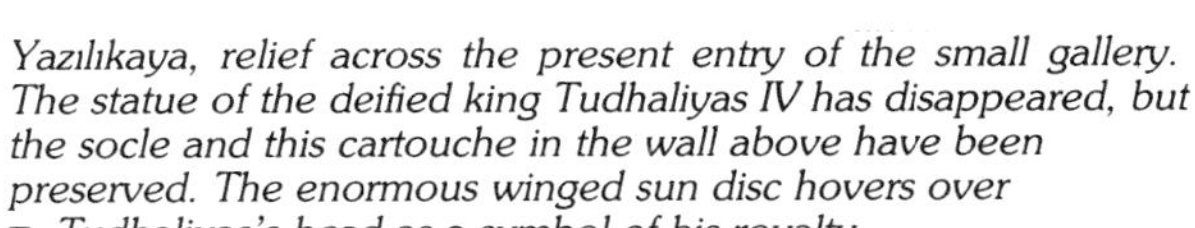

Yazılıkaya, relief across the present entry of the small gallery. The statue of the deified king Tudhaliyas IV has disappeared, but the socle and this cartouche in the wall above have been preserved. The enormous winged sun disc hovers over ▾ Tudhaliyas's head as a symbol of his royalty.

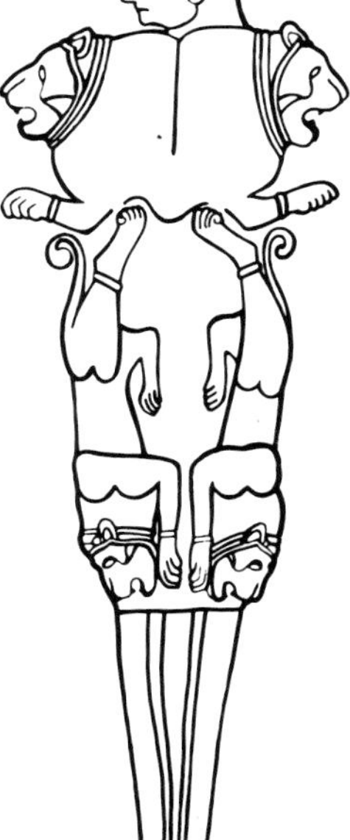

LINE-DRAWING OF THE 'SWORD GOD'

A monumental sword crowned with a head has been stuck in the ground. The significance of this relief is not clear. It could be the symbol of the 'Sword God' or Tudhaliyas's sword.

Manure

Manure has always played an important role in Turkish agricultural life. Archaeologists make grateful use of the fact that in ancient times cattle feed was supplemented with corn. In the remnants of manure, which was used as fuel, the investigators have found the incinerated grains of corn which can be determinated and dated quite well.
In Central and East Turkey manure still serves as fuel for heating the baking ovens. For that purpose manure is first collected and pressed into round turfs, which are then dried in the sun.

Eastern Turkey, a woman in colourful clothing in front of a high pile of manure turfs. ▼

An Arabic woman close to the Syrian border among pressed manure turfs. ▼

During the building of simple farm-houses the walls are coated with a mixture of loam, manure and straw. ▼

The Hittite heritage

Alaçahöyük has already been mentioned in relation with the 'Royal Graves'. It has sometimes been suggested that there is a connection with the later Hittite culture. Yet it is more justified to consider the oldest remnants as exemplifying Anatolian cultural might which had already been established from findings of the Stone Age (Çatal Höyük), the Copper Stone Age (Hacılar) and the Early Bronze Age (Alaçahöyük).
In the fourteenth century B.C. the influence of the Hittite empire was certainly present in the material remnants at Alaçahöyük. This appears from the monumental gate with *sphinxes*, which moreover, was decorated with reliefs both on the two outer sides and on the inside. Just as with the *sphinxes* of the Yerkapı in Boğazkale the two-metres-high *protomas* are hewn out of the side pillars of the gate.
The Sphinxes Gate gives access to a holy area in the urban region of Alaçahöyük. The reliefs are nowadays displayed in the central hall of the museum in Ankara. There, as in the local museums in Boğazkale and Alaçahöyük, the most important objects discovered during the long series of excavations are exhibited.
The pottery is a continuation of the tradition known from the period of the Assyrian trading colonies. Characteristic are the ceramic vessels in the shape of various animals. A Hittite modernization in the range are the painted dishes with humans and animals in relief. On this pottery many rituals and ceremonies from Hittite religion are displayed too. Gods, who can be found in Yazılıkaya on reliefs, are depicted by the craftsmen of Alaçahöyük in gold, ivory, stone and bronze.
In the Hittite art of seal-cutting a similar composition, pose and clothing fashion can be observed as in the other forms of art. Particularly the personal seals of the great kings are impressive.
The king's name is represented in Hittite hieroglyphics and is sometimes accompanied by an image of the deified king himself. The round seal stamps are provided with an edge of cuneiform writing, the inner circle is filled with the winged sun's disc. The use of this disc unmistakably reveals a connection with Egypt and the pharaos. The Hittite great kings were also addressed as 'my sun'.
The great expansion of the Hittite Empire took place in the middle of the second millennium B.C. After a short battle for supremacy and weakening of Hittite power, Suppiluliumas I came to the throne in the fourteenth century B.C. He restored the unity and the position of Hittite power. The ascending empire put an end to the kingdom of *Mitanni* (a region in northern Mesopotamia). Finally Suppiluliumas even managed to conquer East-Anatolia and Northern Syria. The New Hittite Empire that arose out of this grew into a mighty state, equalling Egypt, Assyria and Babylon in power. From royal correspondence it emerges that the kings of these states addressed each other as 'my brother'.
After the fall of the New Hittite Empire (circa 1200 B.C.) large regions in Anatolia fell under the rule of local monarchs. In the use of hieroglyphics and in relief art the material culture of these mini-states clearly reveals the continuation of Hittite traditions. Gradually however, these states became artistically influenced by Assyria. In the collection of the Archaeological Museum in Ankara reliefs from Meliddu (Malatya) and Hatti (Carchemish) bear witness to the Hittite heritage. These

small monarchies managed to survive in the period between 1000 and 750 B.C. among the Phrygian kingdom in the north, the Assyrian Empire in northern Mesopotamia and the Urartian Empire in the east.

▲ The Urartians were masters in hydraulic engineering. This ancient irrigation channel at Çavustepe is still used to irrigate the land.

Urartian fortresses

The kingdom Uriatri, the denotation of the empire of Urartu in an Assyrian inscription of Shalmanasser I (ninth century B.C.), also arose from the heritage of the Hittite period. The centre of this empire was located in Van (the old Tushpa). During the power vacuum after the fall of the Hittite Empire, the Urartian monarchs in East-Anatolia managed to expand their political power enormously, and to give shape to Urartian culture in the area round Lake Van, Lake Çildir, Lake Urmya and Lake Gökçe (in Iran). Expansion into the south took place after the influence of Assyria had diminished due to internal power struggles. In the seventh century B.C. the Medes finished off the kingdom of Urartu.

The homeland of the Urartians, around Lake Van, is extremely desolate and mountainous. The inhabitants have always made skillful use of the natural disposition of their surroundings. Fortresses were constructed on top or against the slopes of strategically located mountains. Dams and waterways allowed for a maximum exploitation of the farmlands. In architecture the Urartians developed new concepts. Temples were built on the basis of a rectangular ground-plan, with a *cella* and a colonnade as reception room. This colonnade was later copied in a grand fashion during the building of the Apadana (audience hall) in Persepolis. Metallurgical industry in particular flourished in the kingdom of Urartu. Parts of furniture in ivory and bronze, bronze weapons, tools, ornaments, girdles and bronze kettles with protruding elements in the shape of winged *griffins* and bulls have been discovered in large quantities in the store-rooms of Urartian fortresses and temples.

▲ *Cuneiform inscription around the entry to the grave of king Arghisti I (786-764 B.C.) on the citadel near Van. In this most extensive of Urartian texts, Arghisti's feats are described.*

The impressive walls of the fortress near Van can be seen from afar. Many peoples, among whom the Urartians and Seljuks, have left their traces at this fortress. ▼

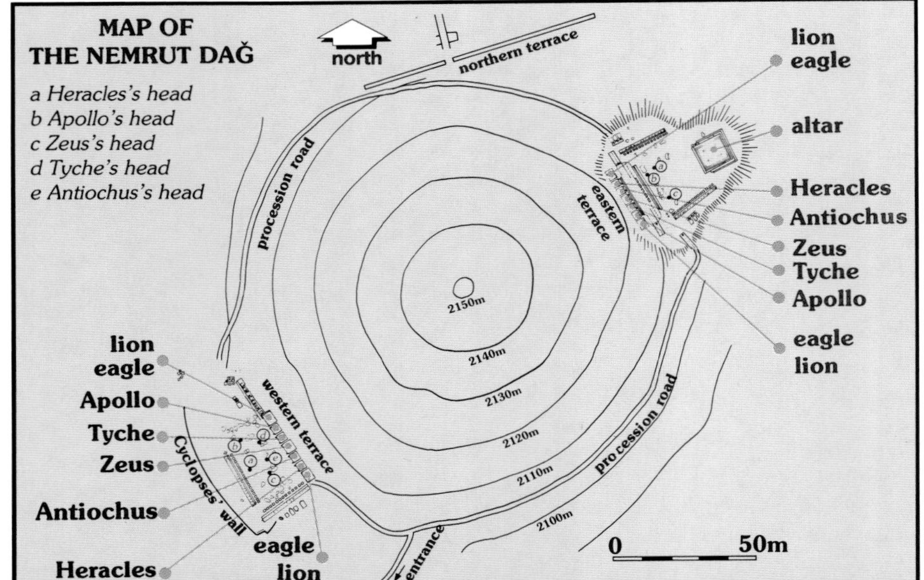

Antiochus I had the sanctuary on the Nemrut Dağ constructed so that, after his death, his memory would live on. ▲

The petrified gods of Commagene

In the rugged mountain regions of Commagene between Elâzığ, Gaziantep, Diyarbakır and Malatya, Antiochus I of Commagene (69-34 B.C.) founded an independent kingdom after the area had been ruled by Assyrians, Persians and Seleucids. Antiochus was the son of Mithridates who descended from the Persian royal family and derived his legitimate royal rights from his marriage to a Seleucid princess. The Commagene Empire lost its independence in 18 B.C. when, after the battle between the Parths and the Romans concerning supremacy in the Near East, it was annexed as part of the Roman province of Syria.
At the top of the 2150 metres high Nemrut Dağ, Antiochus I had a grand grave monument constructed. Enormous sculptures stand on terraces around a 50 metres high burial mound. This mound consists of an artificially elevated *tumulus*; the presence of a grave is presumed but not (yet) determined with certainty. On the northern terrace the remnants have unfortunately been rather badly preserved. Both on the western and on the eastern terrace are five statues of gods: *Apollo*, *Tyche* of Commagene, *Zeus*, Antiochus and *Heracles*. On both sides of the gods stand a lion and an eagle. Insofar as the heads are still there, the giant Hellenistic and Persian statues of the gods reach a height of about nine metres. On the western terrace the colossal heads of the gods lie in a reasonably well-preserved state next to the sculpture group.
More remnants of the Commagene Empire can be found in the surroundings of the Nemrut Dağ. King Mithridates II had a 35 metres high burial mound built on Karakuş Tepe for his mother Isias, his sister Antiochis and his cousin Aka. The mound was originally surrounded by three pairs of columns. The southern pillar with the eagle has been preserved the best.
In the area of Eski Kâhta on Eski Kale the remains of Arsameia, the capital of Commagene, can be seen. A large *stèle* bears the portrait of what is presumably a woman. Then there are two more *stèles*, a monumental staircase, and behind that an opening in the rock leading to a *cistern*. Along the road to the remains of the city on the hill, is a relief showing Mithridates I Kallinikos shaking the hand of *Heracles*. Next to this relief an inscription in Greek has been engraved in which the (divine) law is recorded about the duties of priests concerning government and organization. On the right of the relief is the beginning of a tunnel which, according to tradition, would lead far into the valley.
In contrast to the mountain landscape in the region of Ankara the mountains in the east are more jagged, lacking vast plains. Impressive mountain ranges and old volcanoes give the landscape a grey-brown appearance in summer; a traveller will experience the villages in this region as oases.
In the far east the snow-capped summits of Mount Ararat dominate the surroundings. Mountain nomads migrate through the thinly populated region with their numerous flocks. The economic character is mainly determined by agriculture and crafts. The exploitation of minerals in the soil plays an important role nowadays, just as in ancient times. The oil at Batman (east of Diyarbakır) as well as the copper and chromium ore at Erganı and Maden have caused the main traffic routes to be well-developed. Hotels and restaurants can be found in all medium-size and big towns, eliminating any obstructions for a visit to this rugged mountain region and its art treasures.

▲ The colossal statues of Zeus, Apollo and a lion on the eastern terrace of the Nemrut Dağ. The sanctuary on the top of the mountain can only be reached after a stiff climb, preceded by a trip by landrover or minibus across a steep mountain road.

The 'Lions' horoscope'; ▲ the relief shows the zodiac sign of Leo. Over the back of the animal, Mars, Mercury and Jupiter can be discerned. The constellation possibly indicates the position of the planets and the stars at the time of the coronation of king Mithridates on 14 July 109 B.C.

Kars

The sheep that are kept in the rugged districts of East-Anatolia are of a dark colour. Their thick fleeces can resist the bitter winter cold in this mountain region. Consequently, carpets made from the wool of these sheep are exceptionally strong. The natural dark brown colour of the wool forms the basis of the carpets which are knotted in almost every village and valley around Kars. Many of the patterns used are of Caucasian origin. Along the edge of the carpet shown here, geometrical motives in soft hues have been incorporated; in the middle three stylized eagles can be observed, symbols of freedom.

The giant head of the goddess Tyche. Due to the high and isolated location of the sanctuary the limestone statues remained unscathed for a long time. As a result of earthquakes the heads ▼ have tumbled from the trunks.

3 Burial Mounds and Rock Monuments

A fascinating scenery, dominated by jagged rock masses, once formed the setting for the adventures of king Midas and his retinue. Distinctive rock monuments, graves and churches give evidence of a glorious past on the Phrygian Plateau. Characteristic are the vastness and desolation of the region where the visitor can roam freely.

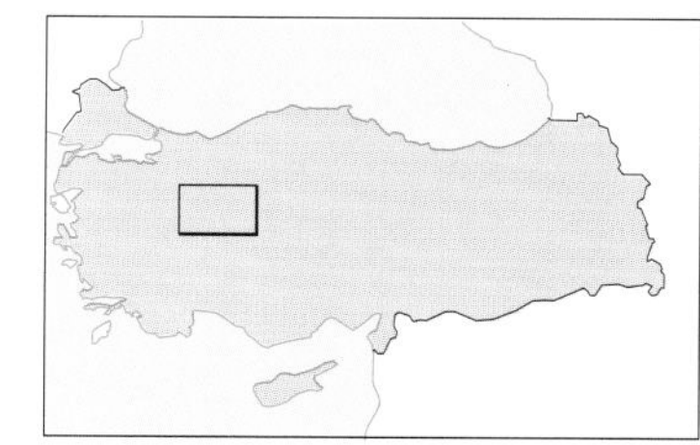

On dusty roads the route leads along Midas City and the enigmatic rock monuments north of Afyon. On the enormous façades of these sanctuaries striking geometrical motives have been hewn out. The adoration of the mother goddess *Kybele* was of central importance in the Phrygian cult.
Just north of the road Sivrihisar-Ankara archaeologists have excavated the ancient Phrygian capital of Gordium. Opposite the museum in Gordium lies king Midas's *tumulus* grave, built of cedar trunks.

Phrygia, hidden places of worship on the Plateau

Phrygia is a name that still rings a bell, although a vague one for most people, due to the proverbial 'Gordian knot'. In the ancient capital of Gordium the chariot of the founder of the city, king Gordias, was kept. The yoke was tied to the pole of the chariot with a very ingenious knot. According to tradition, supremacy over Asia would be given to the person who was able to untie the knot. In 333 B.C. Alexander the Great used his sword to cut the knot with a resoluteness typical of his character.
Phrygia is also renowned for king 'Midas with the donkey's ears', who was humiliatingly punished by the Greek god *Apollo* because he had judged, as a kind of jury-member, that the Phrygian *satyr Marsyas* made finer music than *Apollo* himself.
The Phrygians presumably penetrated into Anatolia from the Balkans around the year 1100 B.C. It is not until a few centuries later that they become archaeologically discernable, mainly through their grey pottery (bucchero) which was used as far as the west coast of Anatolia.

◂ The impressive façade of the Midas Monument in the full morning sun. The façade is sixteen metres high, more than sixteen metres in width and decorated with a characteristic Phrygian 'plaiting' pattern. The monument dates from the beginning of the seventh century B.C.

Thistles

As a result of the various climate zones and the divergent soil conditions in Turkey, hardy thistles can be found in a broad spectrum of growth forms.
In rocky places and uncultivated land the South-European globe thistle (Echinops ritro) is an eye-catching phenomenon. The spherical, small clear blue heads have a diameter of three to three-and-a-half centimetres. The flowering time of this prickly family member of the composites (Compositae) is from July until September.

▾ Globe thistle (Echinops ritro).

Phrygia extended over a great part of Anatolia. The capital Gordium was situated more or less in the middle, 120 kilometres south-west of Ankara. Some important Phrygian settlements are found further to the east, in the great curve of the ancient river Halys, today the Kızılırmak. Here lie e.g. Alisar – where beautiful pottery, decorated with stylized deer, from the eighth century B.C. has been found – and the earlier mentioned Boğazkale, the former capital of the Hittites. To the west especially the hilly country south of Eskişehir is of importance. In this region inscriptions in Phrygian have been found, a language spoken until well into the Roman era. Phrygian was an Indo-European language, related to Greek, Latin and the Germanic languages. The inscriptions, written in a well-preserved script, are, however, for the major part still incomprehensible. Before the end of the eighth century B.C., at the time of the historical king Midas, the Phrygians already used an alphabetical script, strongly resembling that of the Greeks, but containing some letters never used in Greece.

▲ *Museum of Anatolian Civilizations in Ankara: a bronze bucket from Gordium in the shape of a lion.*

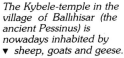

King Midas was married to a Greek woman from Cumae and sent votive offerings to sanctuaries in Greece. He was audacious enough to withstand the power of the Assyrians and was defeated around the year 710 B.C., after which he had to pay tribute. Under his rule the Phrygian Empire reached its height but somewhere around 690 B.C. the empire was overrun by the Cimmerians. The latter moved from the east, leaving a trail of devastation, through the whole of Anatolia. After the attack the Phrygians recuperated quickly. Still in that same seventh century B.C. they were beaten again, this time by the Lydians. In 546 B.C. another subjection followed, now by the Persians. These events did not destroy Phrygian culture; however, the influence of the Greeks did increase strongly from circa 600 B.C. In 333 B.C. Alexander the Great liberated the country from Persian rule.

The most interesting Phrygian remains are found in Gordium, the former capital of the empire, and in the West Phrygian Highlands south of Eskişehir. Near Gordium king Midas's *tumulus* can be visited. To the south-west of Gordium still lies the great *Kybele*sanctuary of Pessinus (Ballıhisar). In the Highlands the phenomenal Midas Monument and other splendid rock monuments are worth a visit.

The Kybele-temple in the village of Ballıhisar (the ancient Pessinus) is nowadays inhabited by ▼ *sheep, goats and geese.*

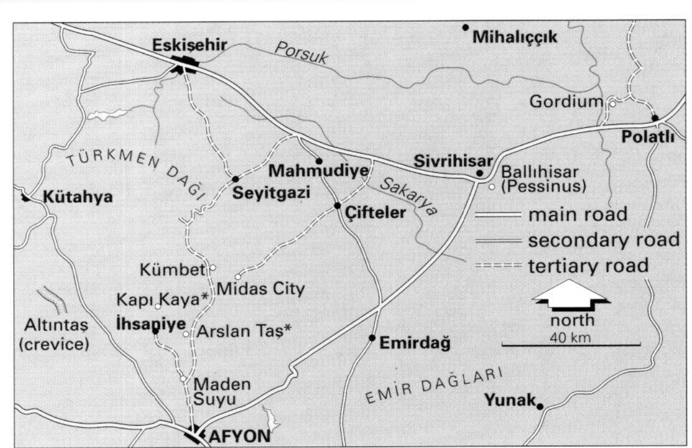

Gordium, a fortress among tumuli

Gordium (Gordion) is located on the vast and totally bare Anatolian Plateau, a plain that in ancient times used to be rich in forests. The city was established near the confluence of two important rivers, the Sakarya and the Porsuk (the ancient Sangarius and Tembris) along an age-old trading route cutting right through Anatolia. Gordium was actually more a majestically planned royal fortress than a city. This was the place where king Midas resided with his court, government and garrison. Apparently the ordinary people lived in the countryside, around the fortress. The city was originally built before 800 B.C., destroyed in circa 690 B.C., and from 546 B.C. magnificently rebuilt under Persian leadership. Shortly after 200 B.C. Gordium was almost completely deserted. American archaeologists have been conducting excavations in Gordium for many years. A monumental city gate with a heavy fortification and a number of large, palace-like houses have been exposed. Most of these remains originated in the time of king Midas or earlier.

The city gate is preserved up to a height of nine metres. When visiting the ruins of Gordium, the walls of this entrance are easily recognizable. The actual gate lies behind a passageway, flanked on both sides by high walls, measuring 23 metres in length and 9 metres in width. This corridor used to serve as a means of extra protection: assailants who penetrated into it in order to break down the gate, were trapped. On both sides, behind the walls, are large rooms which may have served as storage rooms or as barracks. Due to the different kinds of stone used, the building behind the gate is called the 'Polychrome House'. This building served as a gate at an earlier stage. At the time of the Persion domination the city gate was strenghthened and raised.

Right in the middle of the city hill was the 'palace', which consisted of separate houses. Cimmerians destroyed the whole block by burning it down. The 'palace' used to be enclosed by walls inside the fortress itself. The separate houses were designed in *megaron* form: elongated buildings with a shallow front porch and an entrance in the short wall. The large hall behind it contained a round fireplace. All *megara* had a thatched saddle roof. The walls were usually of half-timber: a framework of beams filled up with bricks of unfired clay.

In the so-called Megaron Two, a building with a width of almost ten metres, a floor mosaic has been uncovered of small red, white and blue stones. The pattern consists of geometrical motives. This pebble mosaic, the oldest ever found, now is on display in the

▲ *The floor mosaic with geometrical motives from Megaron Two, now in the garden of the modest museum of Gordium.*

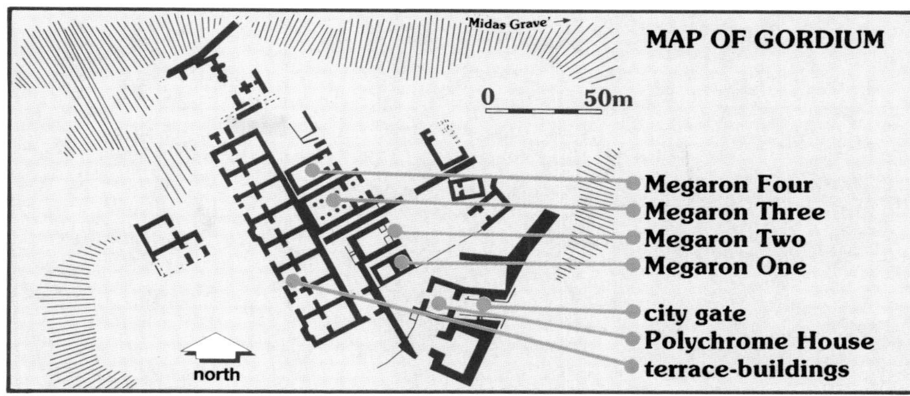

◄ *The well-preserved Phrygian entrance gate of ancient Gordium encloses a narrow passageway. From the towers and walls on both sides of the gate the defenders of the city could harass attackers. In the foreground are the remnants of the huge Persian city gate.*

local museum. The walls of Megaron Two were composed of poros-blocks. These were filled all over with incised, sometimes funny, images, the predecessors of our present graffiti: pictures of houses, birds, a lion and a plough. On top of the façade was an *akroterion* (ridge decoration) and two lion heads of limestone adorned the façade corners. The lion heads have meanwhile been removed to the museum of Ankara.

Somewhat to the north of Megaron Two is the most important building of the city, Megaron Three. It measures 18 by 30 metres. Along three sides of the building rows of wooden pillars were placed forming a gallery. Apparently, this gallery was used as a store-room for pottery and precious furniture. North of Megaron Three, on top of the hill, lay Megaron Four. This building, of a more recent date, may have been a temple.

Just behind these *megara*, with the rear walls towards them and the front portals to the west, are the remnants of a long row of rooms. These were the servants' quarters where, among other things, flour was ground between grinding stones and where ovens were heated. Every room was fourteen metres deep and provided with a round fireplace. The Phrygian city was burnt down by the Cimmerians in 690 B.C.

A smaller city hill to the south-east of the fortress dates from the Lydian period and was conquered by the Persians in 546 B.C. The twelve-metres high wall of clay bricks which has been dug up is full of Persian arrow heads. In a house from the Persian period remarkable fragments of East-Greek murals have been discovered. They date from 525 B.C.

East of the city are more than 80 large and smaller burial mounds, so-called *tumuli*. The oldest date from the eighth century B.C., others are of a much later date.

◄ *View of the excavation at Gordium. Left in the foreground are the terrace-buildings with, behind them, the megara. In the background the interior of the Phrygian gate.*

▲ *A colourful flowering thistle on the dusty Phrygian Plateau.*

These *tumuli* distinguish themselves from those in other regions in that their burial chambers are of wood and have no entrance; they were used for one burial only. The wooden tomb chambers under the *tumuli* were usually sunk halfway into the ground. After the deceased had been put into the grave together with the accompanying burial gifts, the roof was built over the chamber. Then a pile of stones was dumped over the wooden burial chamber and finally a large mound of damp clay and earth was raised over the entire structure. About thirty of these burial mounds have been investigated by archaeologists. Tumulus-P for example was the grave of a young prince of about four years old, who died around the year 700 B.C. In this grave, among other things, wooden toys and amusing ceramics in the shape of geese and the like were discovered. The largest *tumulus*, usually denoted as the 'Tomb of Midas', is open to the public. The mound nowadays measures a height of 53 metres and a diameter of 300 metres, but was once 70-80 metres high with a diameter of 250 metres. After the burial mound of Alyattes at Sardis (Chapter 5) this *tumulus* is the largest in Anatolia. In such immense burial mounds the chamber usually lay deep under the top, the safest place. In Gordium, American archaeologists located the exact spot by drilling down to the stone mound which covers the chamber. Then they dug a horizontal corridor from the edge of the *tumulus* with a length of 70 metres and as an extension of that corridor, a tunnel of 70 metres until they reached a stone enclosure. This wall protects the grave against the enormous lateral pressure of the mound.

The modern visitor still enters the *tumulus* through this corridor and tunnel, constructed by the archaeologists. The grave itself is built with thick, square beams. The inside has a length of six metres and a width of five and a half metres, the walls are more than three metres high. Along the outside of the chamber heavy round beams of cedar wood were piled up and jammed in a bed of stones and rubble between the outer stone wall and the grave chamber. At the same time a part of the clay mound was already raised around the outer walls of the grave. After king Midas had committed suicide (according to tradition) around 690 B.C., at the time of the invasion of the Cimmerians, he was placed into the grave together with a large number of burial gifts (without any gold and silver). A strong wooden saddle roof was constructed over the burial chamber. Then heavy round trunks were piled on the roof in both directions. On top of this a large stone mound was raised, which was finally covered with a tremendous pile of clay. This clay soon hardened and formed a vault taking away the pressure on the roof. This is the reason why the grave chamber is preserved; no grave robber has ever managed to get into it.

The deceased in the grave was a man measuring one metre and sixty centimetres. Among the burial gifts much bronze kitchenware was discovered, such as large basins with beautifully decorated handles. Some of these had been imported from Urartu. Then there were 150 *fibulae* (decorative pins) of brass and inlaid wooden furniture. All this illustrates the special status of the deceased. It is not certain if it was king Midas himself who was buried here; it could also be the grave of his predecessor, king Gordias. The many grave goods of excellent quality can nowadays be admired in the museums of Ankara and Antalya.

Out of the landscape rises the artificial hill of the 'Midas Grave'. The burial chamber in this enormous tumulus is still intact and open to the public. ▼

RECONSTRUCTION DRAWING OF THE 'MIDAS GRAVE'

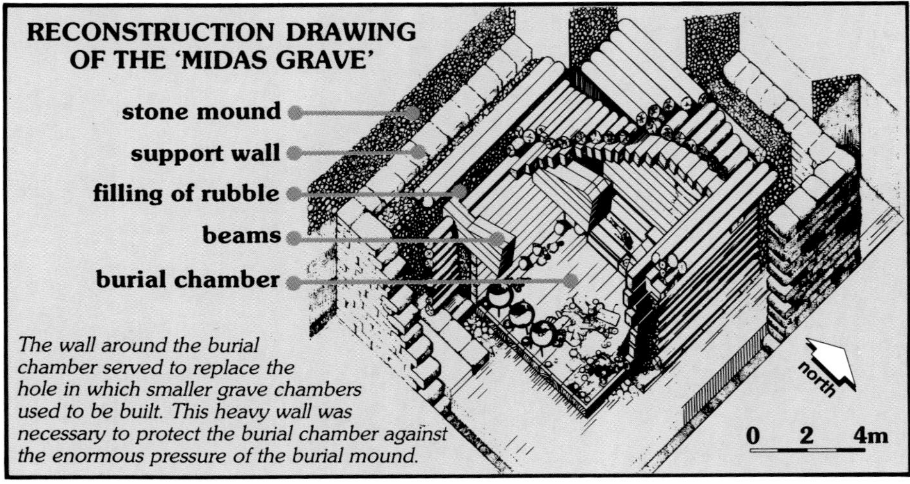

The wall around the burial chamber served to replace the hole in which smaller grave chambers used to be built. This heavy wall was necessary to protect the burial chamber against the enormous pressure of the burial mound.

Mysterious monuments

Some hundred kilometres to the west of Gordium, between Eskişehir and Afyon, lies the Türkmen Baba. This comparatively small tuff mountain range is not easily accessible, but very interesting. Rock erosion has produced peculiar landscape shapes in this region: steep rock walls and almost inaccessible plateaus which were used as fortresses by the Phrygians and later inhabitants. In the Phrygian period many religious monuments were hewn out of these rocks. Innumerable graves from various periods and dwelling caves, monasteries and churches from the Byzantine period are found here as well. As travelling facilities in Turkey have improved considerably in recent years, it has now become more easy to visit a number of monuments in this fascinating Phrygian region.

The archaeologists welcome the tourists and kindly request ▼ *them not to walk on the excavation site.*

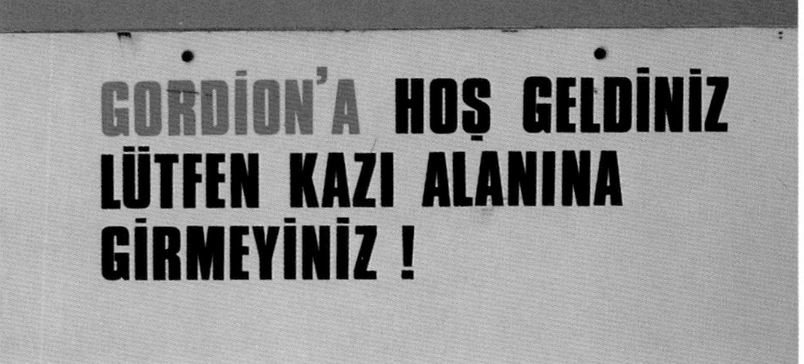

GORDİON'A HOŞ GELDİNİZ
LÜTFEN KAZI ALANINA
GİRMEYİNİZ !

Midas City

In a steep rock wall of an ancient Phrygian city plateau, the so-called Midas City, a huge façade has been hewn out in shallow relief: the Midas Monument. Here the rock wall is twenty metres high; the actual monument is sixteen metres high, more than sixteen metres in width and decorated with regular geometric motives. 'Were there nothing else in Phrygia, this rock would be worth the journey', wrote the famous British archaeologist Ramsay in 1882.
The façade owes its name to an enormous inscription above it, in which the words Midai Wanaktei ('for the ruler Midas') occur. Just like other rock façades in Phrygia this façade is the representation of the front side of a *Kybele* temple. These temples were presumably built with the half-timber technique, in more or less the same fashion as some of the *megara* in Gordium. *Kybele* was the great goddess of the Phrygians, mother of nature and mistress of wild animals. Through the 'door' of the rock monuments one can often see her standing there, sometimes between her lions. However, in the façade of the Midas Monument, a separate statue of wood or stone was placed. The cavity in which this statue was secured is still visible in the lintel of the fake door.
The splendid pattern of the Midas Monument is obviously inspired by plaiting of broad bands and is also reminiscent of the ingenious half-timber found in *megaron* façades. The basic motive is over and over again repeated: it can be seen on either side of the large 'door opening'. This motive consists of four squares with a dot in the middle, which are grouped around a central square.
The letters of the inscription in the Midas Monument are exactly like those found on a bronze bowl from the *tumulus* of king Midas in Gordium. Moreover, the geometrical motive of the façade is also found on an inlaid wooden screen from Tumulus-P of the young prince. On the basis of these similarities, the Midas Monument has to be dated around the year 700 B.C. It is surprising that many archaeologists erroneously date the monument one hundred years later.
A walk around the plateau of Midas City leads past numerous altars, rock façades, reliefs and grave tombs. The quiet stillness of the scenery and the magnificent views across the jagged Phrygian rock masses make this visit an unforgettable experience.

RECONSTRUCTION DRAWING

The rear of the wooden throne in Tumulus-P

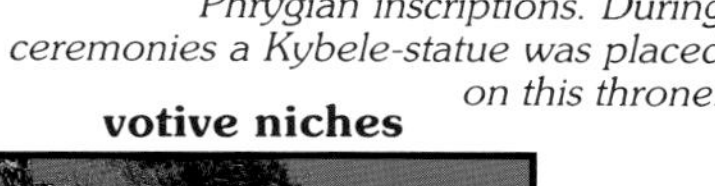

Stepped-altar with, on the left side, Phrygian inscriptions. During ceremonies a Kybele-statue was placed on this throne. ►

throne with inscriptions

Küçük Yazılıkaya

◄ *View across the rock plateau of van Midas City with in the centre of the photograph the façade of Küçük Yazılıkaya (The Unfinished). The width of the façade is nine metres and eighty centimetres and the monument should presumably have been fourteen metres high in its finished form.*

votive niches

Reliefs, votive niches and caves in the mossy rock wall around Midas Town. ▲

altar

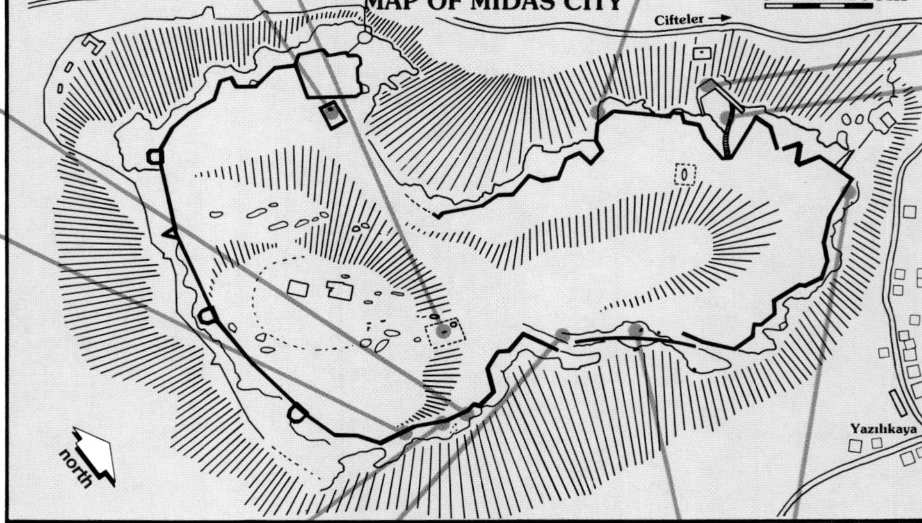

defensive wall

underground stairs

Neo-Hittite reliefs

altar

▲ *Jagged tuff rock formations surround a hill with façades, graves and caves from various periods.*

The Hyacinth Monument is heavily damaged; it is remarkable for its representation of a hyacinth-like flower in the akroterion. In the bottom of the niche a large cavity was hewn out for the pedestal of a Kybele-statue. ►

Hyacinth Monument

Midas Monument

◄ *Along the upper edge of the Midas Monument a Phrygian inscription is carved with the name 'MIDAI'.*

▲ *Dust clouds surround the large flocks which the shepherds lead across the vast plateau.*

Sheep and goats

All over Turkey flocks of sheep and goats trudge along fields and roads. Overgrazing with flocks that are too large and that eat anything that is green, root and all, has led to serious soil erosion in arid regions.
Sheep and goats were domesticated at an early date. Already in the year 9000 B.C. domestic sheep were kept in Anatolia. In the south and east the fat-tail sheep dominates. Both short and long tailed species are found. The fat accumulations serve as reserves for lean times. The historian Herodotus (fifth century B.C.) mentions specimens with such long tails that a cart was fastened behind them to carry their tails. In that way the tail could not be damaged while being dragged along the ground.
It is likely that the goat was introduced in Asia Minor around 700 B.C. A goat can yield three pounds of wool annually if sheared twice a year. The wide-spread angora race belongs to the twisted-horned goat. The famous fine-threaded angora wool is called mohair in the wool trade.
At regular intervals colourful and vivid cattle-markets are held in the villages and towns in the countryside. Depending on species and weight a sheep costs 60 to 100 US $.
Sheep, goats and cows are the pivot of agricultural Turkish society. Agriculture and cattle breeding supply over 28 percent of the total national income and provide a means of livelihood for more than 60 percent of the working population.

▲ *A shepherd clad in a sheepskin coat on the Anatolian Plateau.*

▲ *Sheep's milk is processed into fêta (cheese) and ayran (Turkish buttermilk).*

The tasty fêta ▶ *of the sheep and goats is wrapped in hides. One kilogram of this sort costs 2000 Turkish Lira.*

◀ *This sheep proudly shows off his impressive twisted horns.*

Fascinating rock sculptures

From Midas City an unpaved track leads to the by-road between Eskişehir and Afyon on the other side of the intervening mountain range. Along the route lies the village of Kümbet with monuments worth visiting, such as the Roman Lions' Tomb and a small plateau (Asar Kale) with a stepped-altar and a large subterranean staircase. Kümbet also has a *türbe* (grave monument) from the period of the Seljuks. In this *türbe* remarkable *spolia* from the Byzantine period are incorporated.
Back on the road to Afyon, the next turn leads to the Arslan Taş, the Yılanlı Taş and the Mal Taş. The winding track leading past the three monuments is extremely dusty in summer and the best way to follow it is on foot or on horseback.
The Arslan Taş (Lions' Rock) is a very imposing monument indeed. In an eleven-metres high cube a square burial chamber has been hewn out. The grave is 'guarded' by two huge roaring lionesses which are carved in relatively high relief. Their front paws rest on the small entrance to the grave. The style of the lionesses is very similar to that of the animals in the *tumulus* of the young prince in Gordium. This leads to the conclusion that the Arslan Taş has to be dated around 700 B.C. It is probably one of the oldest monuments in the whole Phrygian region. By the way, this grave too is often erroneously dated much too late.
Some hundred metres further on lies a gigantic overturned lion. This relief used to be part of the Yılanlı Taş (Snakes' Rock or The Broken Lions Tomb), a large grave from the Persian period. From crown to shoulder the head measures more than two-and-a-half metres. The farmers from the neighbouring region called this tomb the Snakes' Rock because they mistook the two lions paws, which used to be visible on one of the fragments, for snake heads.
Another kilometre further on, alongside the bumpy goats' track, lies the Mal Taş (Money Rock). This monument is partly hidden by sand, only the top of the

Arslan Taş. Two huge roaring lionesses face each other with their paws on the frame of the small entrance. The cubs under their ▼ front paws have been heavily damaged by treasure hunters.

▲ The Yılanlı Taş (Broken Lions' Grave or Snakes' Rock) has collapsed into huge fragments. On this fragment, but buried in the ground, are reliefs of a warrior and a Medusa who guarded the entrance to the grave. The Allard Pierson Museum in Amsterdam possesses casts of these reliefs.

Hoca

In 1208 Nasreddin Hoca was born in Hortu, a small village four kilometres outside Sivrihisar. His father was the local *imam*. Hoca also received lessons to become an *imam*, first in Sivrihisar and later in the *medresse* of Konya. After the death of his father Hoca left for Akşehir. He had in the meantime received a good education and became a teacher himself in the *medresses*. Hoca proved to be a philosophical genius and his profound prudence and anecdotes were renowned. His style is unique and brings the truth home to his audience in a humoristic fashion.
Hoca died in Akşehir. The Seljuks built him a grave that became dilapidated during the Ottoman period. Sultan Abdülhamid III rebuilt the grave in 1905. The three doors of the tomb are open, but one of them has a lock. This reflects Hoca's philosophy and humour in essence. His miraculous tales and contemplative anecdotes are still recounted in Turkey and make people laugh and think at the same time.

One day a couple of priests tried to tease Hoca and asked him: 'How did your prophet Mohammed rise up to Heaven?' Hoca reacted by saying: 'The answer to that question is very simple. My prophet climbed into Heaven via the ladder your prophet Jesus had left behind.'

Nasreddin Hoca and his ► donkey travel through Turkish fairy-land. Out of respect for this philosopher the inhabitants of his birth region have placed him face forward and proud on his donkey, and not backwards as in other regions of Turkey.

▲ *The colossal Arslan Kaya (Lions' rock) rises ghostly out of the surrounding landscape. In the deep niche Kybele stands between two enormous lions. This unique sculpture embodies the primeval power of nature. There is a relief of two sphinxes in the pediment.*

Kybele

Kybele is the great goddess of nature and as such part of a longstanding Anatolian tradition. She was also called the Ruler of Wild Animals. For that reason she is often flanked by two lions. *Kybele* is the heiress of a series of Anatolian fertility goddesses. In the Neolithicum the inhabitants of Çatal Höyük and Hacılar already worshipped a nature goddess indeed with very pronounced sexual characteristics, yet also accompanied by lions.
From Phrygia the *Kybele* cult spread all over the Greek-Roman world. As a guardian she was also often portrayed as a city goddess. In that function she used to wear a high crown in the shape of a city wall. *Kybele* was honoured as a mother goddess from the Hellenistic period onwards in ecstatic and orgiastic cults. The worship service was characterized by elated dancing and invigorating music of flutes, castanets and tambourines.

The façade of the Mal Taş bears some old Phrygian inscriptions and is decorated with a geometric-pattern. The site in front of the monument has silted up, only the upper part of the almost ten metres high façade is ▼ *now visible.*

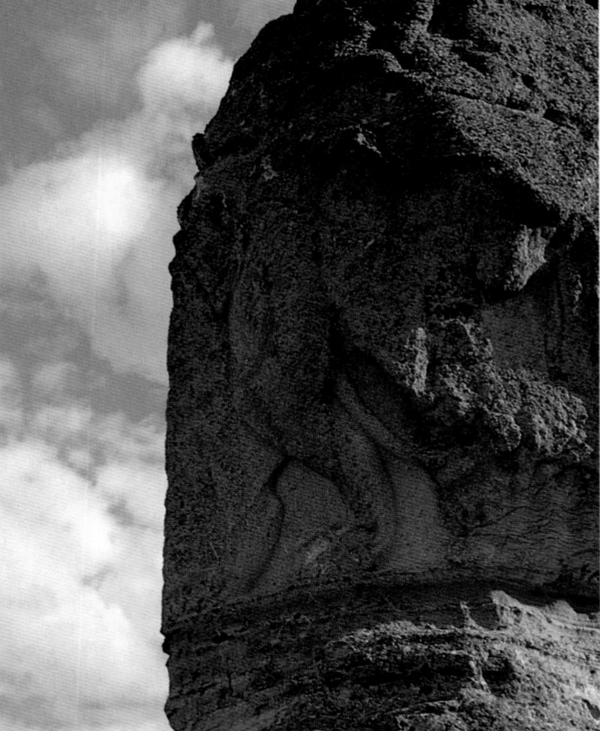

▲ *Detail of the right side of the Arslan Kaya. A seven metres high lion is standing on its hind legs, its front paws resting against the façade.*

façade being visible. Again the pattern consists of bands arranged in regular squares that are repeated time and again.
From İhsaniye an initially passable road leads into the Phrygian mountain region, in the direction of the Arslan Kaya (Lions' Rock). Just before this destination, a village with a beautiful *karavanserai* (trading posts for caravans) from the Seljuk period is passed. After another three kilometres along a rough cart track, the Arslan Kaya is reached. Of all rock façades this is the most amazing one: the rock resembles an enormous petrified wave in the completely deforested landscape. The goddess *Kybele* and her awe-inspiring lions are carved in relief in the rock wall of the deeply hewn out door-opening. On the side of the rock a hefty upright lion is depicted, resting its paws on the right corner of the façade.
Finally, there is the Büyük Kapı Kaya (Great Door Rock), which is situated in so isolated a position that it is hard to find. This monument can only be reached by means of landrover or on foot. The Büyük Kapı Kaya, like the nearby Arslan Kaya, is hewn out of a single outcrop of rock. Both date from the sixth century B.C. This does not only appear from the simpler geometrical patterns, but also from the *sphinxes* which are clearly inspired by Greek art in the *pediment* of the Arslan Kaya. In the Büyük Kapı Kaya not much has been preserved of the sculpture of the goddess. Treasure hunters used to smash such sculptures in search of the gold that, according to their firm conviction, had been hidden in it by magic. Both lions, on the right and on the left, have disappeared. In this case they were not hewn out of the rock, but made separately and fastened with bronze pins.
The road ends in the middle of the desolate beauty of the Phrygian Plateau and so does this journey. The tired traveller has no choice but to retrace his footsteps, back to modern society.

The friendly Phrygian population are always willing to show ▶ *travellers the way to remote monuments.*

4 a Resting-place among the Rocks

Seafarers of olden times built impressive ports and left a magnificent grave culture in the rough landscape. Rock graves and sarcophagi are distinctive features for Lycia and Caria, regions where everyone, including today's visitor, can find peace and quiet. The panorama is dominated by steep mountains and fishing villages in secluded bays.

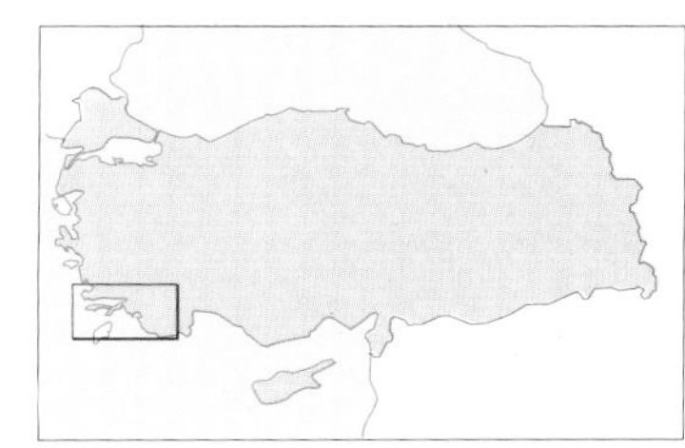

In the port of Bodrum lie the humble remains of what was once one of the seven Wonders of the Ancient World: the Mausoleum of Halicarnassus. From Bodrum a fairly decent coastal road runs in the direction of Antalya. Along that route lie, among others, Fethiye, Xanthus and Kaş. In Myra, the present-day Demre, the bishop's church, the Lycian graves and the Roman theatre are visited. With some difficulty more remote places like Caunus, Cnidus and Pınara can also be reached.

Lycia and Caria, two seafaring nations

The Turkish south and west coasts have always been important for trade in the Mediterranean due to the many natural ports. It is precisely because of that trade that Lycia and Caria belonged to the prominent cultural regions in the second millennium B.C. This can be proved from shipwrecks that have been found along the Turkish coast. The merchandise of such a ship that was discovered near Cape Gelidonya, east of Finike, consisted of, among other things, ingots of copper. This raw material was used to produce bronze tools. The copper had presumably been exported from Phoenician or Palestinian ports. Historians from ancient times mention the Phoenicians as the first colonists of this region. The influence of Phoenician sailors and colonists is still noticeable in place names like Finike, the old Phoinikos.

The interior of Lycia and Caria is extremely mountainous and woody. The cedars from Lycia were much loved in ancient days; the mountains provided beautiful varieties of marble. Agriculture was only possible in the few hilly areas, in the valleys of the lower reaches of rivers and along the coast. Population was mainly concentrated on the coastal area, where large cities arose and where goods were traded. The coastal strip, by the way, was notorious for its many pirates' haunts. Piracy was one of the more profitable practices in providing a livelihood. Often pirate captains filled the power vacuum that was left behind by the great powers. A certain Zenekites occupied a large part of Lycia in the turbulent last century B.C. His empire was quickly terminated, because Rome did not tolerate such infringement on power. Apparently the situation had involved more than just a series of raids by a crafty pirate, for a number of Lycian cities were heavily punished by Rome for having aided Zenekites.

The Lycians and the Carians were skilful sailors and had a good eye for the possibilities offered by trade. The long sea-routes from the eastern Mediterranean to the Aegean Sea required a lot of ports. Of many cities

One of the many sarcophagi in the Lycian landscape. From the imitation of the roof-beams it appears that the wooden construction of a house was copied. ▼

◄ *Caunus, grave monuments from the fourth century B.C. in a décor of beautiful water.*

it is therefore known that harbour works were carried out in order to improve natural conditions. Sometimes even complete cities and artificial harbours were built in places that appeared to be a favourable stop-over on the sea-route. That is how on the peninsula of Reşadiye in Caria the settlement New-Cnidus (the modern Tekir) arose, 30 kilometres west of Old-Cnidus (presumably the present Datça). In ancient days Halicarnassus (Bodrum) possessed a secret port, hewn out of the rocks, which served as a naval base.

Diving into the past

During the recent decades many traces have been discovered of a rich maritime history in the waters along the Turkish coast. Initially mainly American archaeologists, but recently also Turkish scientists, have contributed to the underwater investigations. In the field of underwater archaeology Turkey is quite interesting, for the country has always been located on a junction of significant trading routes.

As early as the Late Bronze Age (1600-1200 B.C.) the ports along the coast were called at by numerous ships. From that period date the two oldest ships ever to have been discovered under water. In 1960 American investigators discovered a ship that had presumably sunk circa 1200 B.C. near Cape Gelidonya. The wreck itself had not been preserved, but a large part of the cargo had. This cargo varied from copper ingots, used among other things as means of payment, to the tools of a travelling blacksmith.

Dr. George Bass, who was in charge of this expedition, argued that the home port of this ship was somewhere in Syria or Palestine. This opinion was criticized by scientists who believed that, in those days, east-west sea routes did not prevail, but a goods-flow in the opposite direction. However, in 1983 George Bass discovered a second wreck from the Bronze Age at Ulu Burun, not far from Gelidonya, this time a specimen from the fourteenth century B.C. Of this wreck also only the cargo had been preserved, but this time very differentiated: copper ingots, glass, Syrian-Palestine vases, man-sized *pithoi* and some gold and silver objects. The contents of the ship give a good picture of the trade from that period and confirm George Bass's theory. If everything goes as planned, the excavation will have been finished in 1992.

The island Yassi Ada (near Bodrum) was the centre of archaeological underwater investigation from 1960 until 1980. At the bottom of a dangerous cliff lay the remains of a great number of wrecks from various periods, two of which have been examined closely; one from the third and one from the seventh century A.D. Both wrecks had a cargo of amphoras, the means of packing for wine and olive oil pre-eminently used in the Roman and Byzantine period. During long archaeological expeditions – the wrecks lay at a depth of more than 50 metres – the cargo was surfaced and the ships were meticulously measured.

At Serçe Limani a wreck was discovered from the eleventh century, a time when South Turkey was in Arabic hands. The ship, which had been discovered at a depth of 35 metres, was mainly loaded with glass. This glass had not survived the blow of the shipwreck and had been broken to pieces. Since there were also weapons on board the ship, the excavators suspect that sea routes in those days were far from safe.

Less spectacular, but just as important, is the harbour investigation along the west coast of Turkey where in classical antiquity various Greek city-states were located. By studying the seabed the location of many ports in ancient times has become clear.

Power struggle in Lycia

The origin of the Lycians is not quite clear. In the eighth century B.C. they came from Crete, and, possibly via Caria, ended up in the region now called Lycia. Lycia is located between the Mediterranean and the line Antalya-Fethiye. The colonists adopted the native language, but kept using the Greek alphabet. Inscriptions in this language, written in Greek letters, can be found in several places in Lycia, especially on graves. In the middle of the sixth century B.C. Harpagos, a general of the Persian king Cyrus, conquered a number of important Lycian city-states. Some cities offered severe resistance to this foreign rule.

The fifth century B.C. was characterized by a power struggle between the Greeks and the Persians. After their defeat against the Greeks, under the command of Athens, the Persians vacated West-Anatolia at the beginning of the fifth century B.C. Archaeological finds from this period reveal an increase in Greek influence. On the basis of their supremacy at sea, the Athenians established an empire in the Aegean region, the Delian-Attic League. Many cities on the coast took part more or less involuntarily. They had to pay tribute and provide harbour facilities. In Lycia this Sea League was less prominent than in Caria. After the Spartans had broken the power of the Athenians in the fifth century B.C., many cities in Lycia again fell under Persian influence.

Lycia was still under Persian rule, when in the first half of the fourth century B.C., at the initiative of Pericles of Lımyra (the present-day Zengerler), the inhabitants united against the Lydians, who wanted to annex Lycia as part of their empire. This initiative is often considered to be the start of the Lycian City League, which would play such an important role in the Lycian unification in the second century B.C.

The Persians reacted by appointing local rulers, *satraps*, who were directly responsible to the Persian king. At Alexander the Great's arrival in 334 B.C., they were permanently expelled and a lot of changes came about for Lycia. Both politically and culturally Lycia was Hellenized. The Lycian language became obsolete and consequently, only inscriptions in Greek have survived from that period on buildings and graves.

The federal governmental system came to its full development. The largest city, Xanthos, became the administrative centre. The Letoon, only some kilometres from and belonging to the City State of Xanthos (Xanthus), served as the religious centre. Within the League the cities had either three votes, two votes or one vote in the federal government, depending on their importance. The six major cities, Xanthos, Tlos, Patara, Pınara, Myra and Olympos each had three votes.

In the period after Alexander's death, Anatolia fell under the authority of the heirs of his empire. The Egyptian Ptolemaeans and the Syrian Seleucids tried to establish power in the region. Around 200 B.C., when the power of these big empires decreased, smaller monarchies such as Macedonia, Pergamum and Rhodes tried the same in their wake. All these attempts were futile due to the great Roman victory over the Seleucid king Antiochus III in the battle at Magnesia in 190 B.C. This victory provided Rome with supremacy in Asia Minor and the Seleucids were forced to accept peace; Lycia was assigned to Rhodes. Yet Lycian national self-

awareness was so strong that the Lycians resisted incorporation into this foreign nation.
In 167 B.C. the protests were successful and Lycia was declared independent by Rome. When in 129 B.C. the Roman province of Asia Minor was founded, the major part of Western Turkey belonged to it, but Lycia remained independent and retained its autonomy.
Roman government was malfunctioning and was characterized by exploitation and corruption. Roman governors considered the areas appointed to them as conquered territory. Even Lycia suffered from this. In the first century B.C. Cassius and Brutus, Caesar's murderers, used the provinces to obtain income in order to form an army. The obstinate Xanthus was occupied by Brutus and he destroyed the Lycian *acropolis*.
In these turbulent times, short periods of occupation by foreign nations alternated with attacks by pirates. This chaos ended when in 43 A.D., under emperor Claudius, Lycia was turned into a province and central government of the Roman Empire improved. For all Roman provinces, including Lycia, a period of economic bloom started.
The period of decline began in the course of the second and third century A.D., after a series of earthquakes and renewed pirate attacks had weakened the region economically. In the next centuries Lycia became part of the Christian world. The many Byzantine churches and monasteries bear witness to this.

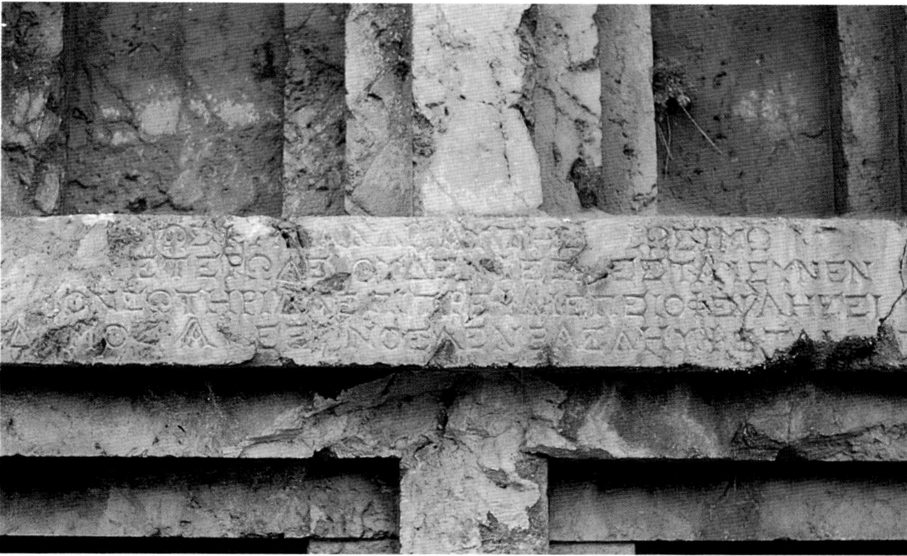

Greek inscription on the ▲ doorpost of a Lycian grave in the rock necropolis of Tlos.

Myra (the present Demre) e.g. was an important early Christian centre. From the seventh century onwards, advancing Islam put an end to this development.

Capers

The thorny caper bush (Capparis spinosa) can be found in the entire mediterranean region. The white or pale-pink flowers with a diameter of five to seven centimetres have lovely violet filaments.
The well-known capers are the still closed olive-green flower buds, which are pickled in vinegar, salt or wine giving them a 'non perishable' quality.
In antiquity the Greeks and Romans knew this appetizer and in the Middle Ages capers were used by herb doctors to stimulate the desire for
Capers have a savoury, somewhat bitter taste and are much loved in Southern European countries. They taste delicious in white sauces, salads and in fish and meat dishes.

Rock graves in the cliffs

Grave architecture is the most characteristic object of interest of Lycian culture. Together with the magnificent mountainous surroundings, the numerous Lycian graves form a fascinating spectacle. Fortunately mass tourism has – not yet – discovered this region, so Lycia can still be explored in peace and quiet.

Public transport in Turkey is well-organized and also easily accessible for tourists. Yet it is convenient to have a car at one's disposal in these regions. In that way remote villages like Üzümlü, Hoyran and Cyaneae can also be reached. The quality of the roads is reasonable, although now and then a little rough country has to be taken in one's stride. The beauty of the unspoilt scenery however makes up for all efforts.

In Lycia various grave types can be observed. For important people pillar graves were erected. These were separate pillars, hewn out of one piece of stone. The burial chamber was hewn out in the top of the pillar and covered with a stone. A number of graves have been provided with inscriptions and sculptured reliefs. It is assumed that there were once sculptures on top of some of the pillar graves. From the inscriptions it appears that the pillars were not just memorials for the dead, but also monuments to commemorate the feats and victories of for example a city-monarch.

About 40 pillar graves have been preserved in more or less original condition. In Xanthus alone there are six specimens. The oldest preserved pillar grave dates from the first half of the sixth century B.C., most pillars however originate from the fifth and the fourth century B.C.

Another, very typical grave form is the grave house. This was a grave in the shape of a house with one room, which was hewn out of the rocks, façade and all, sometimes even detached with walls and a roof, high above the ground. The façade, sometimes crowned by a *tympanum*, is divided into panels which are deepened out. These panels were probably meant to serve as niches to place statuettes or offerings. The burial chamber itself was provided with one or two benches on which to lay the deceased. Some graves were decorated with reliefs and inscriptions. Often the text contains a short dedication and the name of the deceased. A striking feature is that the graves are located together, high in the rock wall, in a kind of dovecote-formation. Most grave houses date from the fifth and the fourth century B.C. A variation on this type of grave, often of a somewhat later date, is the grave temple, which has a façade executed in the shape of a temple front. This façade was hewn out of the rocks as a whole, including pillars and a *tympanum*.

Sarcophagi are of a special type in Lycia. They are in fact coffins placed on a dais crowned by a *tympanum* in the shape of a pointed arch. This *tympanum* is usually divided into four panels which gives the appearance of a cross if seen from a distance. This, of course, is in no way related to Christianity, for these sarcophagi are of a much older date. They can still be found in the fields outside villages and anywhere in a street or among houses.

◄ *Pınara, in this steep rock wall with a height of more than 300 metres hundreds of burial chambers were hewn out.*

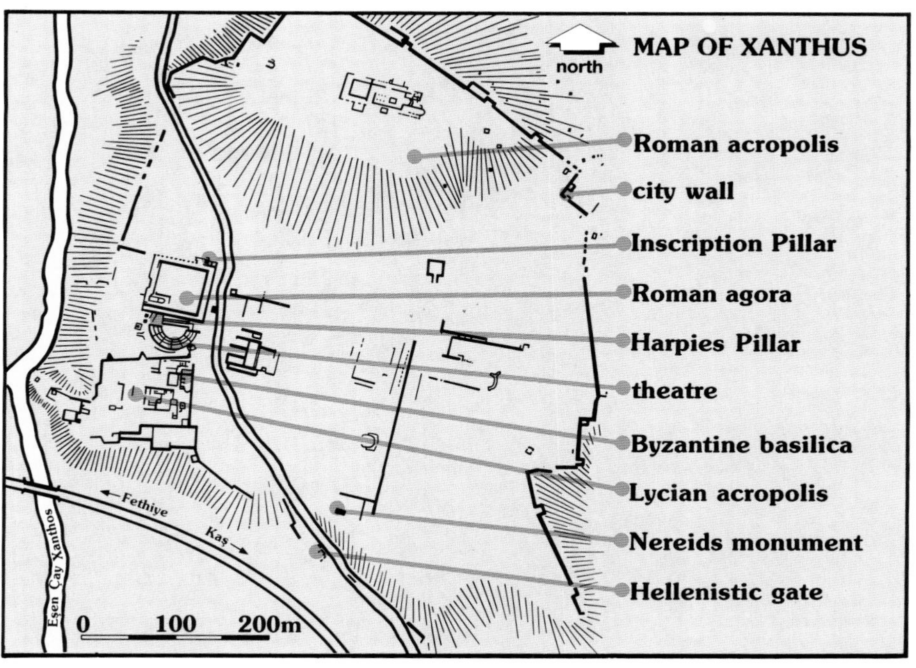

A unique combination of cultures

Xanthus, the modern Kınık, was the largest city in old Lycia and the governmental and religious centre of the City League. The city is worth visiting for its ruins dating from the seventh century B.C. until into the Byzantine period. The city wall encloses an area which has a Lycian and a Roman *acropolis*. The Lycian fortress, in the south-west of the city, is strategically located on a cliff overlooking the river. The earliest period of this *acropolis* ended in the year 545 B.C. with the siege by the Persian general Harpagos.

The historian Herodotus, from Halicarnassus, recounts in the fifth century B.C. how the inhabitants of Xanthus went to face the Persian army and fought a battle. With great losses they were forced back into the city, where they then locked up their wives, children and slaves in the citadel, finally setting it alight. The men themselves perished in a desperate sortie. According to Herodotus, the Xantians of his day descended from some families who had been absent at the time of the siege and had therefore survived.

On the *acropolis* the remnants of some monumental buildings dating from the subsequent classical Lycian period have been excavated, among others a temple for the Lycian *Artemis* and the assumed palace of the local monarch Kheros from the fifth century B.C. Owing to the fact that this period also ended in destruction by fire, the layout of the buildings is hard to recognize. Moreover, the Byzantines used the ruins of the Lycian buildings as a quarry for the fortification of their own stronghold. From the upper rows of the Roman theatre a jumble of small walls and other unrecognizable building fragments can be seen.

The classical period in Xanthus is especially known for its pillar graves, which can be found scattered in the city area among Hellenistic and Roman remains. A particularly interesting monument is the 'Inscription Pillar', a four metres high square column with the oldest known inscription in the Lycian language. The pillar dates from the end of the fifth century B.C. and is the grave monument for the local ruler Kheros, to which the above-mentioned palace on the *acropolis* is also

At an enormous speed ▲ *Lycia and Caria are opened up to tourism. Archaeologists busy working in the Lycian city Arykanda, have placed a sign themselves welcoming visitors.*

The Phlomis fruticosa is found on dry sunny slopes in the entire mediterranean region, but is quite a rare phenomenon in Turkey. ▼

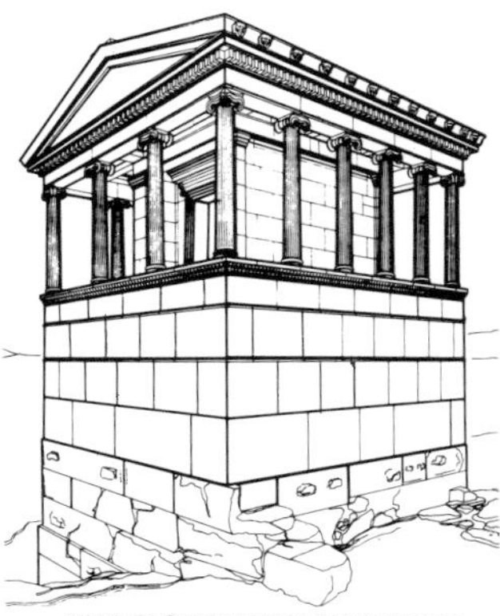

RECONSTRUCTION DRAWING OF THE NEREIDS MONUMENT

A visit to the ▸ British Museum in London is necessary in order to admire the Nereids monument from Xanthus.

attributed. In the nineteenth century the reliefs decorating the outside of the burial chamber of Kheros were taken to London by the British 'researcher' Charles Fellows. Nowadays they are on display in the British Museum. Other fragments of the sculpture are in the Archaeological Museum in İstanbul.

At the edge of the theatre of Xanthus stands the almost nine metres high 'Harpies Pillar', named after a scene with *sirens* – woman-birds – who were supposed to have accompanied the souls of the dead to the hereafter. The originals of these reliefs are also in the British Museum, the specimens on the site are casts. Another grave monument shows the exceptional combination of a pillar crowned with a sarcophagus, having a lid in the shape of a pointed arch.

In the south of the city, immediately above Vespasian's arch and the Hellenistic gate which formed the entrance from the Letoon, was the *Nereids* monument. Most of the reliefs and the sculptures of this building have ended up in the British Museum too. Several architectural fragments at the excavation site and in the excavation depot have made it possible to reconstruct the monument, despite the fact that at the original site only remnants of the socle are left. The *Nereids* monument served as a grave for a royal couple living at the end of the fifth century B.C. The reconstruction reveals to what extent the Lycian artistic idiom of that period had already become the product of a mixed culture. Architecturally the building does fit into the Lycian tradition of burial chambers on high socles, but as far as the finishing and the style of the sculpture are concerned it is completely Greek. The grave building on the socle had the shape of an Ionic temple. In between the pillars were statues of the *Nereids* giving the monument its name. The *Nereids* were daughters of the sea-god Nereus who protected the deceased on the journey to the hereafter. The other reliefs and sculptures show fighting, hunting, and sacrificial scenes as well as the royal couple with their court.

A striking sight is the Roman theatre of Xanthus, which was built against the north slope of the Lycian *acropolis*. The theatre was constructed at the site of a Lycian *necropolis*, which was therefore lost for the main part. Some monuments however were already considered worth preserving in ancient days, among others the 'Harpies Pillar', blocking the west exit of the theatre. The Roman theatre in its turn suffered under later building activities. The upper rows were demolished by the Byzantines and used for the strengthening of their fortress.

The Romans were impressed by the Lycian grave architecture and therefore maintained some of the graves of the Lycian necropolis during the building of the theatre. The enormous weight of the graves made the construction of an entry on the west side impossible. For the sake of symmetry the theatre was provided ▾ with a fake entry.

In the Roman period a new *acropolis* arose on a high hill in the north of the city area. These buildings fell victim to Byzantine construction zeal as well. The large monastery on this *acropolis* for example, is located on the place where there used to be a Roman temple.

A sanctuary full of frogs and terrapins

The Letoon lies four kilometres north of Xanthus and in ancient days belonged to the territory of this city. The religious centre of the Lycian City League was located in the Letoon. The temples were dedicated to gods and goddesses who were worshipped by the entire federation during annual festivals. There are indications that water rituals played an important part in Lycian services of worship. The *nymphaeum*, a building constructed over a natural spring, with altars dedicated to the Lycian national goddess *Leto*, her children the twins *Apollo* and *Artemis* and the *nymphs*, had a prominent place in the Letoon. An inscription from 131 A.D. was found in the building, written by Claudius Marcianus, the high priest of Lycia. In the Doric *stoa* (colonnaded gallery) from that same period facilities were discovered for water rituals, like leaden water pipes and stone basins.
Nowadays the Letoon is the domain of frogs and terrapins. In the museum of Fethiye many architectural fragments of the *nymphaeum* and the *stoa* can be seen, as well as Roman sculptures and inscriptions in the Lycian and Greek language.

▲ *Frogs, toads and terrapins nowadays inhabit the sanctuaries of the Letoon.*

The goddess Leto

The goddess *Leto* was made pregnant with the twins *Apollo* and *Artemis* by her lover *Zeus*. Because *Zeus* preferred *Leto*, *Hera* was jealous. She decided to prevent the birth by banning her competitor to earth. On earth *Leto* was forced to lead a wandering existence, because everybody refused her lodgings. Whoever showed pity was punished by *Hera*. Tormented by acute thirst, *Leto* one day arrived at a small lake in Lycia. At *Hera*'s instigation the farmers, busy mowing there, jumped into the water. They turned up the bottom of the lake so heavily, that the water became too muddy to drink. *Leto* begged *Zeus* to punish the men. There-upon *Zeus* changed the men into green frogs who were forced to live on in swampy lakes. Finally *Leto* arrived at the island Delos where she gave birth to the twins. After the delivery *Hera* kept harassing her rival. However, with the help of her two children *Leto* managed to survive.

Foundations of the temples in the Letoon. These three sanctuaries were dedicated to Leto and
▼ *her children, the twins Apollo and Artemis.*

The picturesque odeion of the, undeservedly, scarcely visited Arykanda. ▲

Fethiye, Tlos and Pınara

Many Lycian cities have remnants bearing witness to the glorious past of the region. The often very extensive *necropolises* have been especially well-preserved. They were after all far less in danger of being used for building activities of later inhabitants than the settlements.

A good 'exit base' for visits to the Lycian cities is Fethiye, (the ancient Telmessos), a pleasant resort with a mediaeval fortress dominating the city. In Fethiye Lycian rock graves with temple façades can be found, among others the Amyntas-tomb from the fourth century B.C.

In the middle of the modern city stands a Lycian sarcophagus. This, by the way, proves that cemeteries were not always safe from later building zeal. The local museum of Fethiye houses a unique trilingual *stèle* with inscriptions, which were crucial in the decipherment of the Lycian language.

From Fethiye a car-drive of about 45 minutes leads to Tlos (the modern Asar Kale). This town is one of the very old settlements in Lycia. The discovery of a bronze axe from the second millennium B.C. proves that long before the Lycian period people inhabited this place. Tlos was one of the cities having three votes in the federal assembly of the Lycian City League. The importance of the city is also expressed by the public buildings, which were constructed in the period from the second century B.C. until the second century A.D. One of these projects concerned the construction of a large stadium along the eastern *acropolis* wall. The rows of benches on the side of the *acropolis* and the vaults on the opposite side can still be discerned among the lush vegetation. The space within the stadium walls is used nowadays to cultivate grain. After each harvest the remains of the

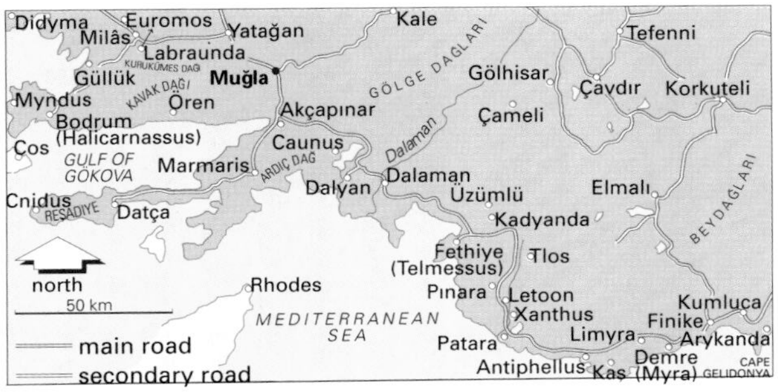

Although in winter a peaceful fishing village, Kaş becomes a crowded tourists' attraction in summer. ▶

◄ *The damaged temple façade of the Amyntas-grave in Fethiye still reveals traces of the original painting. On the door of the grave, metal door furniture is copied in stone. Amyntas was a wealthy citizen who lived in the fourth century B.C.*

The seats of the theatre ▲ in Patara are threatened by an enormous sea of sand.

constructions situated within the stadium become visible. The buildings of Tlos overlap: the stadium uses part of the *acropolis* walls as a side wall and the aquaduct is constructed in the wall of the stadium on the opposite side. The large building blocks of a *basilica* and a bath with an adjoining sports field are, in their turn, built against that wall. During the Ottoman Empire the *acropolis* completely disappeared under new building developments. The most recent building dates from the end of the nineteenth century; a fortress built by a notorious local ruler: 'bloody' Ali Aga. In Asar Kale itself and in the immediate surroundings both Lycian rock graves with various reliefs and inscriptions as well as sarcophagi from the Roman period can be found.
According to tradition, Pınara (the modern Minare) was founded by colonists from Xanthus, 25 kilometres to the south. Pınara developed into an important city, for, within the Lycian City League it was one of the six cities with triple voting rights. The *acropolis* of Pınara was built on a rock with very steep slopes forming a natural defence. Remains of city walls have therefore hardly been found. The entry to the city from the south was formed by a staircase hewn out of the rocks. Pınara was almost completely destroyed during a heavy earthquake in 141 A.D., which accounts for the fact that most buildings date from the period after this event. Of the Roman *odeion*, a kind of concert hall, only parts of the seats have remained. Fortunately the Roman theatre, in the eastern slope opposite the *acropolis*, has been well-preserved.
Pınara is famous for its *necropolises* which are located on the *acropolis* and on the surrounding mountain slopes. Unfortunately the monuments are difficult to reach. The motorist who has found the turning, will come to a parking place via a steep and winding rocky path and can only proceed further on foot. In summer a visit to Pınara is a warm adventure causing quite a lot of discomfort. The stiff climb is however amply rewarded with a breathtaking view across the rocky scenery. Against the slopes west of the *acropolis*, tombs from the Roman time can be found. The Lycian *necropolis* is located on the slope south of the city. Here rock graves in the typical dovecote-formation can be seen. One of them is known as the 'royal grave'. On the door posts are reliefs of humans. Inside, one of the walls depicts a city, possibly Pınara itself. From the rock graves one has an exceptionally fine view of the opposite slope with the theatre.

Ramble past the ruins of Lycian cities

Numerous smaller excavations in Lycia are certainly worth a visit. Limyra (Zengerler) for instance, north of Finike, is known for its well-preserved theatre and the *heroon*, high up on the mountain. The façade of this grave, which is related to the *Nereids* monument at Xanthus, is supported by *karyatids*.
Easy to reach from Finike are, 30 kilometres inland, the remains of the ancient city Arykanda. Theatre, stadium, baths and market place with adjoining *odeion* are in excellent condition due to recent excavations and restorations.
The fishing port of Kaş (the ancient Antiphellos) is a typical tourist resort. As in other places in Lycia, a single deserted sarcophagus can be found standing among the village buildings, at the end of a small ascending road.
The ruins of the port-town of Patara are located in the middle of a row of dunes behind the sunny beaches of Gelemiş. The silted harbour nowadays consists of swamps and dense bamboo woods making the perfectly preserved *granarium* almost inaccessible. The theatre lies half hidden under a sand drift and a little further on tortoises rummage about among the ruins of a Corinthian temple and a Roman bath. On the exit road of the city lies a triumphal arch from the time of Mettius Modestus, the Roman governor of Lycia in the first century B.C.

The solid triumphal arch of Mettius Modestus dominates the entry to Patara. ▼

City of Noel Baba

Myra, the ruins of which can be found some kilometres north of the modern Demre, is well-known for two reasons: in the first place as a Lycian city with many rock graves, and secondly as an early Christian city, the see of Saint Nicholas, the famous children's friend. Myra also belonged to the larger Lycian cities with triple voting rights within the City League.

The oldest settlement on this location dates from the fifth century B.C. The majority of the rock graves can be found in a *necropolis* dating from the middle of the fourth century B.C. The graves are situated high against the rock wall and can be reached via steps hewn out in the rocks. Most of them are of the house-type with façades divided into cassettes. Between the graves altars and niches were built for offerings. A large number of graves is provided with reliefs and inscriptions, most of them simple epitaphs bearing the name of the deceased. Grave 81 has a relief depicting a farewell meal. Even nowadays traces of paint are discernible. In order to get a closer look at this grave, a dangerous climb has to be made across slippery stones and between other graves. From below, at the bottom of the rock, only an impression of the whole is possible. Worth mentioning is the adjoining Greek-Roman theatre of Myra. The audience section, the *cavea*, has been hewn out of the rock slope. The theatre building is still standing up to the first floor and is richly decorated with columns and niches. Also noteable is a *frieze* (decoration edge) with representations from the life of *Dionysos*, the god of wine, dancing and singing.

The *orchestra* has been separated from the audience section by stone slabs on which vague traces are visible of a painting with waterplants and ducks. The theme of these representations was a suitable decoration for the mock fights with boats held in the *orchestra*. All around the theatre lie a number of interesting fragments; out of the high grass theatre masks with hollow eyes gaze at the visitor. The graves which have been hewn out of the rock wall behind the theatre form a typical Lycian décor.

In the centre of the village of Demre is the church of Saint Nicholas, the famous bishop and miracle worker of Myra. Among the Turkish population Saint Nicholas is known as 'Noel Baba', Father Christmas. The church was founded during the third century, but was almost completely rebuilt in the eleventh century. Restorations and changes to the church have taken place up to this present day. To the early Christian tomb of Saint Nicholas the lid of a Roman sarcophagus has been added. This lid is rather peculiar on the grave of a Catholic clergyman, for it bears the representation of a couple! In the church murals from the tenth until the fourteenth century can be seen.

On the coast, five kilometres from Demre, lies the port which belonged to Myra in ancient days. This port-town, Andriake, was not constructed until the second century A.D. This was probably done for strategic purposes. The Parthian Empire was the most important enemy of the Romans in those days. A number of campaigns against this oriental super power

◂ *The rock necropolis in Myra. The fake doors that used to serve as entrances to the houses for the dead were destroyed by grave pillagers. In the inset: a relief over grave number 81. The figures are part of a farewell scene for the deceased.*

Saint Nicholas

Saint Nicholas did not originate from Spain, as many people surmise, but from Lycia, where he was born around the year 280 in Patara. He was already special as a child; it is said e.g. that on fast days he refused the milk from his mother's breast. Nicholas became bishop of Myra. After his death on 6 December 342 he was presumably interred in a tomb in Myra. Nowadays the grave is empty, because in 1087 Italian sailors from Bari robbed the grave of his remains and took these to their city. It was a very lucrative business to have the bones of a saint within the city walls.

From that time on thousands of pilgrims travelled to the Saint Nicholas Cathedral in Bari to worship the remains of the miracle worker. From Bari the posthumous worship of the saintly bishop spread all over Europe. In the eleventh century Bari was part of the Spanish Empire and that has caused the confusion about Saint Nicholas' origin.

Nicholas was the patron saint of sailors, travelling merchants, pawnbrokers, thieves, virgins and prostitutes. The stories about the miracles he wrought became more fantastic in the course of the centuries. One of these stories concerns a poor man who could not give his three daughters dowries. When Nicholas heard about this, he helped the father by secretly throwing a purse filled with gold through the open window three nights in a row. This might have set off the stories about scattering sweets and the chimney. Furthermore Saint Nicholas saved kidnapped children, shipwrecked persons, prisoners, virgins and made the fondest wish of childless couples come true.

In 1970 the Roman Catholic church removed Nicholas from the list of official saints. For the Vatican seriously doubts the historical truth of the legendary aspects of his person. This, by the way, does not make a lot of difference for his faithful followers. In The Netherlands the saint's birthday is celebrated on the fifth of December in the way other countries have Christmas festivities.

Lycian graves

In Lycia are hundreds of graves which can be distinguished into three types: the grave house, the sarcophagus and the pillar grave. The first two grave types were applied both as detached graves and in rock walls. The pillar grave only exists in detached form. These stone monuments show architectural elements derived from wood constructions.
The grave house has a flat roof, such as is often seen on the contemporary Turkish house in the countryside. The entry to the grave was mostly blocked with a *monolith*, a massive lump of stone. In the burial chamber reclining beds for the dead have been hewn out along the sides. Very typical are the projecting beams on the outer sides of the grave house. The front side was divided into a number of panels. A variation on the grave house are the graves with an Ionian temple façade.
Lycian sarcophagi are characterized by the pointed arch-shaped lid lying on the coffin. It is this roof crowning in particular that distinguishes a sarcophagus from a grave house. Moreover, a sarcophagus is usually smaller. The entry has been made in the narrow side or in the *tympanum*. In some cases the lid has to be lifted off the coffin in order to gain entry to the grave. The beam endings on the sides of the lid served to make lifting easier. In the roof construction of the sarcophagi cross-beams are visible too, but in contrast to the grave houses these beams do not protrude from the construction. Sometimes protruding beams have the shape of an animal *protoma*.
Sarcophagi can be found scattered over Anatolia. According to the writer Plinius, the word 'sarcophagus' was derived from the properties of a certain kind of rock in Asia Minor. 'Sarcophaghos' is the Greek word for 'meat eater'. For, in a grave of that kind of rock the body decayed exceptionally fast.
Pillar graves mostly consist of a *monolith*; the grave was hewn out of the *monolith* or was placed on top of it.
The pillars are sometimes nearly eleven metres high. A pillar grave may be decorated with reliefs or sculpture; an example is the Harpies Pillar in Xanthus. The origin of this kind of grave is uncertain. Grain barns or beehives are sometimes considered; the high location served to deter animals of prey from causing damage. A pillar grave could also be a combination of a *stèle* with a burial chamber.
On the basis of inscriptions and decorative style, most Lycian graves are assigned to the fourth century B.C. Only very rarely burial gifts were found, due to the fact that nearly all graves had been pillaged.

◄ *Xanthus, Lycian pillar grave with a sarcophagus placed on top of it.*

were mounted and Myra, in its heyday during the second century, was extremely suitable for supplying the fleet and army units.
The present-day Andriake has a picturesque location at the edge of a swamp where storks find their food. In the port-town one can find remnants of an aquaduct, a market, a harbour street with half-covered mooring places for ships, a watch tower and a large grain storage building. It is above all this *granarium*, 65 by 32 metres, that is in good condition. Over one of the doors busts were placed of emperor Hadrian and his wife Sabina.

Caria, political melting pot

Caria is a region in the south-west corner of Turkey. The east of this province borders Lycia. Just like Lycia, Caria has a mountainous interior and a concentration of cities along the coast. From the eleventh century B.C. immigrants, coming from the islands in the Aegean Sea and the Greek mainland, settled among the native Carian population. These Ionians and Dorians played an important role in Carian political and cultural development. Alongside the existing Carian language Greek dialects emerged. The origin of the Carian language is unknown. It is probably not, like Lycian, of Anatolian origin. The language, of which very few inscriptions have been preserved, has not yet been deciphered.
Six cities where the Dorians had settled, formed the 'Dorian hexapolis'. On the mainland Cnidus and Halicarnassus were members of this League. The religious centre was in Cnidus, which had an annual festival in honour of *Apollo*. Just like the Dorians, the Ionians also joined in a city league. At a very early date, presumably in the sixth century B.C., the Carian cities and villages had also formed a federation with a sanctuary for the Carian *Zeus* in Mylasa (Milâs). These three federations were generally aimed at strengthening their respective identities and at stimulating trading contacts.
The original Carians mainly lived in villages in the interior, a region not penetrated by the immigrants. Some cities, however, known as Greek, like Miletus, Myus and Priene, also had Carians among their population. Furthermore, the Lelegians, who were neither Greek nor Carian, lived in Caria too. Their cities were mainly located on the peninsula of Myndus. The different population groups lived closely together and entered into alliances against mutual enemies.
In the sixth century B.C. the Carians and the Ionians joined their resistence forces against the advancing Persians. Halicarnassus was forced to leave the Dorian hexapolis due to alleged Ionian sympathies. The area known as Caria from the fifth century B.C., was an intensively Hellenized region, where, just as in Lycia, the original language had been ousted by Greek. After the defeats of the Persians at Marathon and Salamis in the beginning of the fifth century B.C., nearly all cities on the Turkish west coast joined the Delian-Attic Sea League. When in 404 B.C. Sparta finally put an end to the Athenian empire and consequently the League, Caria resided under Persian rule again. The region became a *satrapy* within the Persian Empire. Local monarchs could only rule with the consent of the *satrap*, who in his turn was directly answerable to the Persian king. One of these *satraps*, Mausollos, acquired a lot of fame through the grave monument built in his honour, the Mausoleum in Halicarnassus. We owe our

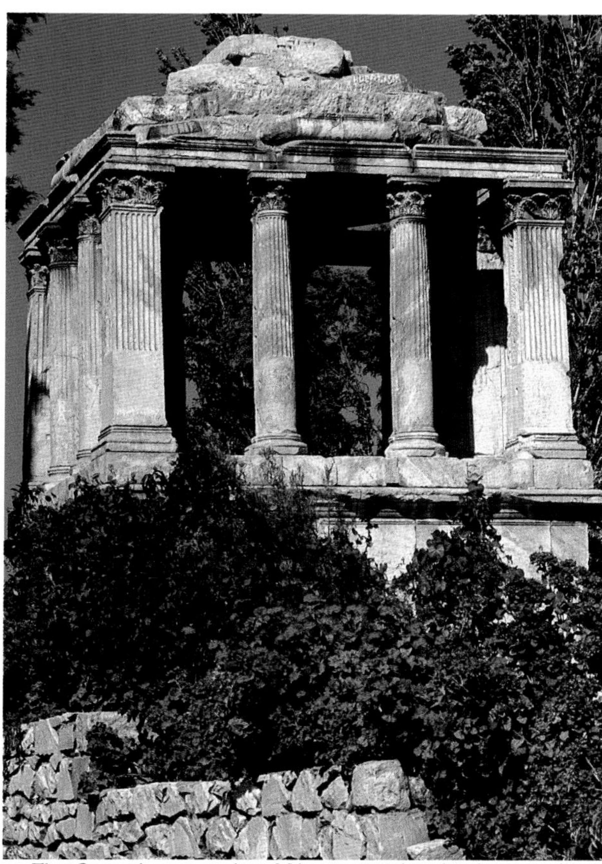

▲ *The Gümüskesen-tomb in Milâs is considered to be a small-scale replica of the Mausoleum at Halicarnassus.*

contemporary term mausoleum to this monarch and his grave. Mausollos had ambitious plans for the region he ruled. He commenced by rearranging the territory of the peninsula of Myndus and realized important military fortifications and public buildings in a number of cities e.g. in Latmos and Caunus. The biggest project was relocating the capital Mylasa to Halicarnassus and moving the population of six Lelegian cities to this new capital.

The arrival of Alexander the Great made Caria part of the Macedonian Empire. After Alexander's death the region, just like Lycia, fell prey to the heirs of his empire: the Egyptian Ptolemaeans and the Syrian Seleucids. In 190 B.C. the Seleucid king was defeated by the Romans at Magnesia, a town not far from Caria on the river Maeander. Rome entered into alliances with the local monarchs. As has already been mentioned in Chapter 1, one of them, the king of Pergamum, left his empire, which included a large part of Western Turkey, to Rome at his death in 133 B.C. Out of this heritage, which also included Caria, the Roman province of Asia Minor arose in 129 B.C.

The Roman governors exploited the provinces as conquered territory, thwarting economical development of these regions. During the Roman Empire the governors were subject to more effective control due to a stricter central authority and gradually the provincial regions gained more independence. For Caria this development signified the beginning of a period of bloom, only ending in the turbulent third century A.D., when the Goths scourged the country with their attacks.

Halicarnassus, grave for a satrap

Halicarnassus (the modern Bodrum) is well-known for its Mausoleum. After the death of Mausollos in 353 B.C., his wife, who was also his sister, had this famous grave monument constructed in his honour. The Mausoleum is considered to be one of the seven Wonders of the Ancient World. Nowadays, only the basis of the monument is visible. In the thirteenth or fourteenth century the building was destroyed by an earthquake. The ruin was thereafter used as a quarry for the construction of the crusaders' castle Saint Peter in Bodrum. The greenish granite of the basis of the Mausoleum can be found in many places in this fortress. A single sculptured fragment has also ended up in the

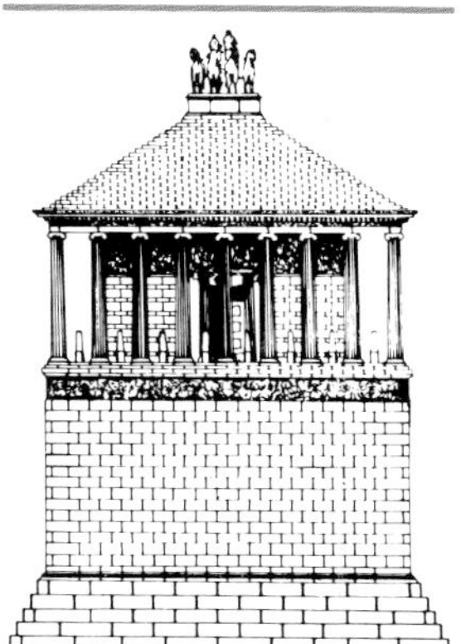

RECONSTRUCTION DRAWING OF THE MAUSOLEUM OF HALICARNASSUS

Nowadays a museum for underwater archaeology is housed in the picturesquely located crusaders' castle at Bodrum. ▼

LINE DRAWINGS OF GRAVES WITH IONIAN TEMPLE FAÇADES

Characteristic elements are the two columns, the tympanum and a shallow forecourt.

castle and is now on display in the museum housed there. Most fragments of the sculpture however, were taken to England by Sir Charles Newton in the nineteenth century. They are nowadays displayed in the British Museum together with many other objects from Turkey. The grave monument which was reconstructed on the basis of finds and remnants, reveals a building somewhat similar to a number of Lycian pillar graves. In essence it is a burial chamber on top of a high socle. The style of the sculpture is entirely Greek. A similar combination can be observed in the *Nereids* monument at Xanthus and in the Gümüskesen-tomb at Milâs.

Since Halicarnassus/Bodrum has been inhabited up to this very day, it is very difficult to reconstruct the old city. Not much is left of all the famous buildings from ancient times, especially from the days of Mausollos and his sister Artemisia. Only part of the city wall is still standing. During the construction of the coastal road through Caria in 1976, the ancient theatre was discovered.

The mediaeval fortress of Saint Peter had been built in several phases over a period of 100 years. From the beginning of the fifteenth century until the beginning of the sixteenth century the crusaders of Rhodes worked on the building, the Turks completed it in the period thereafter. Today the castle houses a museum with finds from the excavations in Bodrum and the surrounding area. An important part of the collection consists of objects obtained through underwater archaeology, such as a series of amphoras and the previously mentioned cargo of copper from the ship that sunk in the thirteenth century B.C. near Cape Gelidonya. The stone anchors in the yard come from the important port-town of Caunus (Dalyan).

▲ Dorian columns carry the front of the nymphaeum of Labraunda. In the background the remnants of the Carian Zeus sanctuary.

A Carian sanctuary in the interior

From Milâs a dusty mountain road of about fifteen kilometres leads to the excavations of Labraunda. Against the pine-covered mountain slopes are thousands of beehives. Heavily protected bee keepers collect the rich honey harvest.

The central sanctuary of Labraunda was dedicated to the Carian *Zeus*. West of this temple lies a reception room, a so-called *andron*. On the northeastern side the temple is bounded by a terrace with a *stoa*. In the Roman period an elegant *nymphaeum* was constructed in the lower southeast retaining wall of this terrace.

Ionian temple façades adorn these impressive rock graves in the lagoon of Caunus. The warm colour of the rock is emphasized by the red glow of the setting sun. ▼

▲ The ancient harbours of Cnidus form the romantic background for the foundations of a round temple. It is assumed that this is where the world-famous statue of Aphrodite made by Praxiteles once stood.

north

MAP OF CAUNUS

temples
thermae
nymphaeum
acropolis
theatre
palaestra
stoa
ancient harbour

Dalaman Çay

To Caunus and Cnidus by boat

By far the easiest manner to reach the ruins of Caunus is by boat. After a 45 minutes' sail from the fishing village Dalyan, the excavation site is reached. A beautiful trip through the swampy lagoon passes thick reed forests and steep rock walls. In these walls many house and temple graves have been hewn out. Coming ashore, a path leads to the Roman theatre. From the top row of seats the glittering dome of the mosque at Dalyan can be discerned in the distance. Having descended the theatre hill, one can stroll along the other ruins, including a *nymphaeum*, a bathing house and a basilica.

The best way to reach the idyllically situated Cnidus, is also by boat. Although a 35 kilometres long track leads from Datça to the very end of the peninsula, this is a very difficult route demanding a special cross-country vehicle. From Bodrum, Marmaris or Datça boats leave for daytrips to Cnidus. On arrival in one of the ancient harbours, the city can be seen lying on terraces against the mountain slope. In ancient times the 'tourists' used to come from far and near to admire the famous statue of *Aphrodite* by Praxiteles here on Cnidus. It is assumed that this statue stood in the temple of which the circular foundations have been preserved.

The small theatre of Cnidus is in good condition, but of the houses and temples only a few modest remnants are left. Numerous excavation trenches mark the area American investigators had to leave, after having been accused of stealing archaeological objects.

◄ In the Glyptothek in Munich this Roman copy of Praxiteles's Aphrodite is housed.

Milâs

Tobacco colours in many shades please the eye while observing the Milâs carpets from southwest Anatolia. Yellow ocre is the dominating colour combined with light brown, dark brown and rusty hues. The high quality of the wool and the vegetable dyes give the carpets a silky glow.

Besides geometrical motives prayer carpets show a symbolic mihrab, a prayer niche, in the middle. Very practical in use, for in that way the believer knows that he always exercises his prayers with his head and feet on the same spot. The stylized tobacco plants along the edges are a typical feature for the Milâs carpets, just like the corner motive which represents a temple with four guardians.

5 Marble Cultures

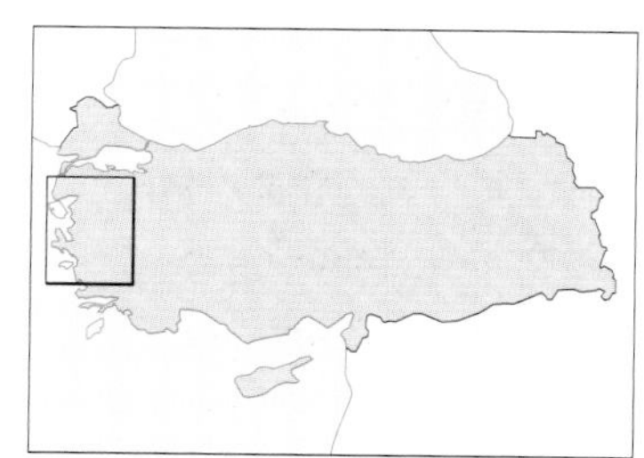

Sunny beaches and pine-clad slopes characterize the Aegean seacoast. In the fascinating landscape of Aeolia and Ionia classical culture revives. Ancient temples and theatres dominate the rural Turkish villages where ruins and houses often blend together. The marble of the archaeological sights glittering in the sun invites the visitor to come on a journey through antiquity.

Çanakkale is the ideal starting point for a tour past the Greek and Roman cities of ruins on the Turkish west coast. South of this vivacious port a turning leads to legendary Troy. Further south the walls of the fortress Assus can already be discerned. Then Pergamum is visited with the remnants of the famous *Zeus* altar.
During a walk through the ancient streets of Ephesus, it is not surprising that the visitor imagines himself to be in the middle of antiquity. In the heart of Ionia lies Priene, the city admired for the quality of its urban development. The ancient harbour-town Miletus, once the site of an important philosophers' school, is nowadays for a large part submerged in a swamp. A sacred road connected Miletus with the *Apollo* sanctuary in Didyma. From the coast numerous interesting places in the inland, e.g. Sardis, Aphrodisias and Hierapolis can be easily reached.

◂ *Near the entrance to the excavations of Troy a large wooden horse commemorates the Trojan War.*

Aeolia

The coastal area south of the Sea of Marmara between Çanakkale and İzmir was known as Aeolia in ancient times. This fertile region had already been colonized from the tenth century B.C. by the Greeks. From Greece city-states had been founded that were politically independent but had strong cultural and economical ties with the motherland. The best known are: Smyrna, Larissa, Temnos, Neonteichos, Kyme, Aigai, Myrina, Gryneion, Elaea, Pitane and Lesbos. The Aeolians made a living of agriculture and nowadays the area still has a wealth of fruit-trees, olive orchards, cotton plantations and corn fields.

The disordered ground of Troy

Legendary Troy became well-known owing to Homer's epos from the eighth century B.C. In his poem, the Iliad, he describes an episode out of the Trojan War, which had broken out after the fair *Helen* from Sparta had been abducted by *Paris*, son of king Priam of Troy. Many famous Greek heroes gathered to punish Troy. They besieged the city and after ten years they finally succeeded in conquering the city through a cunning trick and set *Helen* free. On the initiative of the shrewd *Odysseus* a huge wooden horse was constructed, a hiding place for soldiers. After the Greeks had withdrawn to sea, the Trojans towed the horse inside the city walls. In the evening they had a great celebration and in the middle of the night. when the Trojans were befuddled with alcohol, the Greeks stole out of the

To the north, more and more areas of the Aegean coast are opened up to tourism. After Kuşadası and Pamucak, Gümüldür is next. ▾

◂ *The renowned Celsus library is situated at the end of the Curetes street in Ephesus, which is flanked by marble statues, temples and fountains.*

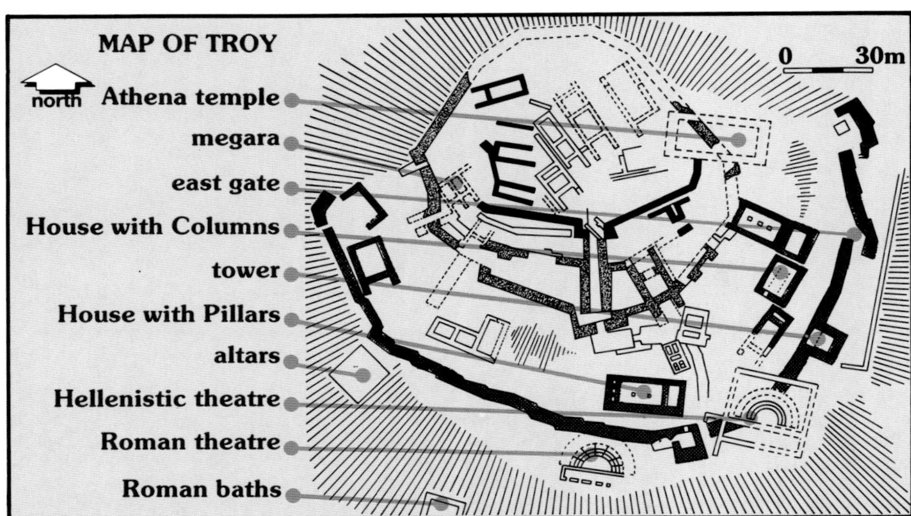

The south-east tower and a part of the city wall from 1300 B.C. (Troy VI). ►

The cluttered remains of the megaron houses in Troy. With his excavations Schliemann dug a trench right through the grounds, ▼ *resulting in a ruin of a ruin.*

horse. Aided by the Greek fleet, which had meanwhile returned, they then conquered the city. According to ancient tradition, Troy was destroyed by the Greeks in 1184 B.C.

Almost as renowned as the history of Troy is the life-story of the man who first discovered the city: Heinrich Schliemann. In October 1871 he started excavations in the village of Hisarlık. As a guide Schliemann used the text of the Iliad, in that way trying to locate the site where the events of the twelfth century B.C. would have taken place. During his excavations Schliemann initially distinguished seven habitation layers. Later another three layers were discovered. The various habitation phases are recognizable from the remains of buildings, fragments of pottery and coin findings.

The oldest habitation layer (Troy I) dates from 3000 B.C. In the top layer (Troy IX) remnants of the Roman period have been found too. The layers of the city such as recited by Homer (Troy VI and VIIa) were not discovered by Schliemann himself. He was digging in a layer full of bronze and gold objects which he erroneously mistook for the 'Treasure of Priam'. For this layer (Troy II) dates from a period 1000 years before the famous conquest. The precious findings unfortunately 'disappeared' for the greater part during the Second World War; only a few objects are kept in the Prähistorisches Museum in West-Berlin.

A visit to the excavations at Troy will be rather disappointing for some people. Little has been left of the glorious city so ornately described by Homer. The remnants of large buildings and houses often lie on top of each other, which makes it rather an intricate business to distinguish the different habitation layers. With signs

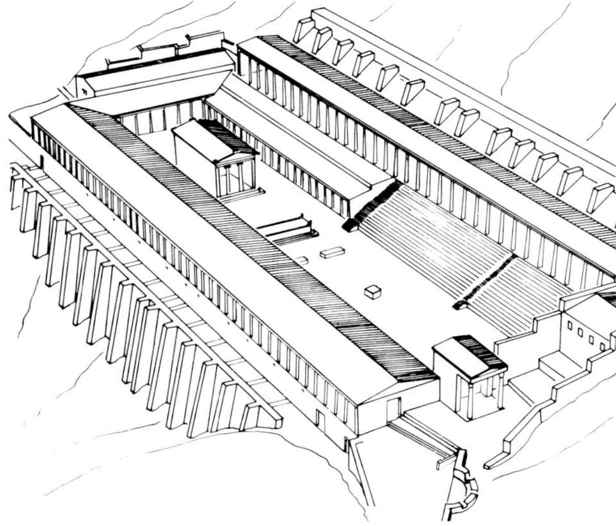
RECONSTRUCTION DRAWING OF THE DEMETER SANCTUARY

The vast buildings of the ▲ Demeter sanctuary in the middle city of Pergamum. According to two inscriptions on the temple and the main altar, the buildings had been dedicated to Demeter by Philetairos and his brother Eumenes in honour of their mother Boa.

city, the most recent excavations are passed: baths and a residential area from the time of Philetairos (281-263 B.C.).
In the middle city are the sanctuaries of *Hera* and *Demeter*. Along the way, houses and public buildings can be observed such as the temple of *Asklepios*, the market, a city fountain and a *gymnasium*.
The Hellenistic-Roman *gymnasium*, extending over three terraces on top of each other, took up most space in the middle city. The upper terrace was meant for senior students, the middle and lower terraces for junior pupils and children respectively.
The Attalos-house, north-west of the lower *agora*, is a beautiful example of a *peristylium* house. It consists of a large court, enclosed by a colonnade, around which a number of rooms is grouped. The Attalos-house dates from the Hellenistic period, but was inhabited during many phases. The house owes its name to Attalos Paterklianos who lived in it around the year 200. This wealthy citizen from Pergamum was consul of Rome.

◄ A large part of the middle city of Pergamum is occupied by the gymnasium, which extended over three terraces. The building block had two baths. In the western bathing building the washing area still preserves water basins.

◄ The stage building blocked the view from the theatre terrace and was therefore dismantled after the play and stored. The wooden poles of the stage house were placed in the stones with square holes.

In Bergama, located as was mentioned before partly on top of the old lower city, are the remnants of a huge temple from the Roman period. The temple, including the court, has a length of 270 metres and a width of 100 metres.
The major hall has been erected out of red brick and is therefore called 'Kızıl Avlu' (Red Hall) in Turkish. The *basilica*-like structure has a nave, two aisles and an *apsis*. The Red Hall is flanked by a building which used to house two elongated waterbasins. This sanctuary is often related to a *Serapeum*, because the Romans worshipped the Egyptian gods Isis and Serapis and this cult involved water. Recent excavations, however, have not provided certainty on this matter. The river Selinus was diagonally channelled under the court through an ingenious construction of two parallel tunnels. The entire building block also had an intricate system of subterranean corridors, basements and *cisterns*.
In the centre of Bergama is the Archaeological Museum, the first museum in Turkey especially designed for local finds. Here a number of objects are on display which were found during the excavations such as tombstones, reliefs, *acroteria*, a mosaic floor and a statue of emperor Hadrian. One of the wings houses a small ethnographical department.

An ancient spa

About five kilometres outside the centre of Bergama, in an area abounding in water, the Asklepieion was erected in the fourth century B.C. in honour of the god of medical science *Asklepios*.
In the second century A.D., under Hadrian, this spa had its major period of bloom. One of the most famous doctors of antiquity, Galenus – the court doctor of emperor Marcus Aurelius – came from Pergamum. In exercising medicine supernatural powers played an important role. The patients had their dreams explained by priests, whereupon they either went home with a prescibed treatment, or were nursed in the Asklepieion itself. The correspondence and writings of Aelius Aristides, who experienced several stays in the spa as a patient over a period of thirteen years, have been preserved and give a detailed picture of daily life at the spa. The treatment consisted of a combination of physical and psychological therapies. Three elements played an important part: dietary prescriptions, hot and cold baths and physical exercise. A typical case was that of a man with bad digestion (dyspepsia). He was put on a diet of bread, cheese, parsley, salad and milk mixed with honey. Moreover, he had to walk barefoot, run every day, cover himself in mud and rub his body with wine before bathing. The treatment was a success!
Between the *acropolis* hill and the Asklepieion lie an *amphitheatre* and a theatre from the Roman period. From this place a two kilometres long, almost completely roofed-over road – the via tecta – leads to the Asklepieion. A *propylon* (monumental entry gate) gave access to the sanctuary. As appears from inscriptions, this gate was built by assignment of consul Claudius Charax. From the stairs on the western side, one has a view of the entire spa. The area is 110 metres in width and 130 metres long and was enclosed on three sides by a colonnade with beautifully sculptured capitals. The floor of both the *stoai* and the court were covered with sand, because some patients walked barefoot during their treatment. Immediately north of the *propylon* was a small library. The building had only one room with niches for the scrolls along the walls. In one niche on the eastern side stood a statue of emperor Hadrian, to whom the library was dedicated.
South of the *propylon* was the round *Asklepios* temple, evidently inspired by the Pantheon in Rome. The round foundations of the temple are clearly recognizable. The building was roofed by a dome with a round opening in the centre, allowing the light to penetrate. Opposite the entry, which, like the *propylon* had a temple-like façade, was a niche, undoubtedly the site of the cult statue of *Asklepios*.
The south-east corner of the spa is filled up by another round structure that was probably used as a sanatorium. The building consisted of two layers; the upper floor had six large *apses* (half round niches) and was roofed with wood. The lower floor, with a gallery, was situated under the ground and for that reason has been well-preserved. The visitor can reach the lower floor via a *cryptoporticus*, an underground corridor, illuminated by openings in the vault. The *cryptoporticus* starts at

At the bottom of the acropolis lies the snug town of Bergama with, in the centre, the Red Hall from ▼ the Roman era.

the middle of the area near the sacred well. This corridor also had a psychological function for patients. Exhausted and dazed by all sorts of hallucinogens, they had to walk through the 80 metres long corridor, heard unfamiliar sounds and experienced strange sensations. This method of treatment was supposed to stimulate the healing process. Near the well were so-called incubation rooms, where strict ritual rules were obeyed. The patient was only allowed to undergo a treatment after he had had a bath and had sacrificed a white sheep while he himself was dressed in white.
In the south-west corner of the building block is a latrine. This public lavatory had a large room for men (40 seats) and a smaller one for women (17 seats). Corinthian capitals decorated the luxurious building. The walls were covered with marble and in the middle, a light and air shaft had been constructed.
The best preserved building of the Asklepieion is the theatre. The typically Roman semi-circular *auditorium* had seats for about 3500 spectators and was certainly also meant for non-patients. The *scaenae frons* originally consisted of three floors with many niches and columns. The lower floor of the façade and the *orchestra* (the dancing area) had marble decorations, while colourful glass mosaics were applied in the niches. The marble arm-rests of the seats of this theatre are in some places adorned with elegant dolphins. From all this it appears that even in antiquity people could 'take the waters', having all conveniences and surrounded by luxury and amusements.

From Artemis to torah

Sardis lies about 100 kilometres east of İzmir. The excavations and ruins are visible from the motorway İzmir-Ankara because the modern road cuts right through the town of Sart, thus more or less splitting up the ancient city.
Sardis was an extremely important city in antiquity. Being the capital of the Lydian Empire, Sardis experienced a first period of bloom at the end of the seventh and beginning of the sixth century B.C. Yet, also later, during the Greek and Roman supremacy and in the Byzantine period thereafter, the city occupied a prominent place. It was only at the beginning of the fifteenth century that Sardis declined.
The ancient history of the city is connected with the river Pactolus. The water of the river carried gold along with it, which was extracted at Sardis. A few hundred metres alongside the motorway, on the west side of the path leading to the *Artemis* temple, lie buildings that go back to a period from the eighth century B.C. until the fifth century A.D. According to tradition, this was the site where the first gold coins were made. Among the ruins are the remnants of a gold forge. On the site (not open to the public) numerous wells have been found where gold and silver (electrum) used to be washed. In furnaces gold was separated from silver through chemical processes already familiar at that time. These forges were in full production during the reign of king Kroisos (Latin: Croesus), who ruled from 562 until 547 B.C. Legend has it that this king was extremely wealthy. Before Kroisos went into battle against the Persians, he consulted the oracle at Delphi. The cunning oracular response was that during his campaign a great empire would fall. Kroisos set out in good spirits on his campaign, not grasping the idea that it concerned his own empire which was doomed to

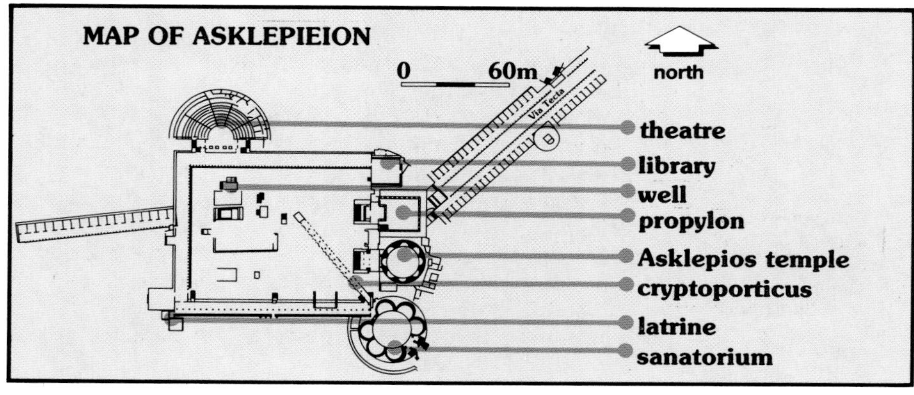

During the annual festival of Bergama (end of May), the theatre of the Asklepieion is still in full use. ▼

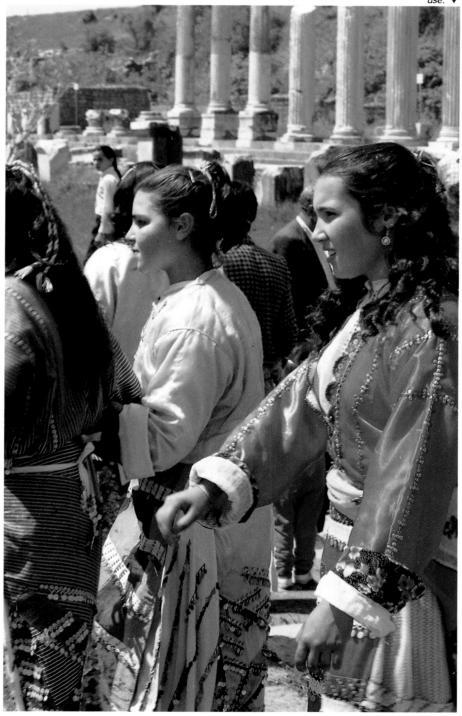

fall. Thus Kroisos was the last king of the Lydian Empire.

The excavations at Sardis extend over a vast area. Past the site of the forges, alongside the former Pactolos and against a décor of steeply rising red-brown mountains, lie the ruins of a huge Ionian temple. In the third century B.C. the building of this sanctuary dedicated to *Artemis* was begun. At this site already stood a red sandstone altar of 11 by 21 metres. During the orientation for the *Artemis* temple this existing altar was taken into consideration. The temple was 23 metres in width and more than 67 metres long. In the beginning of the second century B.C. the building of a colonnade around the temple was commenced. This extension, however, was never finished. The huge columns, column remnants and capitals nowadays surrounding the temple, date from a third building phase, around 150 A.D. At the time of this last building phase a section of the temple was partitioned off to be dedicated to Faustina I, the wife of the Roman emperor Antonius Pius. In the south-east corner of the temple a small Byzantine church was erected in the fourth century.

The impressive ruins of the Artemis temple in Sardis lie at the bottom of an outlandish mountain range. The Ionian capitals bear witness to the great skill of ▾ the sculptors.

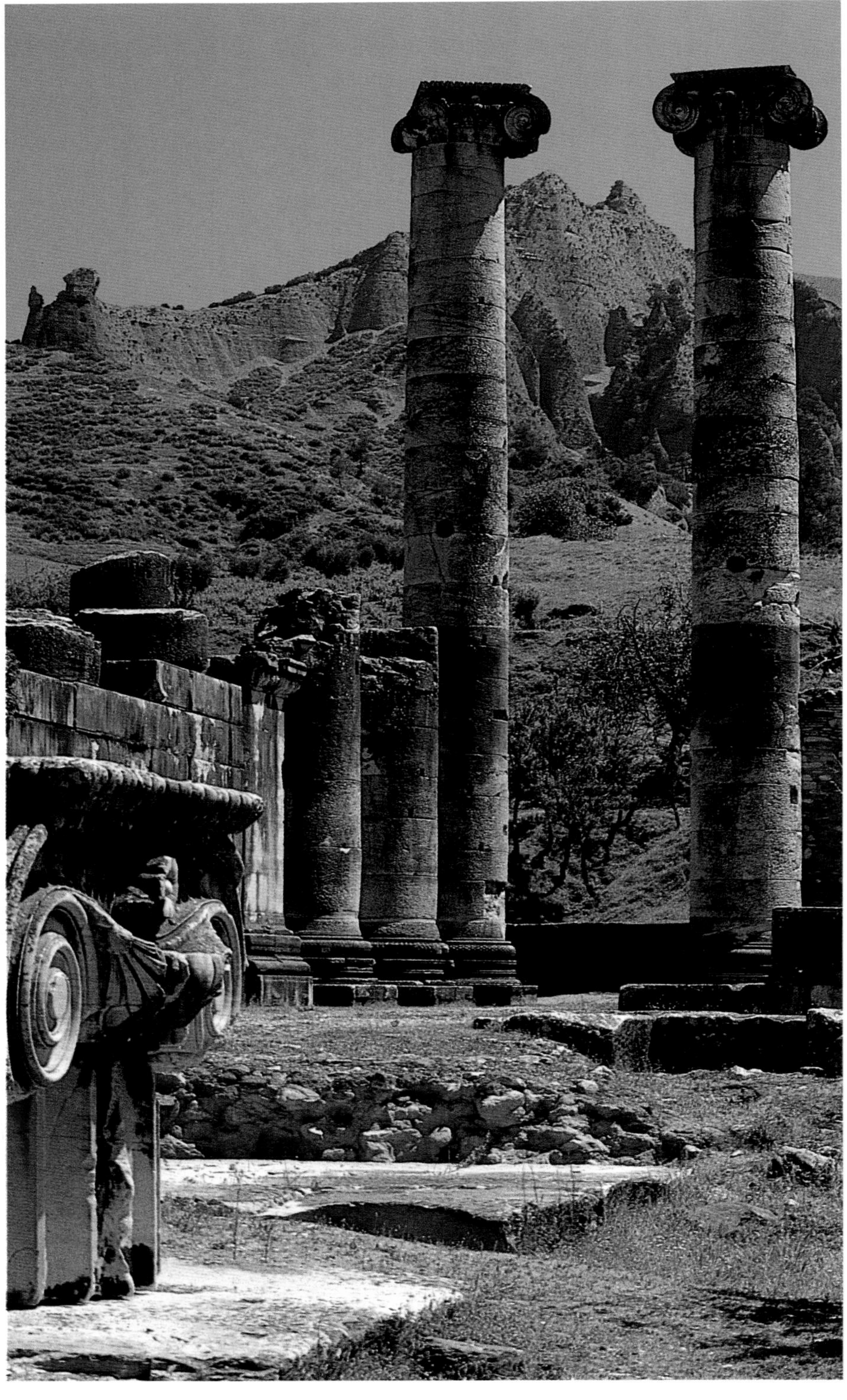

Important and above all spectacular buildings of the Roman period are the baths annex *gymnasium* and the synagogue. These buildings, just north of the motorway, have been partly restored and are striking due to their imposing sizes and rich decorations. In 1962 the synagogue was excavated and thoroughly restored. This largest preserved synagogue from antiquity was built in the third century A.D. and was in use up to the year 616. The synagogue has a courtyard with columns and the walls are embellished with heavily veined marble slabs. The prayer room has mosaic floors with geometrical patterns, marble slabs along the walls and an *apsis* with a gallery for the elders. On both sides of the entrance section two shrines have been constructed in which the torah-scrolls were kept. Greek and Hebrew inscriptions show that the Jewish community consisted of more than 5000 people.

The adjoining baths annex *gymnasium* also date from the third century. The ample space in front of the baths was the *palaestra* (the sports field). The huge and richly decorated façade of the *gymnasium* is an immediate eye-catcher. The deeply drilled out columns, capitals and ridge-pieces have been executed in a baroque style. Near the synagogue, parallel to the modern motorway, is a shopping-street dating from the fourth century. Far into the Byzantine period tradesmen sold their merchandise here. Findings such as coins and residues of meat and fish indicate the existence of small eating-places. In one of the 29 shops the marble basin used for chilling wine can still be seen. At the head of the street, in the south-west, one can see a large ancient latrine. The seats are close together. The water flowing in front of the seats through a trough, provided the necessary comfort.

On the other side of the motorway, American archaeologists carry out excavations every year. During the activities, mostly in summer, they lodge in the completely walled-in house next to the *Artemis* temple. Their garden serves as a depot and the garden shed is decorated with imitation multicoloured Lydian roof-tiles. Objects from both the Lydian and the Roman periods are still being excavated. Many of these finds are on display in the museum of Manisa, a pleasant town north-east of İzmir.

Ten kilometres north of Sardis the kings' *necropolis* can be found. From Sardis a bumpy road leads to the *tumuli* of Bin Tepe (Thousand Hills). This is the site of the largest burial mound of Asia Minor. The *tumulus* of king Alyattes, the father of Kroisos, has a diameter of 355 metres whereas the grave of king Midas in Gordium (Chapter 3) has a diameter of 'only' 300 metres.

▲ *The synagogue of Sardis has a mosaic floor with multi-coloured geometrical patterns. In the niches on both sides of the entrance porch the torah-scrolls were kept.*

A Byzantine street in Sardis with 29 shops. Fishbones, wine barrels and coins provide information about eating places; fragments of beakers and dishes about the trade of a shop selling glass. ▼

▲ *The eighteen metres high façade of the imposing bathing-gymnasium buildings in Sardis can already be seen from the motorway. The columns, capitals and ridge-pieces were executed in the baroque style from the time of Septimius Severus (193-211). The restorers have distinguished old from new by means of subtle colour differences.* ▼

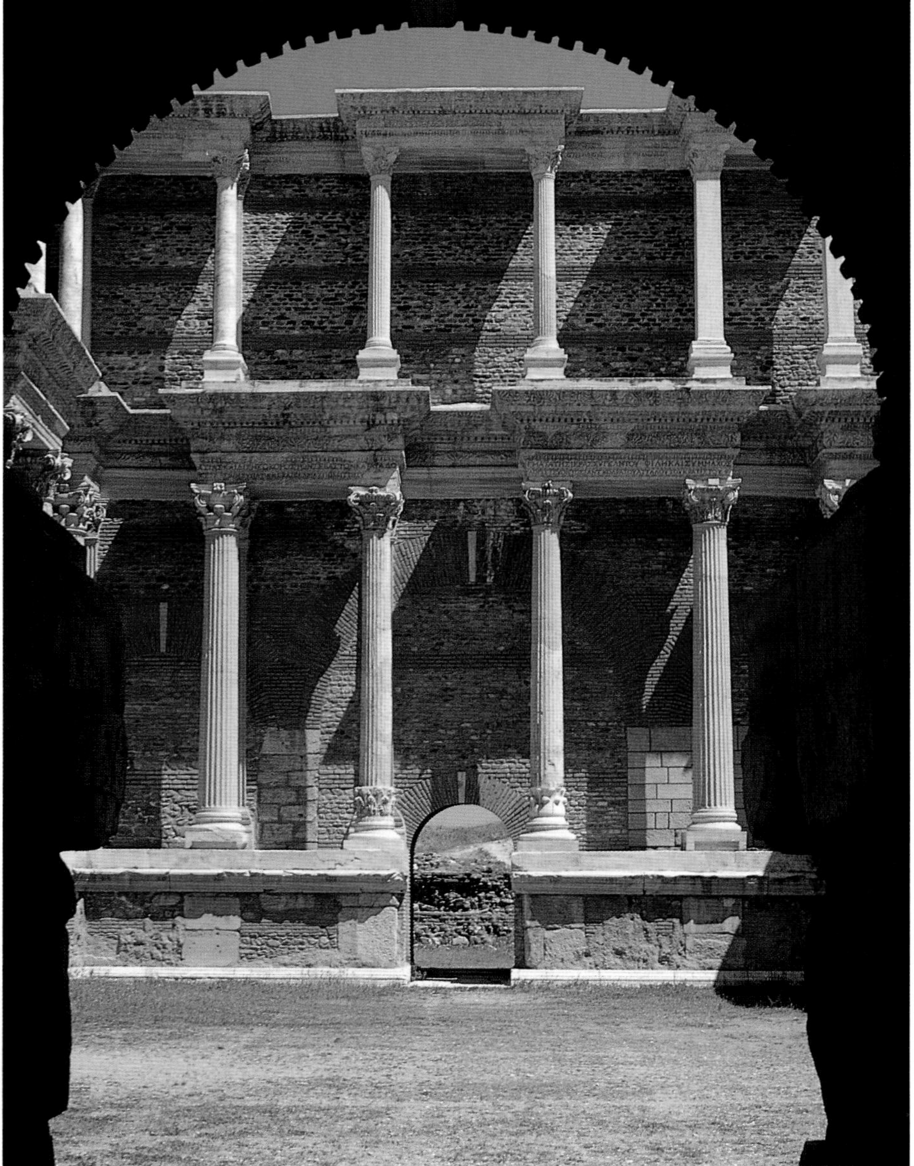

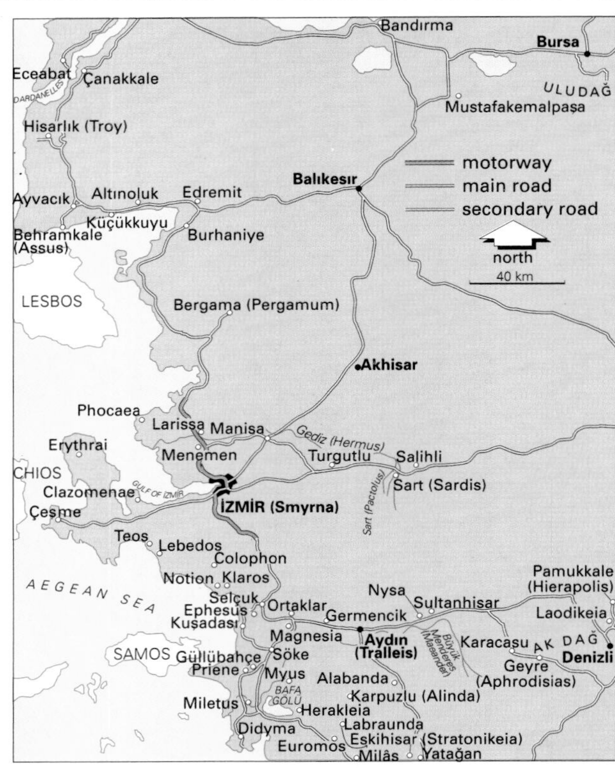

Ionia

The area south of İzmir marks the beginning of the region called Ionia in antiquity. Between İzmir and Didyma the ten cities of the Ionian City League are located: Miletus, Myus, Priene, Ephesus, Colophon, Teos, Lebedos, Erythrai, Clazomenae and Phokaia. The islands of Samos and Chios were also members of this League. Smyrna (İzmir), located on the border of Aeolia and Ionia, initially belonged to the Aeolian territory, but was later considered to be part of Ionia.
The colonists who settled in this region from 1000 B.C., lived primarily from agriculture and trade. In the sixth century B.C. Ionia played a prominent role in science, philosophy, sculpture and architecture. A second cutural period of bloom for the region dawned during Hellenism and when it was part of the Roman province of Asia Minor, Ionia also remained influential.

Prosperity through shipping

The historian Herodotus argued that Smyrna possessed the bluest sky on earth and the geographer Strabo called Smyrna the most beautiful city he knew. Strabo wrote that the streets were paved, a rarity in the Hellenistic-Roman period. With the departure of the Greeks and the arrival of the Turks in 1922, the city acquired its present name İzmir.
To the north of İzmir, the coastal road runs along a former industrial area with a harbour reeking of rotten eggs. For years the chemical sludge has been dredged out of the harbour. The factories are being demolished and huge building developments rise on the outskirts of the city. Along the exit road to Bergama, some eight kilometres outside the centre but still within the boundaries of the city, a turning leads to the district of Bayraklı. Here the remains have been found of the oldest settlement from 3000-2500 B.C. Bayraklı is also the place where the remnants can be seen of one of the Greek colonies founded from the tenth

century B.C. along the coast of Asia Minor. Furthermore, traces of habitations have been discovered from the seventh and sixth centuries B.C. such as the foundations of houses and the ruins of a temple. This sanctuary, dedicated to the goddess *Athena*, is the oldest temple known from the Eastern Greek world. Shortly after 600 B.C. the settlement was destroyed by the Lydian king Alyattes.
From the middle of the fourth century B.C., at the time of Alexander the Great, Smyrna flourished again and remained important until well into the Roman period. The ancient city had wide streets which were at right angles to each other. The main streets ran west-east, in that way benefitting from the pleasant sea breeze. In the centre of the city lies the partly overgrown *agora* from the Hellenistic era. Under Roman rule the city also prospered tremendously. The city square was enlarged, but in 178 a heavy earthquake caused enormous damage. In some places of this so-called state *agora* it is clearly discernible how the streets were laid. Along the main street were 28 shops, some of which had more than one floor. In addition to the state *agora*, Smyrna also knew a commercial *agora*, which however has been completely lost.
With the exception of the state *agora*, little has been preserved from the classical period in the modern city of İzmir. Nowadays the city with over a million inhabitants, situated on the Gulf of İzmir, functions as an important sea port for Turkey. From the fortress Kadifekale one has a view of the hectic metropolis. In the centre of the city is a teeming bazar where 'anything' can be bought in the numerous shops. The nearby Archaeological Museum houses a large number of interesting objects among which remarkable terracotta sarcophagi from Clazomenae.
İzmir has a modern international airport, making the city a convenient starting point for a journey past the many ancient ruins in the neighbourhood.

▲ *The foundations of the colonnade around the Hellenistic agora of Smyrna were supported by solid arches. On the square were statues and in the galleries shops ran their businesses.*

◄ *The head and a part of the left arm of the huge statue of emperor Domitian, which had been exhibited in the basement of the Archaeological Museum of İzmir, were removed to the museum of Selçuk in 1990.* ▼

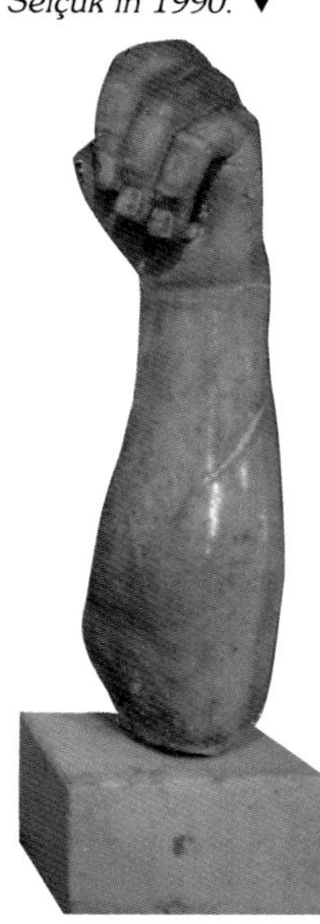

Pomegranate

The pomegranate tree had already been cultivated by the Phoenicians in old Carthage, which can be deduced from the Latin family name (Punica granatum). Phoenician tradesmen distributed the pomegranate across the entire Mediterranean region. Among the Greeks and Romans the pomegranate with its hundreds of seeds was a fertility symbol. The pomegranate is one of the attributes of the goddess Aphrodite and as such refers to her original function as fertility goddess. In the Greek era she developed from fertility goddess to the goddess of love and beauty. Among the Romans she was known as Venus. Presumably it was also the pomegranate which played such an important role as the apple of discord in causing the Trojan War.
A row of thorny pomegranate shrubs often serves as a boundary hedge. The apple-like fruits are very well edible. Sour, pleasant sour-sweet, and very sweet varieties are distinguished. The juice of the pomegranate can be drunk by first kneading the fruit until it is soft, then piercing a hole in it and finally sucking out the juice with a straw. Grenadine, a sour-sweet extract of the fruit-juice, forms the basis for syrups and has a sweet taste in sorbets.
The peel of the pomegranate is applied in medicine as worm expellent. The tannin extracts from the peel are used in tanneries. Furthermore, tea is made from the leaves of the pomegranate tree. From the flowers red dye is obtained and from the roots black pigment.

Ephesus, an image of antiquity

Just like many other ancient cities on the west coast of Asia Minor, Ephesus was founded in the tenth century B.C. During the Hellenistic and Roman eras, Ephesus (Ephesos) was an extremely densely populated city in the Mediterranean region. The *Artemis* cult in particular brought great wealth to the city. Ephesus was not only mighty and prosperous in antiquity, for in the early Christian period a number of buildings were constructed of which some imposing remains can still be seen. At the time of the Seljuks, the inhabitants moved to the place which is nowadays the friendly town of Selçuk. The excavations at Ephesus started as early as 1869 and are still continued this present day by Austrian and Turkish archaeologists.
The secluded sea port of ancient Ephesus was favourably located on a busy trading route. In the Roman period Ephesus was the capital of the province of Asia, numbering about 200,000 inhabitants. Ephesus was not only significant politically and as a trading centre, but also as the city where an influential philosophers' school developed. Religious freedom guaranteed the peaceful coexistence of different religions. Ephesus was visited by the apostles and from the first century Christianity was prominent. After the crucifixion, the apostle John was said to have left for Ephesus with Mary. The house where she lived, high in the hills, is a frequently visited place of pilgrimage. In Asia Minor Mary worship nicely fitted in with the old *Artemis* and *Kybele* cult.
It is not surprising though that the different religions sometimes clashed. Tradesmen who sold small silver idols of the goddess *Artemis*, saw Christianity take the bread out of their mouths. The apostle Paul once narrowly escaped a furious crowd menacing him in the theatre, spurred on by the silversmith Demetrius, shouting: 'great is the *Artemis* of Ephesus!'. At the end of the fourth century the temples were closed owing to Christian influence. As a centre of Christianity the city became important for its St.John's Cathedral, the burial site of the apostle. The ancient city decayed and lost its significance when the water receded and the harbour silted up. Nowadays the sea is about five kilometres from the old Ephesus.
A walk through the impressive ruins of Ephesus forms the climax of a visit to Turkey. Nowhere else can such a complete image of a city in ancient times be obtained. The abundance of monumental buildings, graceful sculptures, richly veined marble and colourful mosaics create an unsurpassed atmosphere.
The best way to set out on a tour of the excavations of Ephesus is to start at the eastern entrance. From this point the walk gradually descends through the ancient streets. The route leads past the most renowned monuments to the main entrance near the theatre.
The vast expanse of grass opposite the eastern entrance used to be the state *agora*. On this square, 160 metres long and 56 metres in width, a number of important public buildings were situated. An *agora* usually had a temple. In Ephesus that temple has almost completely been lost. On the northern side of the *agora* lies a remarkable structure, an *odeion*. This building dates

◄ *The most spectacular building in Ephesus is the Celsus library. The façade is exuberantly decorated with Corinthian columns, egg-and-tongues, acanthus leaves, inscriptions coloured in red and marble statues.*

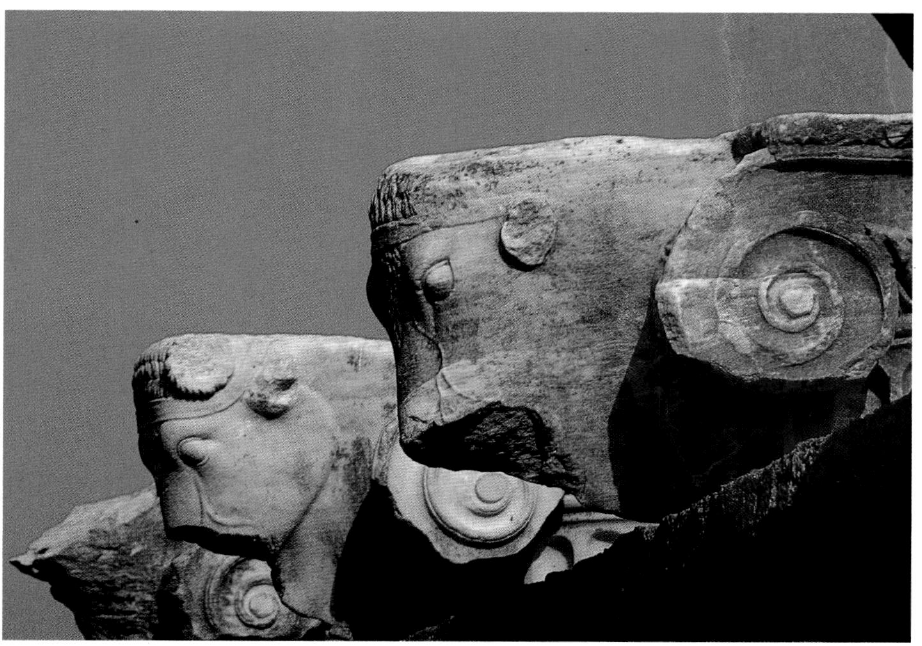

▲ *Consoles with rams' heads on the ledge of the originally two stories high stage building of the odeion.*

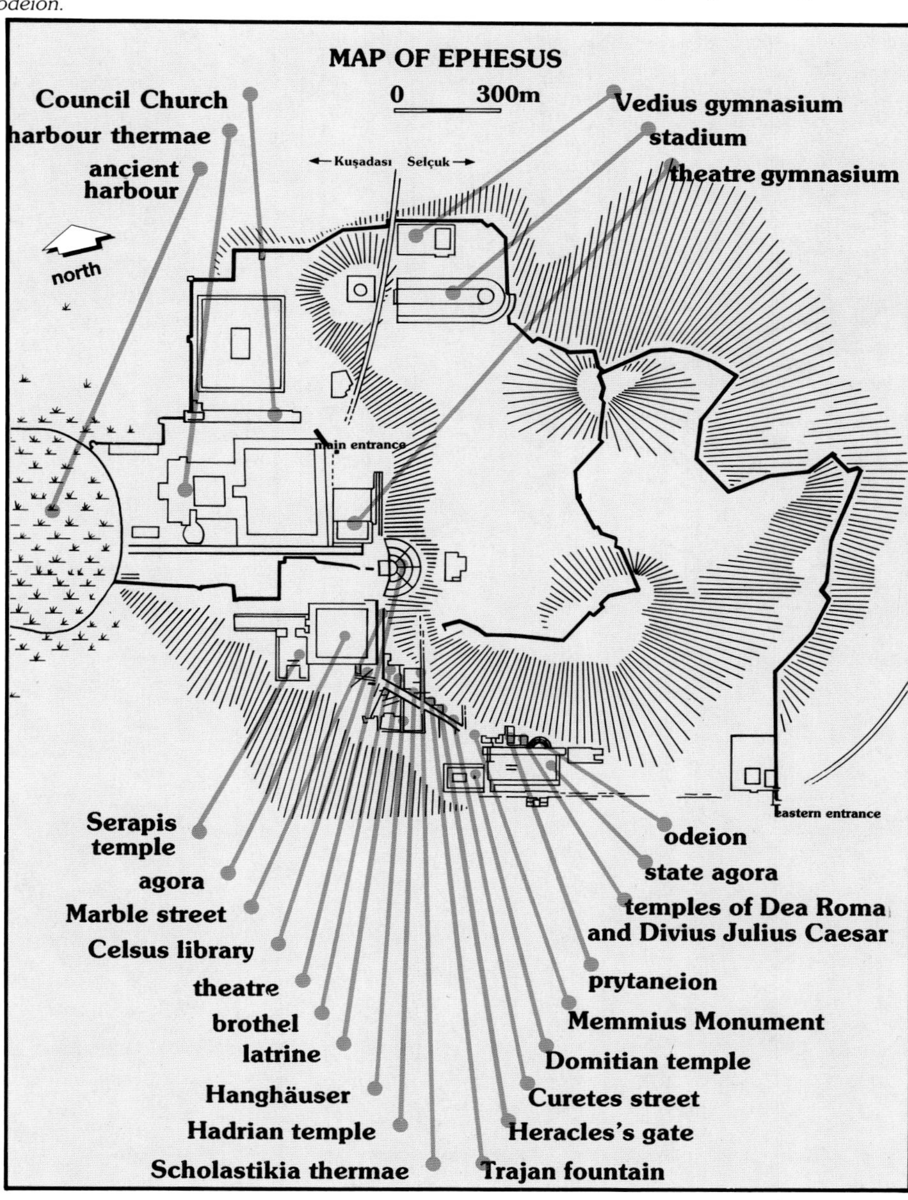

▲ *The odeion of Ephesus had a double function: it served as a music theatre and as an assembly hall. The building is connected with the prytaneion and the large state agora.*

At a junction in Ephesus stands the partly reconstructed
▼ *Memmius Monument depicting this general and his sons in military attire.*

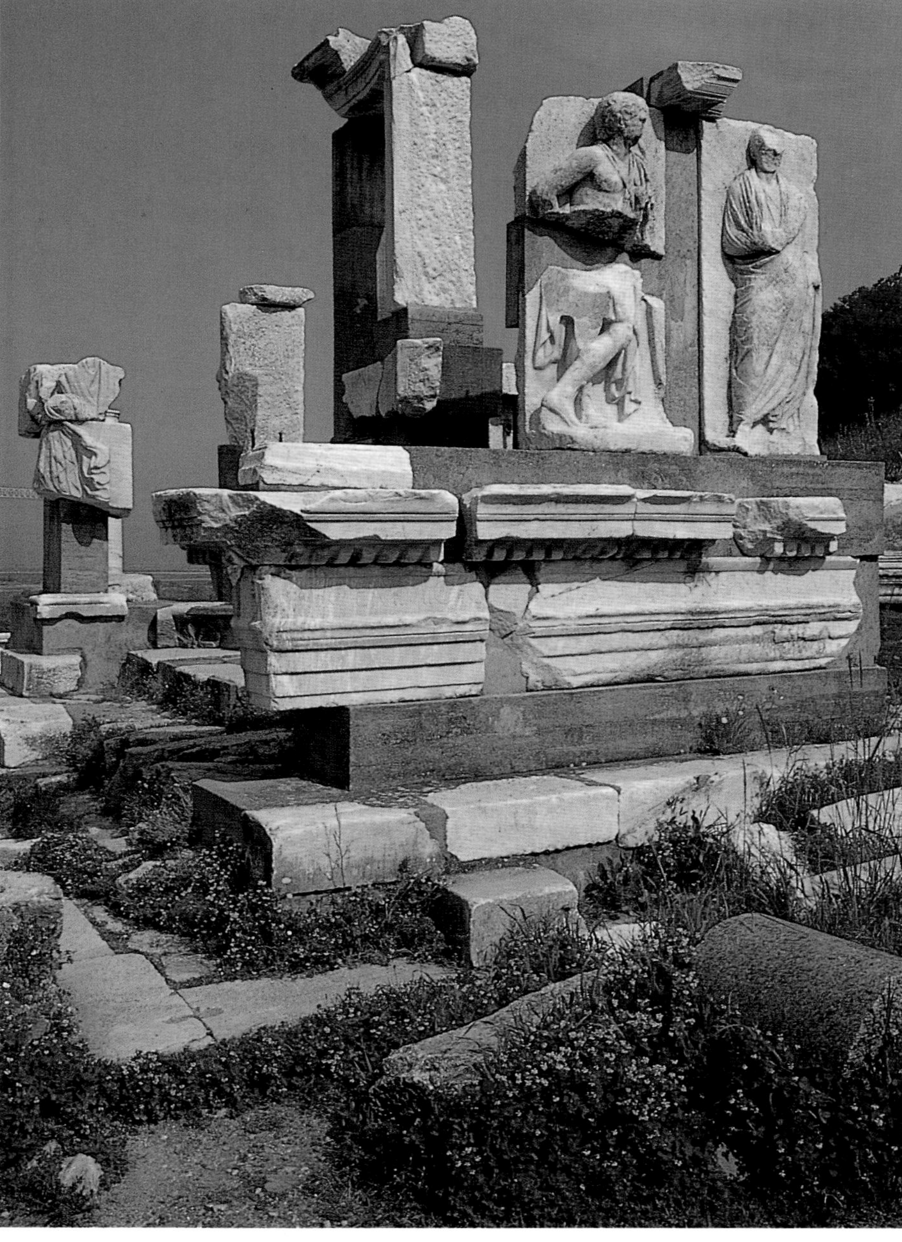

from 150 A.D. and resembles a small theatre. It was not merely used for musical performances but also as a *bouleuterion* (meeting room). The marble benches in the building provided seats for about 1400 people. Next to the *bouleuterion* were two temples dedicated to the Roman imperial cult, the temple of Dea Roma and of Divus Julius Caesar. These temples formed the connection with the adjoining *prytaneion.* In this building, comparable to our town hall, the magistrates held their meetings. A porticus gives access to the hall situated behind it. At this spot the eternal flame of the city goddess *Hestia Boulaia* used to burn day and night. The Dorian columns of the porticus are provided with inscriptions. In the *prytaneion* the famous statues of *Artemis* Ephesia have been discovered, now on display in the Archaeological Museum of Selçuk.

The street running past the *odeion* and *prytaneion*, ends in a small square. A path to the left leads to the arch which is all that is left of a large fountain or well-building from 93 A.D. The fragments of a sculpture group found at this spot depict one of the adventures of *Odysseus*, the blinding of the *Cyclops Polyphemus.* Remnants of the sculpture group can be seen in the museum of Selçuk. Diagonally opposite this well-building was once a temple dedicated to emperor Domitian (81-96). The sanctuary was constructed on an artificial terrace of 50 by 100 metres. A more than life-size statue of the emperor stood in the temple. Only recently, the head and an arm of this statue have been put on display in the Archaeological Museum at Selçuk as well.

At the nearby junction of the main road with a side-road a graceful relief of *Nike*, the winged goddess of victory, immediately catches the eye. This is also the spot where the remains of the Memmius Monument can be found. This Memmius was a grandson of the Roman statesman Sulla. The monument probably served as a tomb and the urn containing Memmius's ashes might have been interred here. The monument consists of a base carrying stone blocks with reliefs of Roman soldiers.

From the junction a beautifully paved road descends. This road is called the Curetes street, after an important class of priests in Ephesus. The priests held functions in the *Artemis* cult. According to mythology, the Curetes were the ones who made a deafening din during the delivery of *Leto*, in order to distract the attention of jealous *Hera*, in that way allowing for the birth of the twins *Apollo* and *Artemis.* In the Roman period the Curetes also had a political function.

Along the Curetes street are socles on which statues of benefactors of the city were placed. At the head of the street lie the remnants of a fountain dating from the time of emperor Trajan. Originally the fountain had a height of twelve metres and was decorated with statues. A number of these statues have meanwhile been transferred to the museum of Selçuk. On the spot itself only a part of the frame and a fragment of a statue can be seen.

Diagonally opposite the Trajan fountain, a path with steps ascends steeply to a number of carefully restored houses. Dwellings from the 'pre-Roman' period have as yet not been discovered in Ephesus. Presumably the city was constructed according to a regular pattern in the Hellenistic era, mainly in the third century B.C. In the Roman period the street plan and the residential blocks were adapted to the orientation of the Curetes street. These recently excavated houses have been built against the slope of a hill in the centre of the city. This

has provided them with their name: Hanghäuser (Slope dwellings). The luxurious design and the location in the city-centre make it likely that these houses were inhabited by the dignitaries of Ephesus. How old the Roman houses exactly are is difficult to determine. A few of the house walls can be dated back to the first century A.D. and there are indications that some houses were inhabited until well into the seventh century. The Hanghäuser have all been arranged according to the same principle: an inner court enclosed by a colonnade behind which lay the bedrooms, the living-rooms, the kitchen and the toilet. The floors were often covered with mosaics and the walls were decorated with paintings deriving from mythology. Nowadays the restored Hanghäuser form a separate museum block.
Opposite this residential district in the Curetes street are the ruins of the Hadrian temple dating from the second century. The entry is formed by an arch supported by two columns. In the middle of the arch a bust of a city goddess has been incorporated. The Greek inscription (during the Roman period Greek was also official language) states that the temple was dedicated to emperor Hadrian. The temple confirmed the ties of friendship between Rome and independent Ephesus. Behind the Hadrian temple lies a bathing building from the first century, still in very good condition. The baths were enlarged in the fourth century, financed by a rich Christian lady, called Scholastikia, hence the name Scholastikia *thermae*. In the *caldarium* (warm water

◂ *Halfway down the Curetes street is a small temple dedicated to emperor Hadrian. A replica of the city goddess Tyche crowns the keystone in the arch of the façade.*

The interior of one of the houses. The rooms around the inner court have splendid mosaic floors and murals. ▾

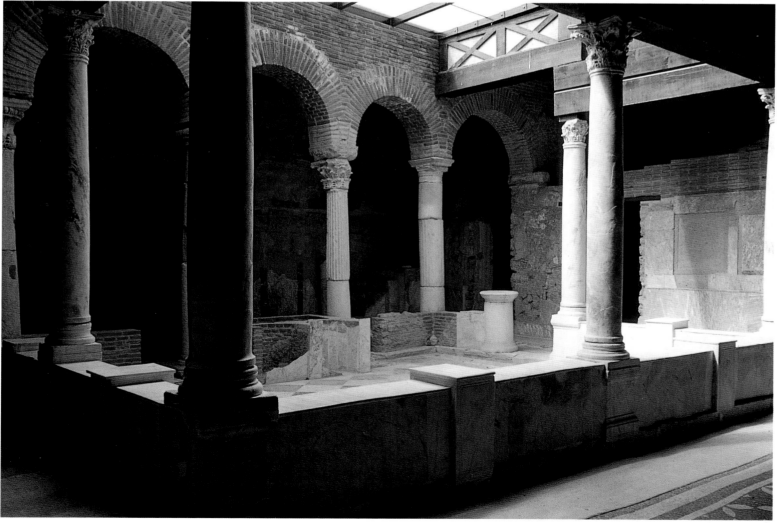

Latrines

Via Mesopotamia and Egypt the toilet was introduced into the Greek world and later adopted by the Romans. Both individual toilets and public latrines were constructed. Often the toilet was situated near the entrance of a house or near the kitchen, but also in an alley behind the house. Public latrines were mostly located in the city centre, close to busy places like theatres and markets. Bathing buildings had their own latrines, sometimes facing the street and probably also for the use of passers-by.

The most important technical facility in a latrine were the water channels. Water flowed through a drainage under the seats, removing the faeces. In front of the seats was a narrower and more shallow trough, through which water flowed as well. Visitors could dip a sponge into this trough in order to clean themselves. People had marble seats with key-shaped openings on the front and upper sides at their disposal. The latrine had an entrance with a porch, where a small amount of money was paid to the attendant on duty, before going in. The door to the room with the seats was constructed in such a way that from the street nobody could look in. The room was provided with a spacious light and air shaft in the middle, the walls were covered with marble slabs and the floor sometimes had mosaics.

◄ *The toilet of a private house in Ephesus bears the picture of the philosopher Solon, uttering thought-provoking sayings concerning bowel motions and digestion.*

In the centre of Ephesus, opposite the residential area and hemmed in between the bathing building and the brothel, lies a public latrine. It had space for well over 40 persons at the same time. ▼

Public latrines at the head of the shopping street in Sardis. The water flowed through a deep drainage channel under the seats and through a narrower trough in front of the seats. ▼

The Urartian palaces were comfortably fitted out, a toilet was part of the basic conveniences. The drainage hole in the ground was connected with a pipe discharging onto the steep slope. ▼

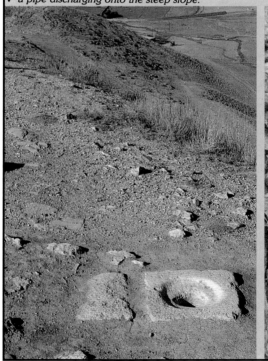

Hidden among the overgrown ruins of a Roman villa in Side lies the marble seat of a private lavatory. ▼

Theatre visitors in Side could make use of a luxuriously designed public latrine in one of the vaulted arches behind the stage building. ▼

bath) the *hypocaust* can still be seen. This is a system allowing hot air to circulate under the floor, in this way warming the bathing water and the room above. An alley next to the baths leads to the ancient public lavatories of this city district. On the seats, which were of marble and had key-shaped openings, people sat snugly together. Water used to flow through a trough in front of the seats. In the middle of the latrine was an open space serving as an air and light shaft. This part of the floor was decorated with a mosaic. A brothel was built west of the toilet building in the first century. The ground floor had a large hall for the visitors while the first floor accommodated the rooms for the girls.

The impressive façade of the Celsus library at the end of the Curetes street dominates the townscape of Ephesus. The building also functions as the mausoleum of the Roman Tiberius Julius Celsus, who was governor of Asia Minor. To honour him, his son had this library constructed at the outset of the second century. The library contained 12,000 scrolls in cabinets along the walls. The façade of the building has been renovated to its former splendour by Austrian archaeologists and replicas of the statues representing wisdom, virtue, intelligence and reason have been placed in the niches. Behind the façade, in the library itself, notice boards have been hung, explaining the building history and the reconstruction.

In the forecourt of the library is the recently restored gate, giving access to a spacious *agora*, the square where trading took place. This square was originally constructed in the third century B.C. and altered in the third century A.D. During the excavations it appeared that the original street-level had been two metres lower than at present. There used to be shops in the colonnades on several sides, some of them with three floors. A big water-clock presumably adorned the middle of the square. On the south-west side of the *agora* are the remnants of a *Serapis* temple. Granite from Egypt has been found in the enormous building dating from the second century and there is reference to an Egyptian cult in the inscriptions. Striking are the columns hewn out of one chunk with a height of fourteen metres and each weighing about fifty-seven tons.

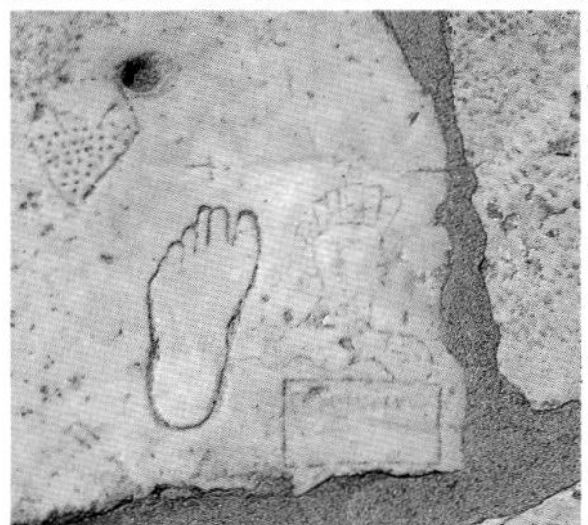

The Marble street runs from the Celsus library to the theatre. The name of this street is derived from its pavement and the statues on both sides. Scratched in one of the marble slabs covering the street are a woman's head, a foot and a heart. This inscription dates from the Byzantine period and served as a 'bill board' and indicator of the brothel!

At the end of the Marble street lies the immense theatre situated against a hill. The structure originally dates from the Hellenistic period, but was rebuilt several times in the Roman era. The theatre offers seats to over 24,000 visitors. The spectators' section, the *cavea*, has a diameter of more than 154 metres and is divided into three compartments by two passage-ways. The façade of the stage building to which the audience faced, originally had a height of eighteen metres and was richly decorated with statues and reliefs. In summer, performances and concerts are still given here. From the top rows of the theatre one has a beautiful view of

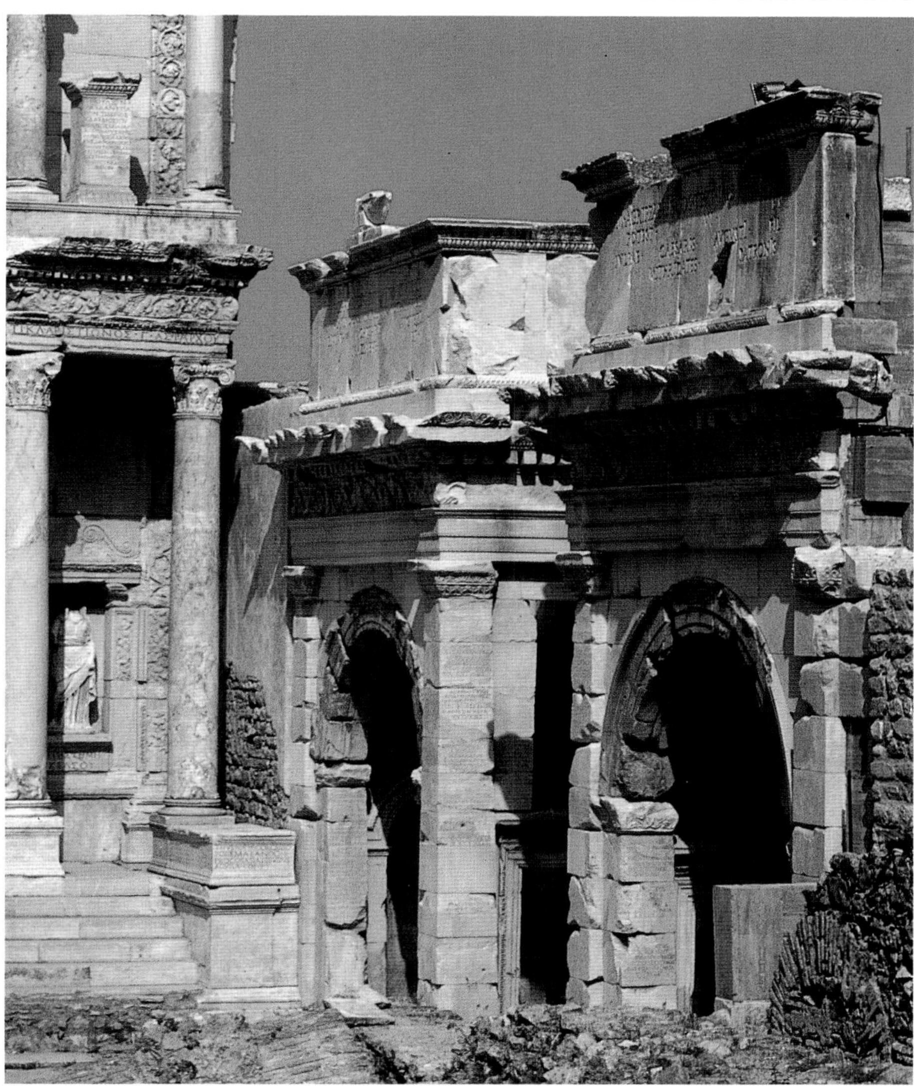

▲ *Next to the library a recently restored gate with three passage-ways gives access to the agora. Niches for water basins have been constructed in the gate. In a niche in the eastern passage-way an inscription reads: 'Whoever urinates in this place will be punished in court'.*

This triangular architectural fragment belongs to Heracles's Gate, which once stood at the head of the Curetes street. The goddess of victory comes flying along in fluttering garments, with a laurel wreath in her extended hand. ▼

▲ *From the upper rows of the theatre one has a splendid view across the stage building, the Arkadiane and the silted harbour of Ephesus. These days the theatre can still seat 24,000 people. During the celebration of Independence Day (23 April) the huge theatre regains its former splendour.* ▼

Ephesus and the surrounding scenery. In the distance the sea, which used to come up close to the theatre in classical days, can be discerned. The outlines of the silted harbour still clearly show in the swampy vegetation.
From the theatre a street leads in the direction of the ancient harbour. This harbour street or Arkadiane used to be 500 metres long and eleven metres in width. On both sides of the street were roofed-over colonnades housing shops. The four large columns nowadays standing on the Arkadiane, once had statues of the evangelists.
On the west side of the road leading to the main entrance of the excavations, the ruins of the theatre *gymnasium* and the harbour *gymnasium* are still visible. This is also the site of the Council Church, where during the council of 431 Nestorianism was forsworn. After having left the excavation site, en route to the village of Selçuk three kilometres further on, the scanty remains of the stadium and the Vedius *gymnasium* are passed. Next to the *gymnasium* are the remnants of a latrine, of which the drainage canals and the entrance with elegant dolphins are still clearly recognizable among the overgrown walls.
The ruins of the Artemision are located along the road from the much frequented sea-side resort Kuşadası to Selçuk. A short walk from the centre of Selçuk leads to the temple, numbered among one of the seven Wonders of the World. At the time of the first Greek colonists, there used to exist a cult dedicated to the mothergoddess *Kybele* in many places in Asia Minor. The Greeks introduced the goddess *Artemis* and a communal *Kybele-Artemis* cult came into being. As a local goddess she was worshipped in different places in Asia Minor in more or less an identical form; this was for example the case in Aphrodisias, Hierapolis and Perge. In the beginning of the sixth century B.C. a new temple for *Artemis* was erected in Ephesus. This was a large-scale project since the idea was to build a temple surpassing the one for *Hera* on Samos. Owing to the swampy subsoil a foundation of alternating layers of charcoal and leather was used. On top of this the first and largest marble structure ever made arose. In 356 B.C. a certain Herostratos committed arson in order to secure a place for himself in history books. He managed to do so. The fire supposedly took place in the night that Alexander the Great was born. When Alexander visited Ephesus, the rebuilding of the sanctuary was almost completed. This temple was not granted eternal life either and nowadays only one column of this Wonder has remained, functioning as a nesting-place for a stork. And even this single column had to be put upright by archaeologists.

MAP OF THE ARTEMISION

0 20 40m

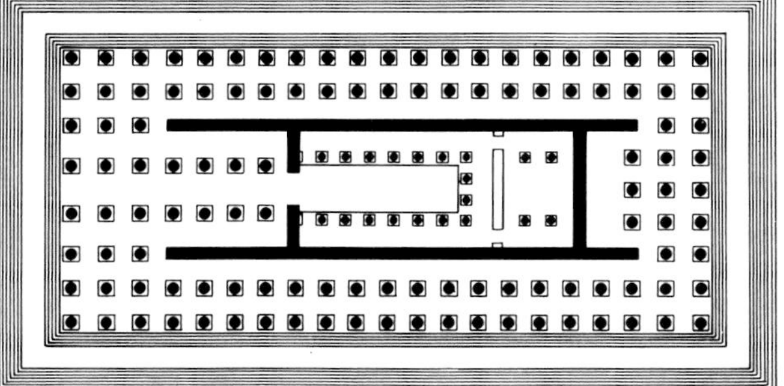

Clattering storks in Selçuk

The friendly town of Selçuk is located at the bottom of the Ayasoluk hill on which the huge Saint John's Cathedral (130 metres long and 65 metres in width) was erected in the sixth century. According to tradition John the Evangelist died at an advanced age in Ephesus. His burial chapel constitutes the centre of a three-nave cathedral with an *atrium*, an *exonarthex*, a *narthex*, a main nave and aisles. The capitals in the nave are decorated with the monograms of emperor Justinian and his wife Theodora. In one of the ante-rooms a baptismal font in an old Christian tradition has been preserved. The building was amply provided with domes: six large ones over the nave and the aisles and five smaller ones over the *narthex*. One of the elevated

RECONSTRUCTION DRAWING OF THE SAINT JOHN'S CATHEDRAL

▲ *The baptismal font of Saint John's Cathedral has steps in the arms of the cross. According to old Christian custom, baptism meant complete immersion.*

▼ *This solid gate gives access to the vast building block of Saint John's Cathedral.*

terraces of the building offers a fine view of the adjoining İsa Bey mosque dating from the fourteenth century.
In the interior of this mosque the remarkably brightly coloured *faience* tiles on the *pendentives* (triangular connectors between columns and dome) have recently been restored. The dilapidated minaret has for many years provided accommodation for a stork family. Somewhat further on, in the centre of Selçuk, are another minaret and a column on which storks have built their nests.
Three large marble statues of the *Artemis* Ephesia are the showpieces of the Archaeological Museum in Selçuk. Opinions are divided about the significance of their striking bossoms. Possible explanations are: an abundance of breasts, eggs, or scrotums of sacrificed bulls. A certainty is that fertility is symbolized. The robe is richly decorated with *sphinxes*, horses, lions and bees. According to a familiar Anatolian tradition the goddess is flanked by two lions.

Priene, silted and deserted

About 60 kilometres south of Selçuk are the ruins of the Greek town of Priene. From the excavation site one has a breathtaking view across the delta formed by the languid Maeander (the present-day Büyük Menderes). The exact location of the first settlement is unknown. As a result of the continuous silting of the bay, this settlement moved more and more inland. In

This statue is one of the three renowned marble statues of the Artemis Ephesia which were found in the prytaneion. One of the rooms in the Archaeological Museum at Selçuk is especially ▼ dedicated to the city goddess of Ephesus.

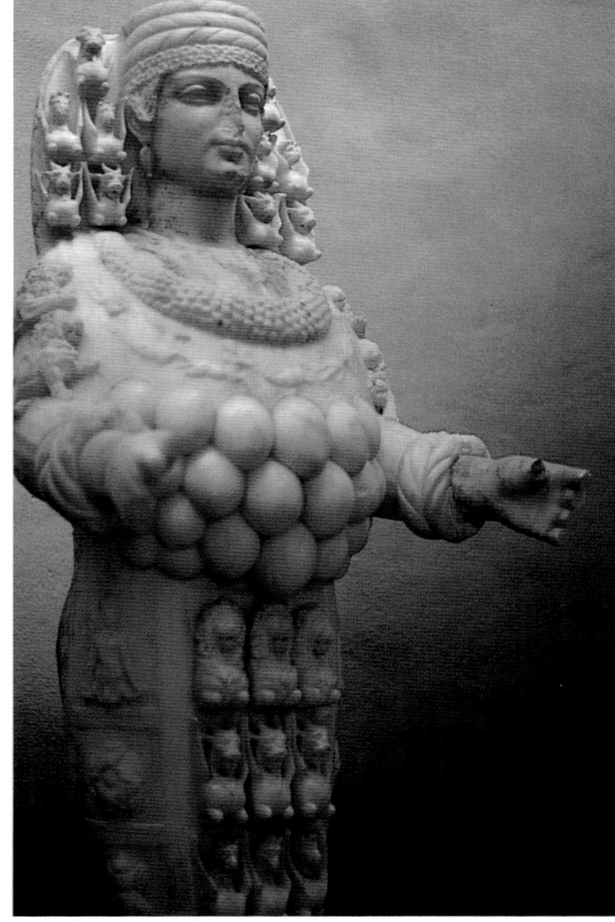

▲ The pinnacle of the minaret of the fourteenth century İsa Bey Mosque is the summer residence of a stork family.

the fourth century B.C. the inhabitants decided to move. Around the middle of that century the new port Priene was founded at the bottom of the Mykale Mountains. When this harbour became silted too, the city lost the competitive battle with the neighbouring Miletus. It was not until the Byzantine period that Priene was definitely deserted.

Nowadays the ruins are located some fifteen kilometres inland. Undeservedly, Priene is hardly frequented. A visit to the remains, mainly dating from the fourth century B.C., is certainly worthwhile. The streets with their public buildings and houses give a good impression of daily life in this former port.

The new city was constructed according to the Hippodamic system in which streets cross each other perpendicularly in a regular pattern. This had led to rectangular blocks of houses, each containing four units. The main streets are orientated east-west. The buildings have their entrances on the south side, allowing them to profit from the sun's warmth in winter. In summer the sun is so high in the sky, that it cannot penetrate inside. Priene is protected by city walls, also dating from the fourth century B.C., fortified in several places by square towers. In the eastern wall water reservoirs were constructed. From these reservoirs the water was distributed through terracotta pipes.

The city was built on terraces against a steep slope. The lower *gymnasium* and a stadium lie at a height of 30 meters. The public buildings such as the *prytaneion*, the *bouleuterion*, the *agora* and the *Zeus* temple are located at a height of about 80 metres. The terrace with the *Athena* temple and the theatre is 100 metres, the temple of *Demeter* 130 metres and the *acropolis* 370 metres above sea-level. Due to differences in altitude the *acropolis* as well as the lower *gymnasium* and stadium are difficult to reach. In the middle of the lower *gymnasium* lies the *palaestra*. This sports-field was enclosed by colonnades. On the northern side of the buildings is the space where young people used to study, the *ephebeion*. On the wall some ancient graffiti can be observed. East of the *gymnasium* lies the 190 metres long stadium. At the beginning of the racetrack a groove has been constructed in the stones at the starting point. It served as a take-off mark for the athletes.

From the entrance of the excavation site a steep path leads to the buildings on the middle terraces. Very well-preserved is the *bouleuterion* in Priene dating from the second century B.C. In this almost square building the 'town council' met. The central hall provided seats for 640 citizens who could gather into the building from three side-streets. They were seated on marble benches, ten rows along the sides and sixteen rows in the back. Around the *bouleuterion* was a corridor and a wooden roof rested on the building. The pillars carrying the roof can still be recognized. It is likely that the building had windows too. In the centre is an altar decorated with reliefs of bulls' heads and laurel leaves.

East of the *bouleuterion* lies the *prytaneion*. Much of the original building has been lost, for it was renovated in the Roman Imperial Age. The *prytaneion* in its present state has a central courtyard and is paved with limestone slabs.

Narrow streets with steps constitute the cross connection between the main streets. One of the series of steps leads to the theatre, which provided seats for about 5000 people in ancient days; people who did not just come for relaxation but also for political meetings. The

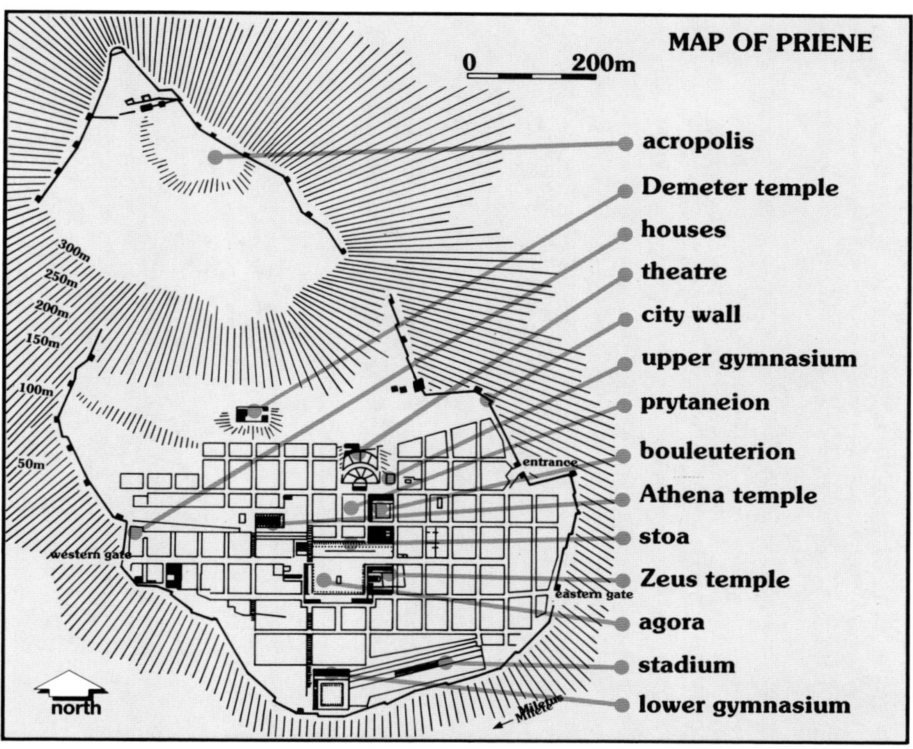

▲ The bouleuterion of Priene.

▲ Bronze statue of a Roman magistrate in the Regional Museum in Adana.

Government

The most important institutions connected with daily government of the *polis* (city state) were the boulè and the prytanis who met respectively in the *bouleuterion* and the *prytaneion*.

The *bouleuterion* in Greek polity represents the town hall The word has been derived from the boulè, which had grown out of the college of elders, the representatives of nobility. The powers of this national assembly comprised supervision of finances, interior relations, preparation of legislation and participation in executing decisions.

The word *prytaneion* is derived from the Greek word prytanis. The main task of the prytaneis was responsibility for daily government. Their functions can best be compared to the council of Mayor and Aldermen. The *prytaneion* was also the site of 'the eternal flame', symbolizing the life of the city. As a metaphor for the hearth in their mother-city, colonists took a sparkle of the fire to the new settlement that was to be founded.

On the restored columns of the prytaneion in Ephesus are inscriptions in which dignitaries make mention of their merits for the city. ▼

▲ *The Athena temple of Priene, with in the background the sheer rising acropolis, has a magnificent location. This Ionian sanctuary with its slender columns and balanced proportions was a source of inspiration for many architects in antiquity.*

The washing room in the lower gymnasium of Priene. From the lions' heads water flowed into ▼ *the basins. Here the pupils could wash after their exercises.*

theatre dates from the fourth century B.C., but was somewhat altered during the Roman era. Characteristic for a Greek theatre was that during construction the natural inclination of a hill was incorporated. The seats have only been partly excavated; the front row of seats has backs. Five honorary seats of marble with lions' paws were inserted into the first row. Opposite the stage is an altar dedicated to *Dionysos*. The stage building used to have two floors. Against the stage house a porticus (*proskenion*) has been constructed. Its front is in good condition and was once brightly painted in many colours; during excavations traces of red and blue paint have been found. The *proskenion* has pillars with Dorian semi-columns above which the *triglyphs* and *metopes* are clearly visible. In the Greek period the actors came into the *orchestra* through three openings. Between these door-openings *pinakes* (wooden panels) were fastened, at the same time serving as a décor. The attachment holes are still visible in some places in the stone. Next to the western door of the stage building a hole can be discerned, which used to contain the lift for the 'deus ex machina', the apparition of the deity. An actor was hoisted up to the roof of the stage building by means of this lift in order to bring the solution in the complicated play as a deity. In the Roman period the action was moved from the *orchestra* to the stage floor (*logeion*) on the *proskenion*. This floor was supported by heavy stone beams, some of which have been preserved.

From the theatre a path leads to the higher situated *Demeter* sanctuary, the oldest temple of the city. Along the southern outer side of the temple a gutter was constructed, serving as a drainage for the blood of sacrificed animals.

On the west side of the middle terraces are the building blocks with houses. The walls, five to six metres high, reveal that the houses sometimes had more than one floor. Often the walls were decorated with stucco, the roofs were tiled. Each house was built around a courtyard providing ample daylight and circulation of fresh air.

The Ionian columns of the *Athena* temple can be observed from afar. This temple served as a model for later Ionian temples. The architect, Pytheos, applied a number of innovations, such as fixed size proportions and columns with 24 *cannelures* (flutes in the column) on square plinths. The temple was surrounded by six columns on the front and eleven on the sides. In the temple, painted over in former times, was a seven metres high statue of the goddess *Athena*, hewn out of local Mykale-marble. In front of the temple the remnants of an altar can be found. The construction of the *Athena* temple took place between the fourth and the second century B.C. The money for building it was made available by, among others, Alexander the Great. In the course of the centuries, the *Athena* temple was severely damaged by several earthquakes. Fallen column cylinders and fragments of the ridge-piece lie chaotically around the sanctuary.

The highly elevated *acropolis* is very difficult to reach. A long climb across a ledge ends at the top where in antiquity a small garrison was quartered. The soldiers were relieved only once every three months. In clear weather, the huge theatre of Miletus can be discerned on the horizon.

Giant fennel

The giant fennel (Foeniculum capillaceum) is an umbelliferous plant, the seed of which is used as a spice. Its appearance is characterized by a long reedish stalk, sometimes a couple of metres high. The yellow flowers at the top form a dense umbel. The marrow of the fennel was sometimes applied in tinderboxes, as it immediately started to smoulder if a spark was dropped on it. Greek mythology tells the story of Prometheus stealing fire from heaven with the aid of this marrow. The plant played an important role as an attribute of the god Dionysos. The giant fennel served as a thyrsus rod in Dionysian processions. The crowning then often has a heart-shaped appearance and the stalks are tied together.

▲ *In the stadium of Priene a row of stones marks the site where the athletes 'were off'. An ingenious system with levers provided the means for a fair start.*

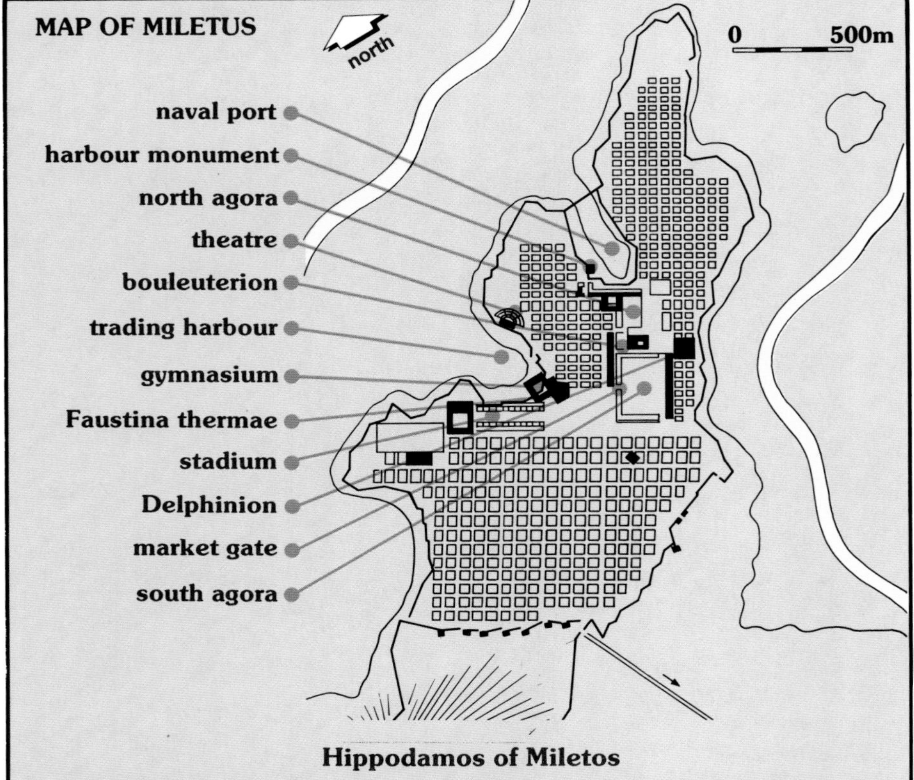

Hippodamos of Miletos

Hippodamos, the city architect from Miletus, designed a new regular map for his birthplace in 479 B.C. This model had already existed for some time, but Hippodamos is considered the theoretician behind it. The map of the area within the city walls was based on an oblong street plan, within which the buildings were systematically ordered. Important main streets, perpendicularly intersecting each other, were alternated with parallel running minor streets, dividing the city into a network of equal blocks. Squares and public buildings were assimilated into the system by combining a number of blocks. All houses in the blocks were similar and had their entrances facing the street. This uniformity also reflects equality as an expression of democratic principles. The orientation of the streets was determined by hygienic and topographic considerations. Often the broad streets ran east-west and the narrow ones north-south. In this way, wind and solar heat were optimally exploited. Miletus was not constructed on the basis of a central axis, but the straight-lined city plan was flexibly adjusted to the topographical situation. A finer example of the application of Hippodamos's ideas is the map of Priene.

Submerged into the swamp

Miletus (Miletos), located on a peninsula on the Anatolian west coast, used to be the largest and mightiest Ionian port. The imposing buildings of olden times have now crumbled down to ruins. The four harbours, surrounding the city in ancient days, have silted up due to sedimentation of the river Maeander and are now situated way inland. As a result of earthquakes, the groundwater level is higher than in antiquity, providing the reason why the major part of Miletus is nowadays submerged into a swamp.

In the second millennium B.C. this was already the location of an important trading colony, inhabited by native Carians and immigrated Cretans. The Ionians gained supremacy in the eleventh century B.C. and developed Miletus into a flourishing city. According to ancient tradition, the city possessed about 90 colonies, mainly in the Black Sea area. Through trading activities, these colonies brought tremendous wealth to their mother-city Miletus. Material prosperity was accompanied by exceptional achievements in the scholarly field. The city brought forth famous philosophers, such as the natural philosophers Thales, Anaximander and Anaximenes. This was the birthplace of western philosophy. Other famous scholars were the historian and geographer Hekataios and the city architect Hippodamos.

In 546 B.C. Miletus was captured by the Persians, who razed the city to the ground in 494 B.C. The immediate cause for this was Miletus's solidarity with Athens during the Persian wars. The city managed to recuperate fairly quickly however, and achieved great fame again in the field of trade and art during the Hellenistic era. From 133 B.C., when the whole of Asia Minor was incorporated into the Roman Empire, the Romans granted the city many favours and presented it with numerous splendid buildings. Eventually, as was the case in Priene, Miletus's harbours also silted up, causing the city to fall into decay comparatively early in the Byzantine period.

Due to its elevated position and its impressive walls the

▾ *Resembling a massive chunk of stone, the theatre of Miletus rises from the plain of the Maeander. Here 15,000 spectators could enjoy the performances.*

theatre is the most striking building of the city. The oldest remains date from the fourth century B.C., but the present shape of the theatre, consisting of the semi-circular *cavea* and the stage house, is Roman. The sizeable *cavea* has about 15,000 seats, among which very special ones reserved for the emperor and other prominent guests. The remains of two small columns are the only visible evidence of the imperial box with canopy. The *scaenae frons* consisted of three floors and was richly decorated with reliefs and statues.
From the high theatre hill the urban construction, based on the regular city plan of the architect Hippodamos, can be clearly observed. In the centre of the city a number of plots were reserved for public buildings. Here are e.g. an *agora*, a *bouleuterion*, a stadium, sanctuaries and baths.
Along the theatre hill a road leads through wet-lands to the old city-centre. Between the north *agora* on the right and baths annex *gymnasium* on the left, the *bouleuterion* of the city is reached. This meeting hall was built between 175 and 164 B.C. judging by an inscription in the entrance hall. This mentions that Timarchos and Herakleides dedicated the town-hall to *Apollo* of Didyma, *Hestia Boulaia* and the people, in honour of king Antiochos IV Epiphanes (175-164 B.C.). The buildings consisted of a *propylon* with behind it a large court enclosed by colonnades and the assembly hall. From the court four doors provided access to the semi-circular *auditorium*. The assembly hall offered seats to 1500 people and was covered with a wooden roof.
The *bouleuterion* adjoins the south *agora*, which has a size of 164 by 196 metres and is by far the largest of the three market places in Miletus. The south *agora* dates from the Hellenistic era and was provided with a monumental access-gate in Roman times. Nowadays this market gate can be admired in the Pergamum Museum in East-Berlin. The gate has two floors and three passage-ways, the façade is embellished with Corinthian columns. The south *agora* was enclosed by colonnades of the Dorian order. In the eastern gallery 79 shops were housed.

Even in the middle of summer the northern agora of Miletus is nearly completely flooded. The steps and columns of the stoa along the square can generally just be discerned. ▲

West of the south *agora* are the *thermae* of Faustina, of which the remains are in excellent condition. These baths were erected by asssignment of Faustina II, the wife of emperor Marcus Aurelius (161-180). The *thermae* are situated asymmetrically in relation to the other buildings and disturb the austere arrangement of the entire city plan. The *palaestra*, in size about 77 by 79 metres, was surrounded by colonnades of the Corinthian order on four sides and was connected with the *apodyterium* (the changing room). This room consisted of a long corridor with smaller rooms on both sides. From the *apodyterium* the other bathing rooms could be reached. The entrance hall of the changing room, the so-called Muses Hall, had a broad *apsis* and many niches, accommodating man-sized statues of *Apollo* and the nine *Muses*.
In contrast to the Faustina *thermae*, the stadium was again constructed according to the Hippodamic system. The stadium originally dates from 150 B.C., but was rebuilt many times in the course of the centuries. The track is 191 metres long and 29.5 metres wide. Many

◄ *The swampy vegetation in Miletus is an ideal biotope for numerous special species of tortoises.*

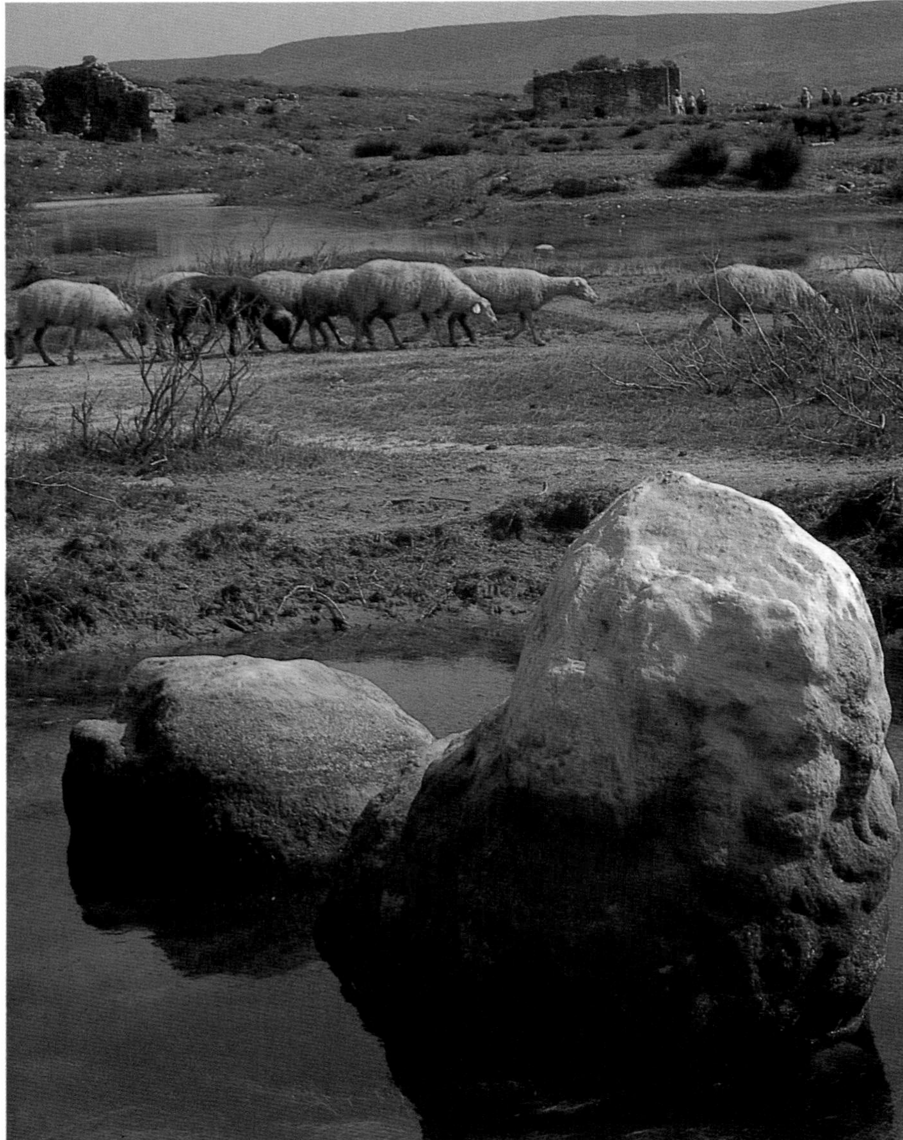

▲ Half submerged in the swamp this huge lion still guards the naval port of Miletus. At the threat of war a cable could be stretched between the two lions in the harbour entrance.

sports activities and ceremonies took place here. On both sides are the stands, twenty rows high, which could seat about 15,000 spectators. Remarkable is the absence of the semi-circular ends, also called *sphendonai*. Instead, monumental gates with Ionian and Corinthian columns had their place at the west and east end of the stadium. These gates obviously served an esthetic purpose. Nowadays a motorway has divided the stadium into two parts.
On the west side of the peninsula on which Miletus was located, two harbours were incorporated into the city plan. The west harbour in the Theatre Bay served as a trading harbour. The most northern harbour was located in the so-called Lions' Bay and was a naval base. The naval port was flanked by two huge stone lions between which a cable could be stretched to close off the harbour mouth at the threat of war.
Near the Lions' Bay lies the once very famous Delphinion, a temple dedicated to *Apollo* Delphinios as the protector of ships and sailors. The Delphinion consisted of a large temple court, enclosed by *stoai* on three sides. These days the sanctuary is mostly flooded, and due to algae growth the architectural fragments have a reddish hue. The Delphinion was connected with the *Apollo* temple in Didyma by a fifteen kilometres long Sacred Road. On both sides of this road, used for processions, were statues of *Branchides* (a class of priests). Nowadays these statues can be found in the local museum and in the British Museum.

Ionian natural philosophers

Philosophers' sarcophagus in the garden of the Regional Museum in Adana. On both sides of the door to the hereafter philosophers ▼ stand in line.

The Seven Sages are considered to be predecessors of the Greek philosophers. A number of these Seven Sages came from the Ionian region. They had set down a practical life-philosophy in brief proverbs. Their names tend to differ, as every city eagerly wanted to claim the fame of one of these Seven Sages. The most famous ones are: Thales of Miletos, Bias of Priene, Pittakos of Mytilene, Solon of Athens, Kleoboulos of Lindos, Chilon of Sparta and Periandros of Corinth. They lie at the root of sayings like: 'Carpe Diem', 'Know thyself' and 'Too much of ought is good for nought'.
Thales was the teacher of Anaximander and Anaximenes. These three philosophers from the sixth century B.C. became famous as the Ionian natural philosophers and the founders of the School of Miletos. They had a rational approach to the world surrounding them and are considered as the founders of western philosophy and science. The Ionian natural philosophers occupied themselves with meteorology, cosmology, mathematics and astronomy. Thales for example, was the first to predict a solar eclipse on the basis of mathematical calculations, namely the solar eclipse of 28 May 585 B.C.

Next to the Delphinion lies an elegant monument to commemorate the naval battle in 31 B.C. at Actium. The base of this harbour monument has been decorated with reliefs of ▼ mythical sea creatures.

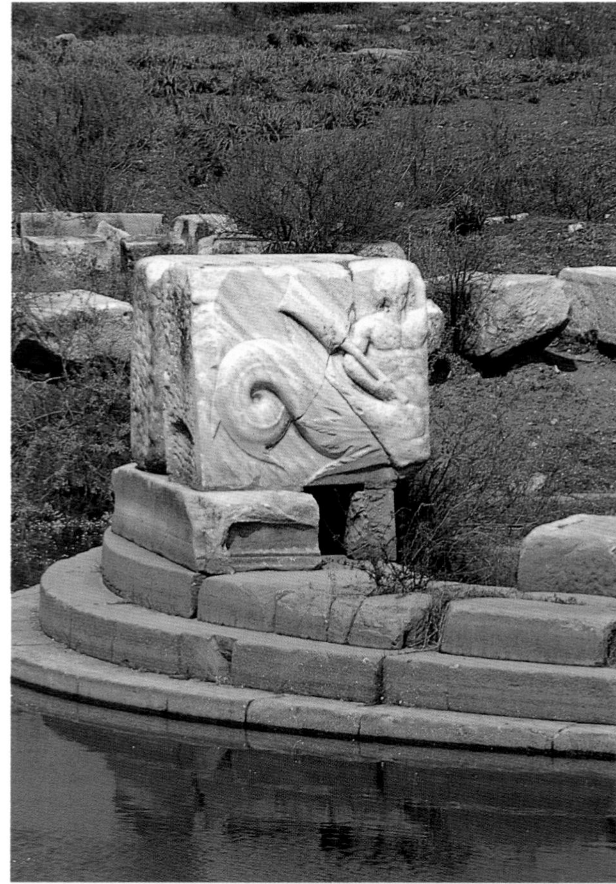

The Apollo sanctuary of Didyma

Didyma is renowned for its imposing ruins of what used to be a very famous temple, dedicated to *Apollo*. This Hellenistic temple measures more than 109 by 51 metres and its size makes it one of the largest of the Greek world. The *Apollo* sanctuary of Didyma was an important oracle site, enjoying great fame in antiquity. The sanctuary is located among the houses of the small village of Eski Hisar (Old Palace). In the 1960s the Turkish government founded a new village, Yeni Hisar (New Palace), with the intention that the inhabitants could settle there, allowing the area around the sanctuary to be examined. Many people, however, stayed in the houses around the *Apollo* temple.
The word Didyma is derived from the Greek 'didymoi', signifying twins. In most cases this is related to the famous twins *Apollo* and *Artemis*. In Didyma only a temple dedicated to *Apollo* was found. The oldest remains date from the seventh century B.C. and lie within the present temple. A sacred well, an altar and presumably a laurel tree were part of this sanctuary. It is likely that there was already a sanctuary on this location before the Greek period.
The present-day remnants for the greater part date from the Hellenistic period. Alexander the Great made money available to erect the temple. During the construction it was taken into account that the sacred well of the oracle had to remain under the open sky. The construction started around 332 B.C. and continued until well into the Roman era, but the temple was never completely finished. This could clearly be

In the grass, not far from ▲ the temple, lies a remarkable fragment of the frieze. It bears a Medusa-head, a malicious looking woman with wild, thick hair.

MAP OF THE APOLLO TEMPLE
0 25 50m

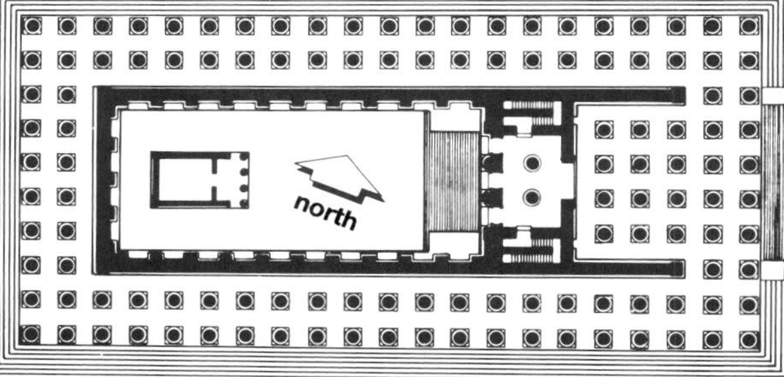

The huge inner court of the Apollo temple at Didyma was the seat of a famous oracle. Despite financial aid from Alexander the Great and several Roman emperors the sanctuary was never finished. ▼

The column bases in ► Didyma show a great variation of decorations consisting of scales, palmettes, sea-creatures and geometrical patterns.

proved from three columns, standing upright when German archaeologists started on the reconstruction of the oracle sanctuary. The two columns on the north side were connected by an *architrave* (roof beam) and were completed. The single column on the south side however lacked any finishing. The *cannelures* e.g. were only hewn out just under the capital. The capital itself had already been finished on the ground and had then been hauled on to the column.
On the east side of the sanctuary high steps lead to a wood of huge columns. After the front two column rows, one enters the *pronaos* (entrance hall), the roof of which used to be supported by twelve columns. The *pronaos* and the 'Two Column Room' behind it, were later employed for the storage of oil and straw. A fire in the tenth century devastated this part of the temple. From the entrance hall two arched corridors lead to the inner court. In antiquity these corridors were used exclusively by the oracle priests. In the immense court was a small temple for the cult statue of *Apollo*. The inner walls of the court served as a drawing table during the construction period. With favourable skimming light, the construction drawings of the temple are vaguely observable on the greenish efflorescent and weather-stained walls. From the inner court broad stairs lead to the 'Two Column Room', a room used to record and announce the sayings of the oracle. At the rear of the sanctuary the fallen column cylinders lie neatly in a row. In the high grass at the south side of the *Apollo* temple tortoises lead an undisturbed existence among the remains of a small stadium.

The slender columns of the Zeus temple of Euromos are in remarkably good ▼ condition.

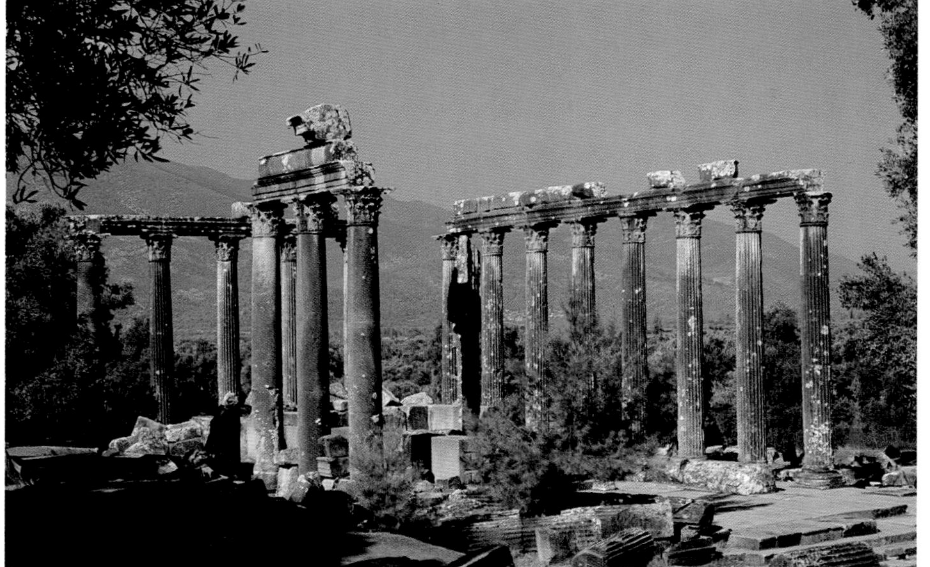

▲ *Klaros was the site of an important oracle sanctuary, which, just like Delphi and Didyma, was greatly renowned. The thousands of inscriptions are not oracle texts, but the names of visitors. Columns, porches, benches, a sun dial, any stone material was employed as a writing table.*

Oracle places

Famous from antiquity is, of course, the oracle at Delphi, but other places, such as Didyma and Klaros also had a sanctuary where the gods were consulted through priests and priestesses. It was not just a matter of simply addressing a question to the god *Apollo*. A questioner had to cleanse himself at a well in front of the temple and, perhaps of prime importance, had to pay for the advice. Private matters were eleven times more expensive than public affairs. Before the deity could be consulted, a sacrifice was made by slaughtering a goat on the altar in front of the temple. The question was then posed to a priest, who thereafter entered the temple. This priest served as an intermediary who conveyed the question to the priestess seated in the holy of holies of the temple. Before pronouncing an oracle, the priestess had been fasting for three days, had been subjected to a ritual cleansing with water from a sacred well and had chewed on laurel leaves. The priest proclaimed the oracle. Most times practical advice was given but the oracle sayings were often ambiguous, as in the case of king Kroisos.

A Corinthian sanctuary

In Euromos the best-preserved Corinthian temple of Asia Minor can be found. This sanctuary dedicated to *Zeus* lies only about ten metres beside the main road, twenty kilometres south of Herakleia. The graceful columns with their Corinthian capitals can be observed from afar. The *architrave*, the beam connecting the columns, is also largely in perfect condition. Inscriptions have been applied on twelve of the sixteen columns still standing upright. From the wording of the texts it appears, that the columns were presented by prominent citizens.
The other buildings of ancient Euromos lie hidden in the landscape among pine trees and olive orchards. Of the theatre only the bowl-shape remains against a mountain slope.

The city walls of Herakleia

The modest remains of Herakleia have an idyllic location along Lake Bafa on the border of Ionia and Caria. In ancient times the city had a sea connection, but river sediments have reduced the estuary to a lake. Especially during the Hellenistic and Roman eras Herakleia held a prominent trading position and in the early Christian and Byzantine periods the city was of considerable importance too. On some of the islands in Lake Bafa the ruins of small churches and monasteries can be found. In the course of the centuries the water level of the lake has risen, as a result of which the harbour works and some burial tombs from the classical period have been flooded.
The ancient Herakleia was famous for its city walls, which were erected around 287 B.C. and initially had a length of more than six kilometres. This was later reduced to about four kilometres. One can walk along the ancient walls and towers and enjoy the view across the lake and the olive orchards in the surrounding area. Just like Priene, Herakleia had been constructed according to the so-called Hippodamic system. Little remains to be seen of the architecture of the classical period. The most remarkable ruin in Herakleia is the late Hellenistic temple of *Athena*, not far from the *agora*, which, by the way, is partly hidden by a potato field.

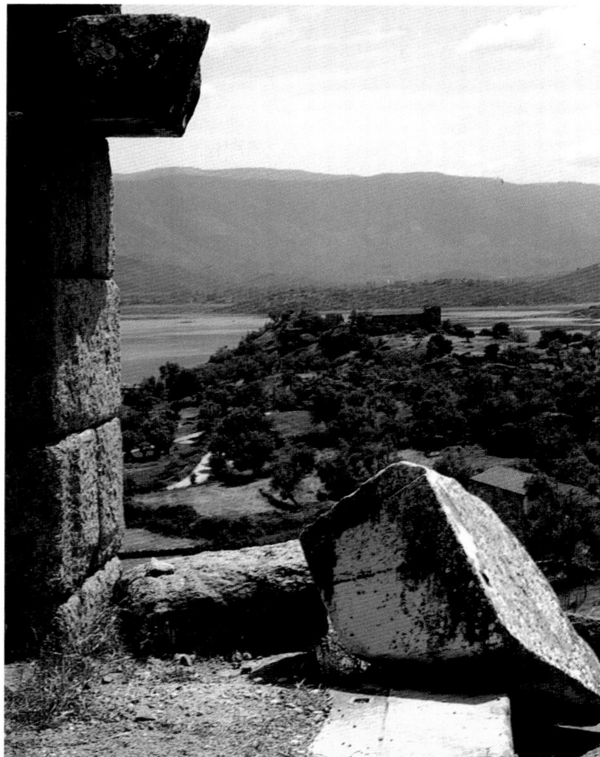

◄ One of the more than 50 towers in the city wall of Herakleia with, in the background, Lake Bafa.

Forgotten cities

The main road to the south leads from İzmir via Milâs to Yatağan. Just before Yatağan large-scale brown coal digging threatens the remnants of the ancient Stratonikeia. In the present-day village of Eskihisar numerous *spolia* are visible in streets, walls and back gardens of the houses. The modern main road has swallowed up the theatre for the major part.
In the northern direction from Yatağan to Aydın are two small excavation sites in the dreamy Carian interior: Alabanda and Alinda.
Cotton shrubs flank the by-road to Alabanda. The walls of the *bouleuterion* from the Hellenistic period are in remarkably good condition. The vast plain in front of the building is scattered with the remains of the *agora*.
Alinda can be reached by a winding rural road among corn fields and cotton plantations. Just outside the village of Karpuzlu a path ascends to the rocky *acropolis*. The impressive terrace walls of the *agora* are partly standing upright. The market building was more than 90 metres long and 15 metres high and consisted of three floors in which the warehouses were situated. In 334/333 B.C. Alexander the Great spent the winter in Alinda. He aided queen Ada in defending her small kingdom and she looked upon Alexander as her son.
In Aydın the road from Yatağan to the north joins the main road from the coast to the interior. Aydın, the former Tralleis, had been an influential town from the time of around 400 B.C. In 334 B.C. Alexander the Great also visited this town. The boy from Tralleis, the statue of a young athlete, is one of the showpieces of the Archaeological Museum in İstanbul.
Not far from Aydın lies the village of Sultanhisar. From the centre, one arrives at the excavations of Nysa after two kilometres. The picturesque ruins of this ancient city, including a theatre, a *bouleuterion* and a library, are hardly ever visited. Nysa, assumedly founded in the first half of the third century B.C., was a well-known city in antiquity, providing education to, among others,

The bouleuterion of Alabanda used to be decorated with pilasters on the outer side. ▼

The aquaduct of Alinda is situated on the acropolis against a small slant of the mountain slope.
▼ At the bottom of the four remaining arches sarcophagi lie chaotically together.

▲ One of the reliefs embellishing the stage building in Nysa. Dionysos, the god of wine and theatre, is led away in inebriated condition by two satyrs.

the geographer and historian Strabo. Much of the knowledge of the buildings in Nysa has derived from Strabo, who described the city in his Geographia.
The charming theatre from the Roman period has been well-preserved. On the left and right side the building is still entered through the original *vomitoria*. Such arched corridors in a theatre are a typical Roman characteristic. The stage house is richly decorated with reliefs depicting mythological stories concerning *Dionysos*. By means of an intricate channel system the theatre was sometimes filled with water, allowing even sea fights to be performed.
On the east side of the theatre a path descends to a ravine. This is the starting point of a 150 metres long tunnel from the Roman era, which can be walked through in dry periods (a torch is recommended). This tunnel diverted the water coming from the mountains around the theatre and transported it to the ravine. A masterly example of Roman engineering!

Romantic city of ruins

Emperor Augustus considered Aphrodisias the most beautiful city in Asia Minor. Although only ruins give evidence of this once so glorious city, one can still vividly picture its beauty nowadays. Aphrodisias is located among cypresses and pomegranate shrubs in a hilly area south of the road İzmir-Aydın-Denizli. Under Roman rule the city flourished exceptionally. Before the Hellenistic period the place was known as Ninoë, a name related to the Mesopotamian goddess of war and love *Ishtar*. The Greeks associated her with the love goddess *Aphrodite*, of which the name Aphrodisias is a derivative. The cult in honour of *Aphrodite* was extremely popular and drew thousands of pilgrims annually. Moreover, the city was renowned as a centre of sculpture. The beautiful cream-coloured and blue-veined marble from the nearby quarries was not only just utilized in Aphrodisias, but was also exported to various other cities in the Mediterranean region.
From the third century A.D. the position of Aphrodisias steadily decreased. The bishopry founded by the Christians caused strife with the local cult. Gradually the heathen name Aphrodisias was banned and replaced by Stavropolis (city of the cross). After centuries of affliction by earthquakes and attacks by foreign peoples, the city finally failed to hold its own in the thirteenth century. Among the old ruins eventually a small village arose, Geyre, which now, little by little, has to clear the way for the excavations under supervision of the American-Turkish archaeologist Kenan Erim, who passed away recently.

The odeion of Aphrodisias where frogs give a concert ▼ and pond tortoises listen.

The main building structure of Aphrodisias is the *Aphrodite* temple. The origin of the sanctuary goes back to the seventh century B.C., yet there is a minimum of evidence to prove this. More is known of the present-day (Hellenistic) temple.
This temple consisted of a *cella*, an entrance court and a *peristasis* of presumably eight by thirteen columns. The beautifully decorated *temenos* with niches and small Corinthian columns dates from the time of emperor Hadrian (117-138). In the fifth century the temple was radically renovated. The *cella* was removed, the columns relocated and in this way a three-nave *basilica* was created, of which nowadays about fourteen columns still stand upright. By accident, three heavily damaged fragments of a huge statue of *Aphrodite* were discovered south of the *temenos* in the foundations of a wall. Small replicas of this statue have been found in large quantities in, among other places, Rome. Close to this spectacular discovery, the remains of a sculptor's workshop with numerous sculptures of exceptionally good quality were found. Of special interest are the unfinished fragments, telling something of the working methods employed. It reveals that not all statues were perfect at the first attempt.
About a hundred metres east of the temple is a group of columns belonging to a monumental gate. Such a construction of four by four columns is called a *tetrapylon*. The east side of the *tetrapylon* was provided with a richly decorated façade with spirally grooved columns and a lovely *pediment*. With a similar idea of refinement the *odeion* in the city-centre had been built. In the soft hues caused by the afternoon sun, this music theatre is of a serene beauty. The building originally had a roof, but during an earthquake in the fourth century it collapsed together with the upper rows of seats. In the *orchestra* lies a mosaic of white and dark blue stones. Earthquakes brought the groundwater closer to the surface, as a result of which the *orchestra* is almost permanently flooded. On the stage of the *odeion* minor performances took place. The back wall was formed by niches, providing space for statues of poets, philosophers and magistrates. In the corridor behind the stage, which gave access to a porticus of the *agora*, a lot of graffiti bears witness to the complaints and sense of honour of those days.
The best-preserved building of Aphrodisias is the stadium. Nowhere in the Mediterranean region has a similar building been so perfectly preserved. The stadium has a length of 262 metres and a width of about 59 metres and seated as many as 30,000 spectators. The long sides do not run parallel, but have a somewhat elliptical shape, providing an optimal view for every visitor. The eastern part of the stadium was rebuilt in the Byzantine period into a small *amphitheatre*. This probably took place in the seventh century, when a section of the large theatre, situated at another location in the city, had collapsed due to an earthquake.
On the southern side of the city-centre lies the *acropolis*. This refuge fortress is actually an accumulation of settlements. The final habitation layer from the seventh

century entirely covered the theatre, which proved to be in good condition after excavation. The horse-shoe shaped audience section with the seats, had room for about 8000 spectators. In the second century the *orchestra* was deepened, making it suitable for the gladiator games, so popular among the Romans.
The *scaenae frons*, which had already been erected around 30 B.C., consisted of simple Dorian columns between which *pinakes* were placed. The most striking find the archaeologists experienced was at the northern wall of the stage building. For this wall is covered with Greek inscriptions, among which are copies of letters of Roman emperors. Hadrian for example, exempted the city from tax on nails. In a letter from emperor Augustus it is mentioned that the ambassadors were assigned special seats in the theatre.
Between the *acropolis* and the *thermae* of Hadrian is the Porticus of Tiberius on the southern half of the *agora*. Remarkable and characteristic for Aphrodisias are the *friezes*, which are decorated with masks and garlands. The Porticus of Tiberius is connected with the *palaestra* of the *thermae* buildings of Hadrian by means of steps. Marble walls, floors, statues and basins gave the bathing rooms a magnificent appearance. The Turkish government originally intended to turn these baths into a museum, as has been done in Hierapolis and in Side, but further investigations and reconstructions proved too costly. That is why it was decided to build a new museum near the storage depot of the archaeologists. This museum was officially opened on 21 July 1979 and acknowledges the significance of the ancient city of Aphrodisias.

The sumptuously ▲ overgrown stadium of Aphrodisias. On the east side the remnants of a small amphitheatre lie within the stadium.

◄ This sarcophagus is on show at the entrance to the museum of Aphrodisias. On the left Eros extinguishes the torch of life. Hermes with his heralds' stave in his hand accompanies the souls to the hereafter.

Laodikeia

This place is situated on a hill, about two kilometres north-east of Denizli. The city was founded by Antiochus II around 255 B.C. and was given the name of his wife. Laodikeia owed its prosperity to the trade in very soft, black wool and was already renowned in Roman days. Laodikeia is furthermore famous as one of the seven cities of John's Apocalypse. Although very few buildings have been excavated, the city is important from a historical point of view.
The stadium dating from the first century A.D. can clearly be recognized by its shape. As both ends are rounded off (normally one side is straight), it is assumed that this stadium also served as an *amphitheatre*. East of the stadium are a *nymphaeum*, a small *odeion*, a small theatre from the Roman period and a considerably larger, but less well-preserved, Greek theatre.

A relief of the nymphaeum in Laodikeia depicting Theseus and the Minotaur. ▼

Limestone falls

The limestone rocks of Pamukkale, fourteen kilometres north of Denizli, are a natural phenomenon, which have attracted visitors ever since antiquity. Pamukkale, 'cotton castle', owes its name to the white limestone sediments glittering in the sun. For thousands of years the mineral-rich water from the nearby warm water springs has deposited calcite and created the most miraculous shapes.

Behind the frequently visited and water-filled limestone terraces lies the ancient spa of Hierapolis. The city was founded by the Pergamene king Eumenes II, who called it after Hiera. Hiera was the wife of Telephos, the legendary founder of Pergamum. As part of the Pergamene Empire Hierapolis fell under Roman rule in 133 B.C., like so many other cities in Asia Minor. In the first century A.D. the city was struck by two heavy earthquakes, but after a fast rebuilding programme Hierapolis flourished more than ever. Owing to the warm water springs a significant wool and textile industry developed. The water was employed both for washing the raw materials and for fixing the dyes. This industry was mainly in the hands of the Jewish community.

In the Byzantine period Hierapolis received an episcopal see and a church dedicated to Saint Philip who had died a martyr's death on the cross. During the following centuries the city gradually passed into oblivion. The final noteworthy and at the same time tragic event is the destruction brought about by the Seljuks in 1097. Today's ruins still bear witness to this.

Hierapolis was constructed according to the Hippodamic system, which divided the city into a austere street pattern of regular oblongs. The main street, hemmed in by colonnades, had monumental city gates on the north and south sides. The two gates on the north side are still standing for the greater part. The outer gate dates from the Roman era and consists of three arches with two round towers on both sides. An inscription on the *frieze* of the gate mentions that it was erected by the proconsul of Asia, Julius Sextus Frontinus, in honour of emperor Domitian (81-96). The inner gate is Byzantine and was incorporated into the city wall.

In the centre of the city is the public fountain, not just indispensable but also a very representative structure. The water used to flow through a pipe from a higher reservoir and not, as would perhaps be expected, from the warm water springs.

Just behind this *nymphaeum* are the remnants of the temple of the city god *Apollo* and the small sanctuary of *Pluto*, the god of the underworld. The exact location of this so-called Plutonium had been a mystery for a long time and was accidentally discovered when archaeologists were busy digging up the south side of the *Apollo* temple. According to ancient sources, here, hidden in a small room, lay the entrance to the underworld. It consisted of a deep crevice with an underground river producing a strongly stinging gas. The gas, probably carbon dioxide, was very irritating for humans and could in high concentrations even be

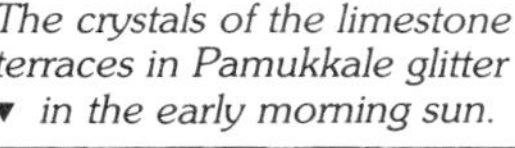

The crystals of the limestone terraces in Pamukkale glitter ▼ in the early morning sun.

lethal for small animals. Only a special group of priests had access. These people were supposed to be immune to the poisonous vapours. Presumably they just held their breath. The Plutonium was 'world famous' in antiquity and was an important place of interest in Hierapolis.

The theatre lies against a hill in the eastern part of the city. It was built in the second century and has been exceptionally well-preserved. The view from the upper row is breathtaking. The large audience area contains about 50 rows of seats and covers a little more than a semi-circle. The marble honorary stand in the middle was embellished with lions' claws and provided with foot-benches. The *orchestra*, the place where the notorious gladiator games were held, is typically Roman and is an exact semi-circle. In the opulently decorated back wall niches have been incorporated with shell-shaped cupolas and small columns with spiraled *cannelures*. The middle niche gave access to the storage rooms for stage props and the changing rooms under the platform. The most beautiful part of the theatre is the *scaenae frons*, which is abundantly decorated with reliefs, columns and statues. The reliefs depict scenes from the myth of *Dionysos*, *Apollo* and *Artemis* with among others *Niobides*, festive processions and a sacrificial scene. In several places a representation of *Artemis* Ephesia can be discerned. Many of the stage building decorations were never finished, thus providing a good picture of how sculptors used to work.

Outside the northern city gate is the largest *necropolis* of Asia Minor with over 1200 graves. During the course of many centuries different grave types have been applied here: house-shaped graves with flat roofs, structures resembling temples with fake doors and decorated façades in the shape of a *tympanum*, sarcophagi and *tumuli*. Most graves bear inscriptions, giving an impression of the social life of the citizens of Hierapolis. For instance the text on the grave of the Jewish trader Flavius Zeuxis mentions that he had travelled to Rome 72 times to sell his products.

A second and much more simple *necropolis* is located east of the city. It was apparently meant for the less well-to-do. Small burial chambers were hewn out in the rock wall, which unfortunately have almost completely collapsed due to earthquakes.

Climbing the hill north-east of the city, the Martyrium of the apostle Philip is reached, an ingeniously constructed building of the fifth century. It presumably served as a commemorative church and an inn for the pilgrims.

On the southern side of Hierapolis, near the limestone terraces, are the Roman baths dating from the second century. The bathing areas were fitted out with wall slabs of finely veined marble. The holes in the pockmarked walls show where these slabs had been fastened with metal clamps. The main hall of the building block consists of three parallel rooms, covered with vaults. Nowadays the building serves as an archaeological museum and the former bathing rooms contain a collection of reliefs and statues worth seeing. The style in which these objects have been executed strongly resembles that of the sculptures from Aphrodisias.

Hierapolis is the final stop on the tour around the marble cultures of West Anatolia. Along a decent minor road the route can be continued to the turquoise coast of Pamphilia.

▲ *In Hierapolis the stage building with its columns, reliefs and arches, gives a good impression of a theatre from antiquity.*

Kız Bergama

Bergama is the centre of the age-old carpet production in West Anatolia. The pure sheep's wool is dyed with natural colours, made from flowers, leaves, roots and fruits. Every region has its own specific colours and the recipes are secret. The deep red colours, together with the geometrical patterns and the practical sizes, are typical of the Bergama carpets. The motives and colours applied are rooted in the traditions of the nomads. The women know these motives by heart and this knowledge has been passed on from mother to daughter for hundreds of years. A Bergama carpet of medium size takes about six weeks' work.

6 the Turquoise Coast

Crystal-clear water and sun-drenched beaches form a subtropical décor along the Turkish south coast. The oleanders flower and rare bird species have their habitat among colourful rock masses. On the fertile coastal plain bananas, figs, citrus fruits and tobacco are cultivated. In addition to this, the Turkish Rivièra offers a surprising diversity of historical places of interest. Inland lie the breathtaking tuff formations of Cappadocia.

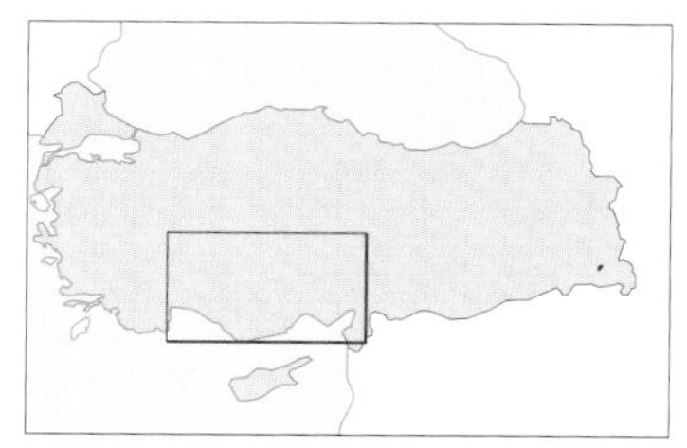

The numerous excavation sites with monuments from the Greek, Roman and early Christian periods lie scattered among the mountains and forests of Pamphilia, Pisidia and Cilicia. In the surroundings of the historical provincial town of Antalya the remarkable remains of the cities of Side, Perge and Aspendus can be found. A winding mountain road through a nature reserve leads to Termessus, an archaeological surprise enclosed by rugged rock formations.
Along the unspoilt coast are stalwart castles, built by crusaders. In Cappadocia Byzantine rock churches, underground cities and the fascinating lunar landscape compete for attention.

Pamphilia, Pisidia and Cilicia

The south coast did not constitute a governmental union until the foundation of the Turkish state by Atatürk. In the geographical field there is no union either. Three landscapes can be distinguished: a fertile flat strip of land between Antalya and Alanya, north of this the plateau of Pisidia and from Alanya to Silifke the western Taurus Mountains, which run down to the sea. Beyond Silifke the mountains recede, and the coastal strip is flat again.
Farmers settled in the fertile coastal plain at a very early date. A legend recounts that groups of Greeks, led by the legendary heroes Mopsos, Kalchas and Amphilochos founded cities on the coast after the Trojan War. As a result of the foundation of Greek colonies the population increased considerably from the twelfth century B.C. Up to this day however, nothing has been found of these colonists' settlements. The archaeological finds which have been discovered all along the south coast, mainly date from the Roman era.

◂ The romantic atmosphere in the theatre of Perge is made perfect by the reflection in the water. The audience section was screened off from the stage floor by small stone fences. Wild animal games and sea fights could be performed in this theatre as well.

◂ The Bougainvillea (Bougainvillea spectabilis) was imported from Brasil in the nineteenth century. The climber appears to flower the entire year. The striking violet leaves are not flowers however, but bracts. The fig cactus (Opuntia ficus-indica) in the foreground is often cultivated for its fig-like fruits.

The Romans divided the region into the provinces of Pamphilia, Pisidia and Cilicia. Especially in the second and third centuries A.D. a lot of building activity took place. This was the period of the Pax Romana, an era of stability in the Roman Empire.
During Byzantine rule the cities, which had been founded by the Greeks and Romans, remained inhabited, just as during the Seljuk supremacy. This was succeeded by a period of decline; only a few places remained populated. The villagers sometimes literally built their farms among the ruins, often utilizing the ancient remains. Most people moved to big cities like Antalya.

Antalya is a very busy trade and tourist centre. The harbour and the nearby international airport have shaped this modern city into a traffic junction where numerous guests come and go. ▾

The provincial capital Antalya

Antalya has grown into the largest city of Pamphilia. The provincial capital is favourably located on rocks around a bay and enclosed by the Taurus Mountains. It is a luxurious place with modern palm-tree boulevards and characteristic streets with restored wooden houses. Especially in the busy harbour district many old Turkish houses have been preserved. On the first floor they usually have a wooden bay, with pear-shaped extruding lattice-work. This provides the women with an unobstructed view of the street. The houses on the opposite side of the narrow street have been built in a similar fashion, so neighbours do not have to yell at each other in passing on the latest news.
Antalya, the ancient Attaleia, is not just as old as for example the cities of Side, Perge and Termessus. The city was founded by the Pergamene king Attalos II (159-138 B.C.). The Pergamenes had not succeeded in conquering the strategically located port of Side and were therefore in need of another naval base. Pergamene rule over Antalya was short-lived, however. The city was captured by pirates, who in their turn were expelled by the Romans in 66 B.C. The next centuries of Roman and Byzantine government brought Attaleia peace and prosperity.
From the seventh century A.D. Pamphilia became the target of Arab attacks and Antalya was conquered in the year 860. During the following turbulent centuries the inhabitants of Antalya lived under Arab, Byzantine, Seljuk, Cypriot and Venetian rule.
In 1391 the city was occupied by the Ottomans. Once again the Venetians lay at anchor in the roadsteads of Antalya; the chain sealing off the harbour was shot away, houses outside the city walls were destroyed, but the city itself was not captured. The Venetians took the harbour chain back to Saint Peter's in Rome, where it still remains.
During the period of decline of the Ottoman Empire many refugees came to Antalya: in 1822 and 1823 Peloponnesian Turks, in 1897 Cretan Turks and in 1913 Üsküp Turks. After the Great War, Antalya fell under Italian supervision for a short time.
Not much is left of the ancient Attaleia, as the modern city has been built on top of the old one. The most exceptional monument in Antalya is Hadrian's Gate, erected as a triumphal arch for emperor Hadrian at the time when he visited the city in the year 130. In 1959 the columns and capitals were repaired and the entire façade has recently been restored to its former splendour. During the Byzantine period the rooms under the vaults were used as chapels, after the arches had been walled up. In the Turkish period these walls were removed again. The gate is hemmed in between two towers of the city wall. The remaining part of the city wall was demolished between 1935 and 1940, allowing the cool sea-breeze to blow unhampered through the city. At Hadrian's Gate the difference between the street-level of ancient days and the higher position of the modern boulevard can clearly be discerned.
The tower of Hıdırlık, in the northern corner of the Karaalı Park, was constructed in the second century A.D. The lower section is square and the upper one round. On both sides of the entrance, twelve fasces (bundles of rods tied round an axe) are depicted in relief. From these honorary signs it appears that the tower served as a tomb for a Roman magistrate. The burial chamber was accessible through a low-lying door on the north side, which is nowadays half-covered by rubble. Possibly the building functioned as a lighthouse in later times.
In the city-centre one finds the so-called grooved minaret of the Yivli Minare Camii. This minaret is the symbol of Antalya and is pictured in many leaflets about the city.
On the western exit road lies the renowned Archaeological Museum of Antalya. The beautifully appointed rooms display among other things prehistoric pottery, Phrygian burial gifts, marble sculptures and a large number of sarcophagi. The statue garden with palm-trees and exotic plants is an oasis of peace and quiet in the boisterous harbour town.
Antalya is a good starting point for a visit to the numerous excavations in Lycia, Pamphilia and Pisidia.

Hadrian's Gate in the centre of Antalya. Wagon wheels have worn out tracks in the pavement of the central passage-way. The vaults of the three arches are embellished with fine coffer-▾ ceilings and rosettes.

A bastion in the mountains

Termessus (Termessos) lies about 30 kilometres north-west of Antalya. Through a vast coniferous forest a new road meanders upwards along the northern slope of the Gülük Dağ. In antiquity this mountain was called Solymos, explaining the name Solymi for the inhabitants of Termessos. At an altitude of 1050 metres lie the remains of the ancient Termessus, half submerged under thick overgrowth. Yet, it is more than worthwhile to make the journey. On a clear day the view is spectacular; due to its location, however, Termessus is often hidden by clouds.

The city was founded by the original inhabitants of the region, but is only mentioned for the first time in the report of Alexander the Great's campaigns. Alexander did not succeed in conquering the city and gave up the siege after a short time. Termessus experienced periods of great bloom, first in the Hellenistic and later in the Roman period, when the inhabitants were called 'friends and allies of Rome'. The ruins of Termessus have not yet been closely investigated. That is a pity, for this city has never been inhabited again since it was deserted in the fifth century.

Although Termessus was not large, the city had its own *agora*, surrounded by colonnades, a shopping street, a *gymnasium*, temples, a theatre and a small roofed-over *odeion/bouleuterion*.

In Termessus the theatre, seating 4200 spectators, is a building particularly worth visiting. It is a Greek theatre, the public stand is built against the slope of the hill and covers more than a semi-circle. The space in front of the stage, the *orchestra*, is circular and between the stage house and the stands were entries, *parodoi*. The stage house was erected in the Roman period. Greek theatres did not have high stage houses, often a tent sufficed.

To the south-west of the theatre is another well-preserved building, its function being rather obscure. It might have been an assembly hall for the town council (*bouleuterion*) or a small roofed-over music theatre (*odeion*). These days the walls are ten metres high. The interior is covered in rubble, but one side clearly had an ascending public stand. Among the rubble pieces of yellow, green, violet and white marble have been found, presumably from the wall coverings. The marble slabs were fastened to the wall with pins; holes in the walls of many ruins betray the former presence of this kind of wall covering.

◂ *The ruins of Termessus compete with the beauty of the surrounding mountain scenery. Among the sumptuous vegetation lie the remains of the theatre.*

Termessus still awaits further archaeological examination. ▾

◂ *In the teeming bazar of Antalya pickled vegetables are colourfully displayed. The sour-sweet peppers, cucumbers and paprikas taste delicious as a snack or as a side-dish with the main meal.*

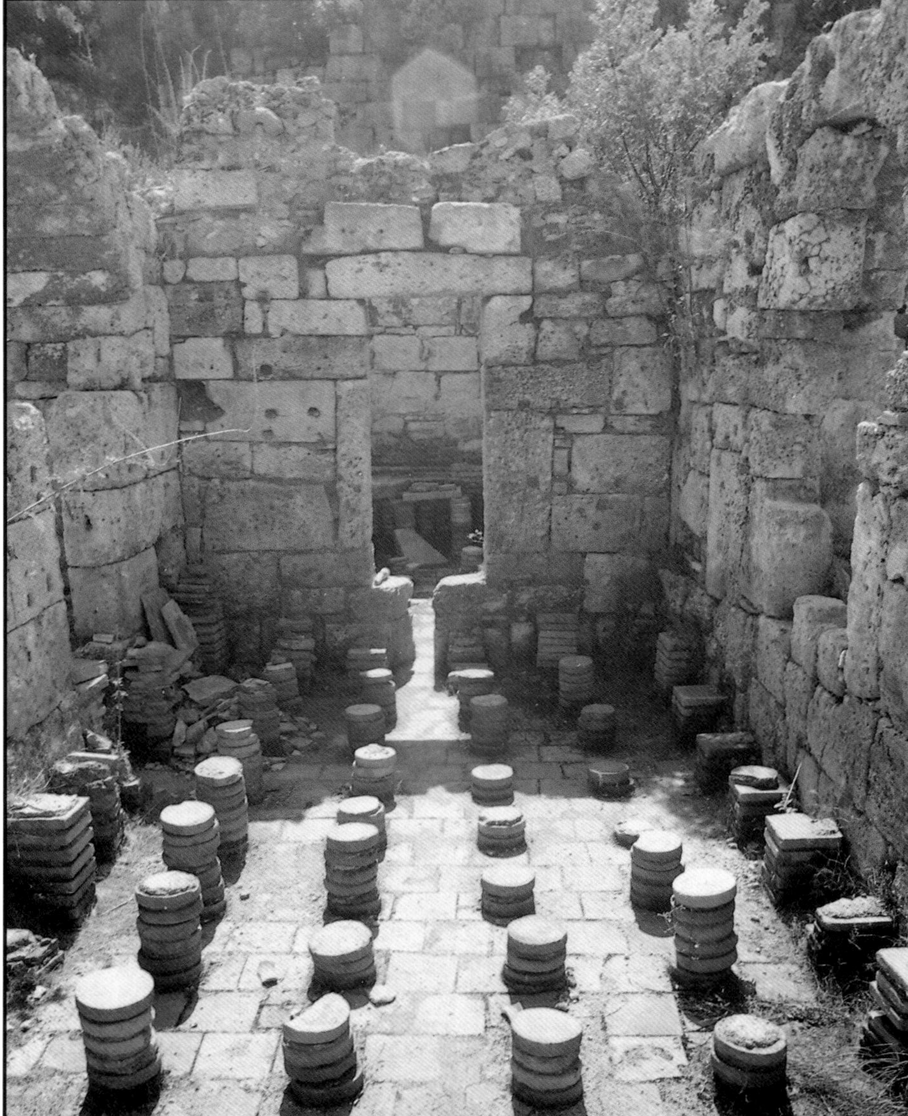

▲ *A hypocaust floor in the thermae of Phaselis. In the underground fireplaces wood was burnt. The hot air circulated among the small brick columns and warmed the bathing area above. The floors were water-proof and had drains with tapering stoppers of baked clay.*

Baths

Bathhouses played an important role in the public and social life of the Roman citizen. Here appointments were made, business was done and friends were met. In the second and third centuries the *thermae* became more numerous and more luxurious. The floors were covered with marble or mosaics and the walls with marble slabs. There were also marble statues and washbasins in the bathing rooms.

The main rooms were the *caldarium* (warm water bath), the *tepidarium* (luke water bath) and the *frigidarium* (cold water bath). Entrance fees were paid in the *apodyterium* (changing room) where shoes and clothes were also left behind. There was often a latrine near the entrance, separated from the other rooms by an air shaft. A *palaestra* (sports field) did not lack either. The necessary bathing water was supplied via aquaducts. The warm water baths were heated by means of a *hypocaust*, a heating system allowing hot air to circulate among small poles under the floor and transporting it via flat pipes along the walls. These terracotta pipes were hidden from view by marble panels. The closer a room was situated to the fire, the warmer it was. Cleansing of the body was done with water and oil. The oil was scraped off the body with a *strigilis* (scraper). The result however was a slippery floor and a broken leg was not an imaginary injury. The floors were regularly scrubbed, the excess water was drained through holes in the floor. The drains could be closed off with stoppers. Bathing gear and oils were brought in by slaves or were bought in the building, usually in the *apodyterium*. Roman baths can be compared to the present-day Turkish *hamam*, which can be found in nearly every city.

RECONSTRUCTION DRAWING OF A HYPOCAUST

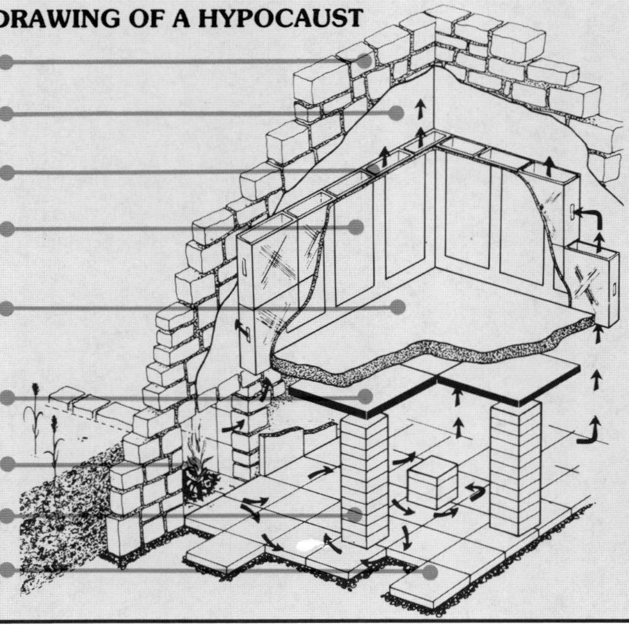

outer wall

layer of plaster

wall heating

layer of stucco

mortared floor

tiled floor

fireplace

pillars

supporting tiles

On the pillars of this hypocaust system still lies a part of the original floor. Left, in the foreground, a stopper can be seen ▼ *with which the drainage in the marble floor was closed off.*

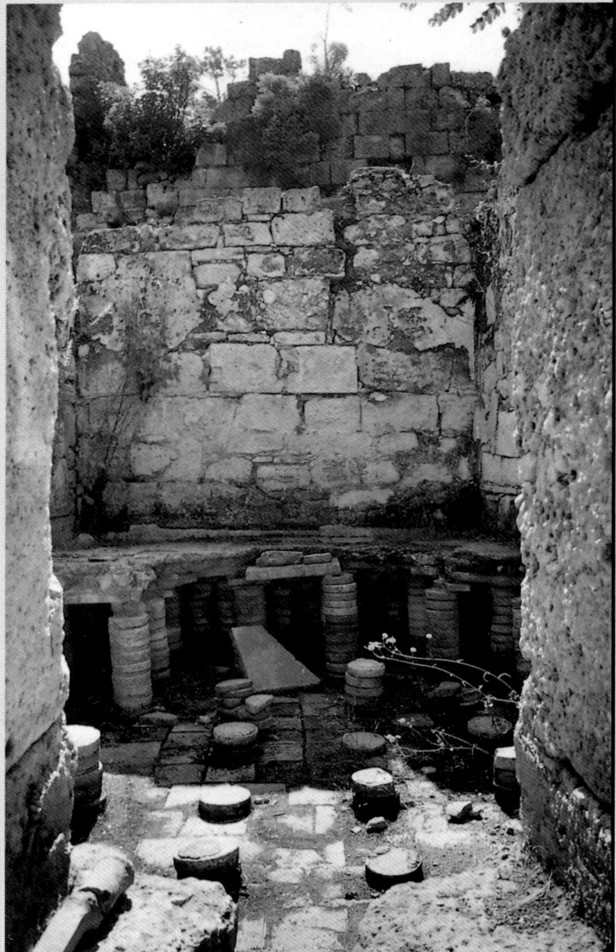

Natural ports

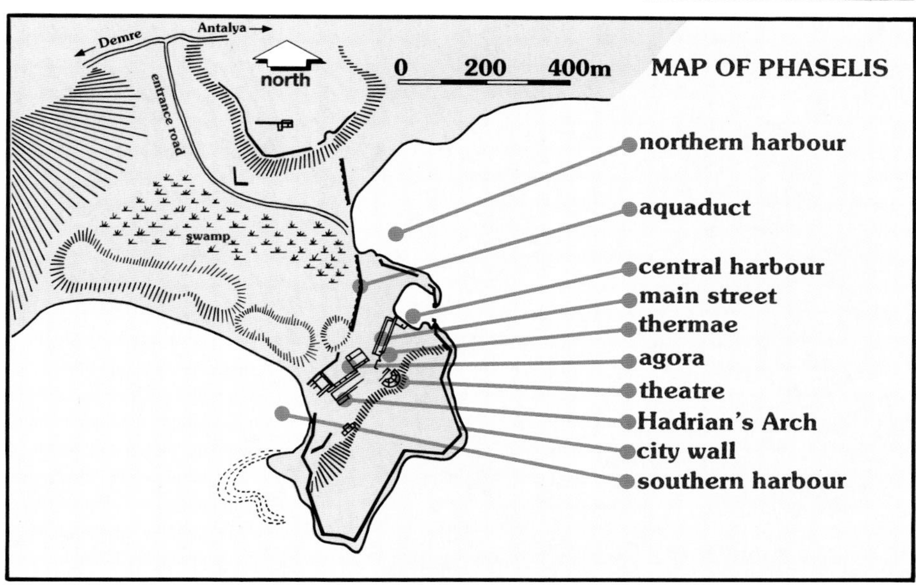

South-west of Antalya lies the ancient harbour town of Phaselis, which used to be part of the province of Lykia. The ruins of the city are covered with pine-trees and a wealth of rock plants; this is one of the reasons why Phaselis is one of the most idyllic places in Turkey. Here a visit to an excavation site can perfectly be combined with a dip in the sea, sunbathing on the beach or a picnic under the pine-trees of the peninsula.
Phaselis was founded by colonists from Rhodes in the beginning of the seventh century B.C. The city had three harbours: one in the north, one on the north-eastern and one on the south-western side of the tongue of land. In antiquity the harbours were protected against the beating of the waves by piers and ships were hauled onto the beach. Little remains to be seen of the ancient harbours except stone piers in the sea and column remnants under the surface of the water.
On the neck of the peninsula, between the north-eastern and south-western harbours, the ruins of houses and public buildings are sumptuously covered with vegetation. A paved street connects both harbours. There used to be shops on both sides of this arterial road. At the south-western harbour was a triumphal arch in honour of emperor Hadrian. The remaining fragments lie chaotically scattered among the pine-needles.
The inhabitants of this relatively small city had two bathing buildings at their disposal, which can nowadays clearly be recognized from the floor-heating system.
On the west side of the main street lies the collapsed theatre, hidden under the overgrowth. From the upper rows, however, one has a splendid view across the city and its bays.

View from the theatre of Phaselis across the densely grown city of ruins and the shady lagoon. ▼

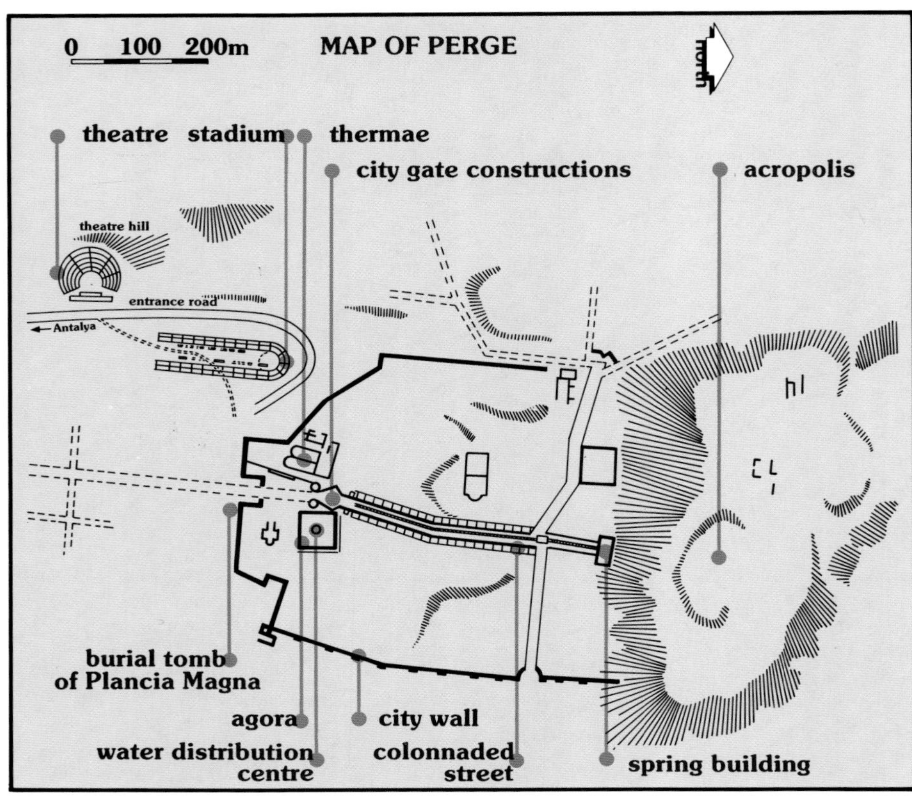

Ingenious waterworks

In the fertile plain east of Antalya lie fascinating cities of ruins. After fifteen kilometres along the main road Antalya-Alanya, a narrow minor road leads to the excavations of Perge. Although it is assumed that the original settlement was located on the *acropolis*, no remains from before the Byzantine period have been discovered there. The city was supposed to have been founded after the Trojan War by Greek immigrants from Argos led by Kalchas and Mopsos. The names of these legendary founders occur on the bases of statues found near the city gate. Little else is known of the earliest history of Perge. The name Perge appeared first in a description of Alexander the Great's campaigns. The inhabitants of Perge cordially received Alexander, which might be explained from the fact that the city did not have any defence walls at the time, making it impossible for the inhabitants to defend themselves against attacks. Only later were walls constructed around the city. Until 188 B.C. Perge was governed by Alexander's heirs, the Seleucids. Thereafter the city was incorporated into the Pergamene Empire. *Artemis* Pergaia was the local tutelary deity. From the third century B.C. she has been depicted on coins, minted in Perge. This *Artemis* Pergaia was presumably the Hellenistic version of a mother goddess. The mother goddess was worshipped by primitive farmers, because she symbolized the fertility of the earth.

The impressive stadium of Perge viewed from the nearby theatre. In the background lies the Hellenistic city gate and the columns of the shopping galleries ▾ *around the agora are visible too.*

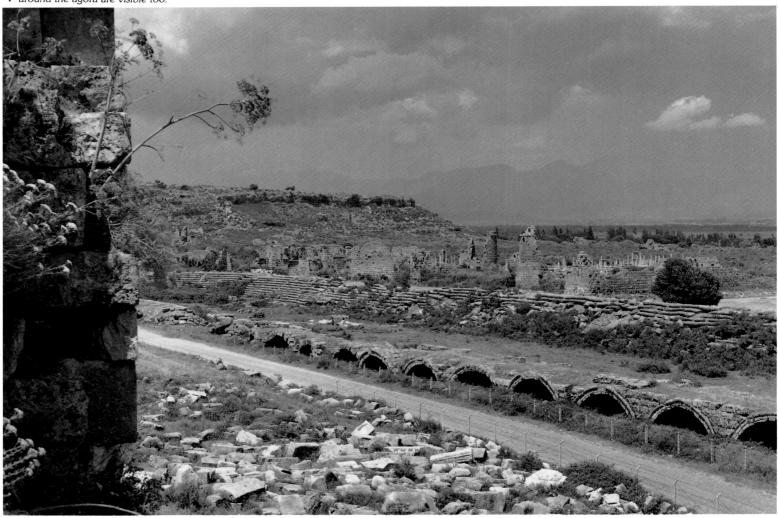

According to ancient sources, the temple of *Artemis* was located outside the city, but up to this day it has not been discovered.
Perge is also mentioned in the old annals of the Christian church. In the Acts of the Apostles it says that Paul and Barnabas sailed to Perge from Paphos in the year 46. After visits to Antiochia and Iconium (Konya) they returned to Perge to preach there as well.
The second and third centuries, the time of the Pax Romana, signified a period of prosperity for Perge. In these peaceful times the defensive works had become useless and the city outgrew its walls. Wealthy citizens had large public constructions executed. That is how the theatre, the stadium, the colonnaded street and the *thermae* were built; monuments still dominating the cityscape. During the Byzantine period the episcopal see was in Perge and a second period of bloom followed. In the seventh century the city was conquered by the Arabs and most of the population left for Antalya. Slowly Perge fell into oblivion and nowadays only a few houses remain at the excavation site. The goats and sheep of the inhabitants graze among remnants worth visiting.
The ancient Perge lies hemmed in between the *acropolis* and the theatre hill. The city has not been completely excavated, yet the main contours can be distinguished. The Greeks and later the Romans constructed their cities according to a regular pattern, provided the ground condition permitted it. Such a systematic lay-out has also been applied in Perge. Two intersecting main roads run through the city, the narrower streets and alleys all lead to them.
Just outside the city walls lies the large ancient theatre of Perge, seating 15,000 visitors. It was built in the middle of the second century and financed by a wealthy female citizen, Plancia Magna. This is apparent from an inscription on a bust of her, found in the theatre. Greek and Roman theatre building techniques were combined in constructing the theatre. The seats were built against the slope according to Greek tradition and form more than a semi-circle. According to Roman tradition the high stage house was connected to the public stand by vaulted entries and the upper half of the seats was supported by vaults. Along the top was a gallery, of which some arches have been preserved. The graceful *frieze* on the partly collapsed stage house depicts scenes from the life of *Dionysos*, the god of wine, and in his honour ancient play-acting arose.
The 234 metres long stadium of Perge has remained in very good condition, just like the one of Aphrodisias. It could seat 12,000 to 15,000 visitors. The seats were partly of wood and partly of stone and rested on sloping vaults in which shops were housed.
It is assumed that the southern side of the stadium originally had a large monumental wooden entrance. In the third century, when gladiator fights were popular, the round part on the north side of the arena was closed, creating an *amphitheatre*. The footpath from the theatre to the city gate leads right through the stadium, which nowadays serves as a dépot for architectural fragments.
The largest gate constructions can be found, just like the stadium and the theatre, on the southern side of the city. These buildings actually consist of a double entrance gate. The front gate is Roman and was built at the end of the third century A.D. This Roman entrance has two square towers and a receding court with behind it the first gate. In this way attackers could

◄ *On the east side of the main street stand three marble columns with remarkable reliefs. The city goddess Tyche carries a cornucopia. On an adjoining column Artemis stands with her bow and arrows.*

Dionysos

In the theatre of Perge the marble *frieze* of the stage building has been partially preserved. The scenes in relief have the adventures of *Dionysos*, the god of wine and theatre, as their subject. To the far left the god of the river Cestrus (now the river Akşu) is depicted. On the second relief the birth of *Dionysos* as the son of the mortal *Semele* and the highest god *Zeus* is shown. *Hera*, *Zeus*'s wife, was infuriated when she found out that her husband had had yet another of his affairs and decided to avenge herself. *Hera* asked *Semele* if she would not like to see her lover *Zeus* the way he appeared before the gods of Mount Olympos. When *Zeus* manifested himself as fire in front of *Semele*, she was burnt. However the child she was carrying was saved from her body and sewn into *Zeus*'s thigh. The relief shows the 'birth' of *Dionysos* out of his father's thigh.
Hermes thereafter sent *Dionysos* to the *nymphs* of Nysa for his education. The most devastated part of the *frieze* shows the good life with these *nymphs* with dancing *satyrs* and *maenads*. *Dionysos* was educated in the knowledge of wine by *Silenos*, a bearded old man. After he had grown up, *Dionysos* travelled through many countries in order to propagate his wine-knowledge. His departure on a wagon drawn by two panthers has also been depicted.

◄ *On this relief in the theatre of Perge the young Dionysos is being washed by the nymphs.*

◄ *Detail of the frieze of the theatre in Perge. Accompanied by two Erotes Dionysos sets out into the wide world on a wagon drawn by two panthers.*

▲ *The city gates of Perge. The horseshoe-shaped inner courtyard was covered with marble and in the niches were statues of Kalchas, Mopsos and Plancia Magna.*

▲ *This console rests on the bottom of the water distribution centre in Perge and has been finely decorated with acanthus leaves and volutes.*

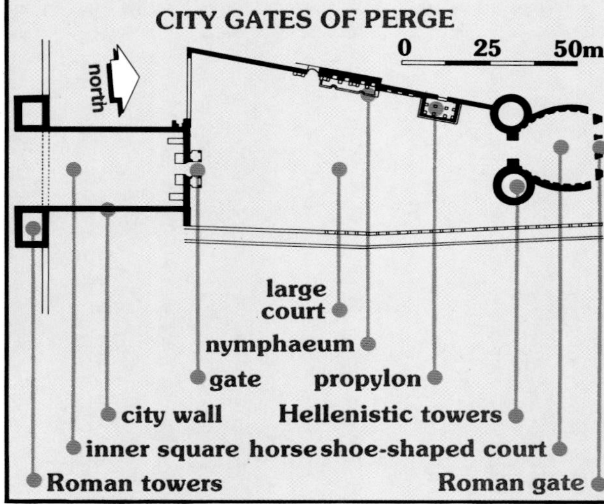

In the middle of the agora lies the former water distribution centre. Through terracotta pipes the water was transported to several places in the city. The pipes were connected to different ▼ *levels and this determined the hierarchy in the water distribution.*

be harassed from three sides. Initially the gate had been built as a triumphal arch, but after some alterations it was assimilated into the defensive system. In front of the gate were Corinthian columns; the walls were covered with marble slabs, which can be deduced from the holes in the walls.

The second gate had already been constructed in the Hellenistic period. The two round towers of this gate still have their original height. The stones consist of alternating rows of short and long stretcher faces, a characteristic of the building method in the third century B.C. Through this gate an oval court was entered, half of which was demolished in the Roman era, leaving a horseshoe-shaped space. In the high walls were niches filled with statues of Greek gods and the founders of the city. Pin-holes indicate that these walls had also been covered with marble slabs. In 121 the Romans built a triumphal arch with three passage-ways, resembling Hadrian's Gate in Antalya, on the north side of the Hellenistic court. The triumphal arch of Perge was once again a gift of Plancia Magna, as appears from the inscriptions on architectural fragments and statue socles. She had the gate decorated with statues of the Roman emperors Nerva (96-98), Trajan (98-117) and Hadrian (117-138). In the period of emperor Septimius Severus (193-211) the square between the Hellenistic and Roman gate was given its final shape. On the square remnants of statues of *Artemis* Pergaia, *Aphrodite* and her *nymphs*, emperor Septimius Severus and his wife Julia Domna have been found. Furthermore, an inscription was discovered, stating that the inhabitants dedicated the square to their beloved city of Perge, to *Artemis*, to the emperor and his sons Caracalla and Geta, and to Julia Domna. Along the east side of the Septimius Severus Square is a colonnade, behind which were shops. On the west side is a large *nymphaeum*. It has a pretty façade with four niches, in which statues and columns with *aediculae* (small niche-shaped crownings) were placed. The *nymphaeum* had a large basin with two semi-circular inlets, from which the inhabitants of Perge could get water. The water for the *nymphaeum* was supplied through waterworks and came, partly, via the *thermae*. These baths were provided with water by an aquaduct. Via a monumental *propylon* one can walk to the bathing buildings, situated against the city wall. The baths consist of four parallel rooms connected by narrow, low doors. The *caldarium*, decorated with marble, has been well-preserved and the *hypocaust* system can also be clearly discerned.

East of the Hellenistic gate lies the large square *agora*. The square was enclosed by a colonnade and numerous shops. In the middle of the *agora* is a round building with a diameter of more than thirteen metres. The tiled roof was supported by a centrally placed column. The building used to house an ingenious water distribution system. In times of abundance, the water flowed from this *castellum* through a system of pipes to all city districts. In times of drought, however, water had to be used more economically. The first to lack water were the upper pipes; they led to the houses in the poorer districts of Perge. The houses of the wealthy inhabitants were then still provided with running water. As the water level dropped, fewer and fewer places in the city got water. The bottom pipes were fed to the last moment; those pipes were connected to the public fountains, where all citizens could fetch water. Lengthwise the main street is divided in two by a

▲ See-through from the nymphaeum across the main street of Perge. From this spring building at the bottom of the acropolis runs a wide water-channel. ▲ The division plates in the channel regulated the flowing rate of the water.

channel which is part of the water-supply system. The two metres broad channel had division plates every eight metres, regulating the waterflow. On both sides of the street was a roofed-over colonnade with mosaic floors. Along this colonnade were shops.

A pretty *nymphaeum* is situated at the head of the street, at the bottom of the *acropolis*. This spring building, from the middle of the second century, was the first to be provided with a façade to the front and back. In the central hall lies the statue of the river god *Cestrus*. Furthermore there were statues of *Zeus*, *Artemis*, emperor Hadrian, a nude youngster and important female citizens.

Lizards and salamanders nowadays live among the bounteous vegetation of the dried-up Perge. Only the baths, spring buildings, channels and terracotta pipes bear witness to its watery past.

◂ The separate parts of the water-channel could be closed off to remove silted dirt and calcifications. The waste water was drained off through openings in the bottom of the channel to the underlying sewage system. The openings were closed off by stoppers.

◂ Half-hidden among the vegetation lies this huge waterbasin next to the waterchannel in the main street.

▲ *The stage house and a part of the seats of the theatre in Sillyum have fallen into the ravine due to a landslide. The rest of the theatre hill could collapse any day.*

Destructive landslides

Sillyum (Sillyon) lies on a hill in the plain of Pamphilia between Perge and Aspendus and can be seen on a clear day from Perge. The city had already been discovered in 1884, but has not been excavated yet. According to a Greek legend Sillyon was also founded after the Trojan War by Kalchas and Mopsos. The city name on coins from the second half of the third century B.C. is 'Selyviys'; on coins from the Roman period it says 'Sylliu-me'.
Alexander the Great tried in vain to conquer Sillyum. In the Hellenistic period the inhabitants moved from the top of the hill to the lower terraces. During the subsequent period Sillyum fell into disrepair. In the Christian period an episcopal see was established at Sillyum. During the rule of the Seljuks several buildings were erected on the hill.
Among reed forests a rural road leads across a fertile plain to the slope of the *acropolis*, studded with building fragments. There a steep climb to the top starts. Beyond some farms are the ruins of the stadium dating from the middle of the second century. The western wall of the stadium can be recognized by the slant in the landscape, but remains of seats have not been found. In front of the stadium was the spring, part of the *nymphaeum*, the only water-supply of the ancient city. Behind the stadium lies a *gymnasium*, also from the second century. In the Byzantine period it was restored with stones from older buildings and was then probably used as a palace.
The *acropolis* can be climbed in two ways. The first – short – route is along steps, which have been hewn out of the rocks. The longer path starts at the northern bottom of the hill and leads upwards via a talus. Originally the long road was covered with a wooden roof. This road formed a weak spot in the defence system of the city and was protected by towers. The path ends at a square tower gate with two floors. On the *acropolis* is a small Seljuk mosque, a *mescit*, with a square lay-out and built of re-used material. The dome is undamaged and rests on the *pendentives*. Behind the mosque is a monumental access gate.
The Seljuk fortress is the largest building on the *acropolis*. For their settlements in Pamphilia the Seljuks opted for easily defendable sites, such as Sillyum. They restored the old walls of the *acropolis* and according to Turkish tradition they built an inner fortress. The Graeco-Roman theatre on the southern side of the *acropolis* has partly collapsed. However, when the archaeologist Count Lanckoronski visited and described Sillyum in 1884, the theatre was almost unscathed. Since then landslides have largely destroyed the theatre, and the adjoining *odeion* as well. Landslides are quite common in this region, so the remaining parts of the theatre are not really safe either.

The castor-oil tree

In the subtropical coastal region of Southern Turkey grows the one to three metres high castor-oil tree (Ricinus communis). This tree or shrub had already been used by the ancient Egyptians to obtain oil for their many lamps. The seeds of the castor-oil tree contain the poisonous ricine; this substance remains after extraction of the oil. The pure oil does not contain this poison. Nowadays medicinal castor oil and its industrial variety are extracted from the Ricinus. Castor oil is applied, among other things, in the processing of leather and in the production of soap and candles.

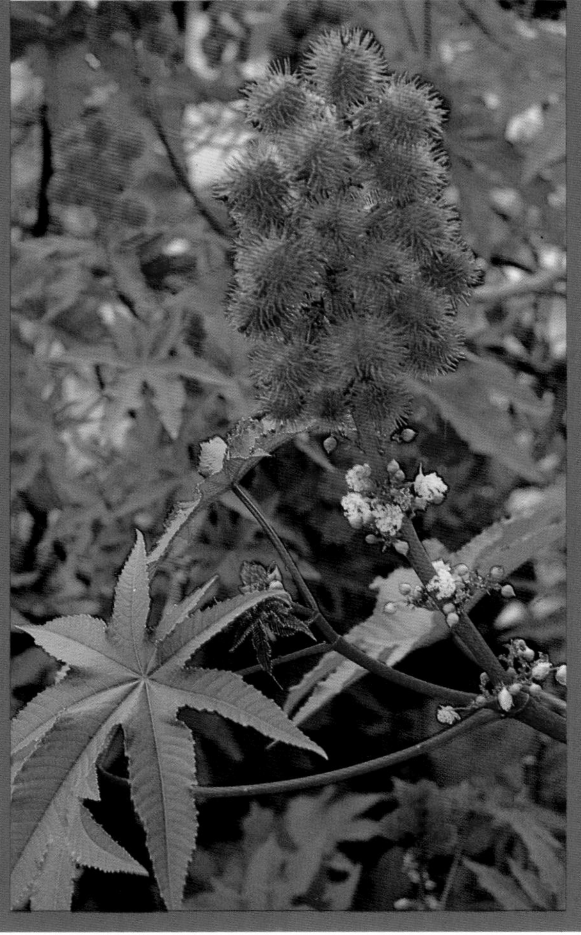

Hydraulic engineering and theatre architecture

The ancient Aspendus (Aspendos), 44 kilometres east of Antalya, lies along the river Köprü (the ancient Eurymedon). The old name for the city, Estwediiys, is probably related to the Hittite king Asitawada. The name Aspendos has been derived from the Persian words 'aspa' (horse) and 'spanta' (sacred place). In antiquity Aspendus was renowned for horse trading.

There are silver coins from Aspendus dating from around 450 B.C.; only an autonomous city with sufficient power was allowed to mint its own coins.
A Greek legend mentions the Argives, in particular the hero Mopsos, as founders of Aspendus too. The remains of the city are on the *acropolis*, where the population has continued to live for a considerable time. This in contrast to the inhabitants of other cities, such as Sillyum, who moved to the plains as from the Hellenistic period. According to historians, Aspendus was the third-largest city of Pamphilia in Roman days. In the second and third centuries Aspendus developed into a commercial centre, owing to the fact that the river Eurymedon was easily navigable; trade extended across the entire Mediterranean region. Important export products were horses, corn, wine, rosewood statuettes and salt from the old Lake Cabria (the present-day Karagöl Gölü).
The large theatre of Aspendus is the best-preserved theatre of the ancient world and well worth a visit. The auditorium could seat 15,000 persons. The upper part of the seats rests on vaults, the lower part has been built against a slope. Stairheads on the left and right of the stage house connect it with the auditorium, making a closed unit of the theatre.
The *scaenae frons* has been decorated in an exceptionally attractive way. The two floors had 40 columns: with Ionian capitals at the bottom and Corinthian capitals at the top. The columns were crowned by a richly decorated ridge-piece with alternating triangular and semi-circular *pediments*. Between the columns of the stage house five doors give access to the stage floor. In the niches between the columns were statues; the central niche presumably had a life-size statue of the emperor. The large triangular *pediment* in the middle has a relief of *Dionysos* with garlands.
The walls of the *nymphaeum* on the *acropolis* of Aspendus can be seen from afar. On the hill remnants of a market hall, a three-nave *basilica* and a semi-circular *bouleuterion* can be found.
The inhabitants of Aspendus did not have water-wells at their disposal on the *acropolis*. Initially, water had to be hauled up from the river Eurymedon. In the middle of the second century an aquaduct was constructed from the mountain range north of the city to the *acropolis*, 40 metres above the surrounding plain. The distance from the hills to the *acropolis* is considerable and a normal aquaduct would have to be 40 metres or more in height the entire way. That is why at Aspendus an ingenious system was applied, transporting the water under pressure through a low aquaduct. For this purpose pressure towers were constructed on both sides of the valley, in which the water, running through closed pipes in the entire system, could be drained at the right height due to the law of communicating vessels. Although the Romans seemingly had enough technical knowledge, they rarely applied such a cost-reducing system in practice.

Fight over a royal daughter

A legend exists about the building of the impressive theatre of Aspendus. As the king of Aspendus did not know whom to marry his daughter off, he organized a competition. His daughter was to marry the person who could construct the most beautiful building for the city. Two applicants remained: the engineer of the aquaduct and the architect of the theatre. The king first examined the aquaduct and drank some of its water. He was greatly impressed and considered the building extremely useful. Thereafter he visited the theatre. While the king admired the theatre from the gallery, he heard whispering sounds. He looked back, but could only see someone all the way down on the stage. The whispering easily reached the upper rows of the theatre. The king was also very content with the qualities of this building.
The king could not choose and decided to have his daughter 'split' in two, leaving each of the two young men their deserved half. Thereupon the architect of the theatre withdrew his marriage claim. As this magnanimity revealed true love, the king gave his daughter to this man in marriage.

▲ *The northern pressure tower of the aquaduct at Aspendus. The waterworks could not be conducted along the ground of the valley, as it was flooded both in winter and in spring. That is why the aquaduct is fifteen metres high in the valley itself.*

In Aspendus water was conducted to the city via an ingenious system. ▲ *An aquaduct and two towers on both sides of a steep valley provided constant pressure, so that the water could be brought up to the level of the acropolis.*

LINE DRAWING OF THE AQUADUCT AT ASPENDUS

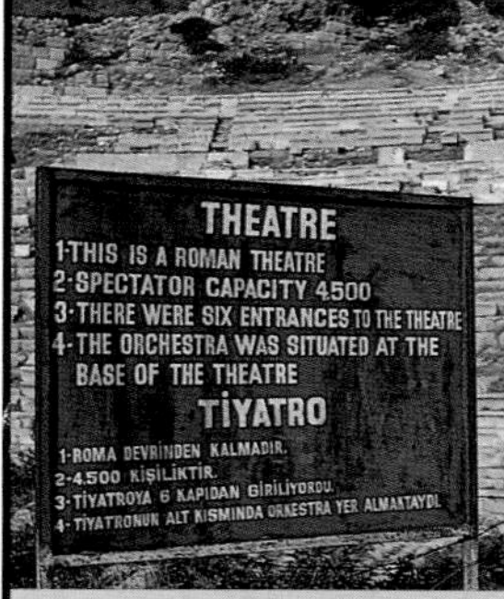

▲ *This sign can be found in Cnidus at the entrance to the theatre.*

▲ *The theatre of Side lies in a narrow bend where many tourist coaches daily create a traffic chaos. According to Roman custom, the seats of the theatre rest on vaults. In the north-eastern vault is a public latrine.*

Theatres

The best-preserved Roman theatres can be found in Orange (France), Bosra (Syria) and Aspendus. In Turkey theatres form an inextricable part of the archaeological landscape.
A theatre consists of three important sections: the *orchestra* (round dancing area), the *scaenae frons* (stage house) and the audience section. In the theatres plays were performed and, from the Roman period more and more gladiator fights and wild animal games were organized. Greek architects made use of a natural hill in constructing theatres, so that the seats could be built against the slope. A Roman theatre however is a detached building with seats resting on vaulted constructions. In Turkey often a combination of Greek and Roman elements can be found. This is not surprising in view of the long habitation history of many cities. The auditorium is divided by steps in wedge-shaped sections, the horizontal lay-out is shaped by galleries, which are accessible from the arched vaults (*vomitoria*).
In the Greek period actors played in the *orchestra*, in the Roman period the action moved to a stage floor (*logeion*). The wall of the stage house served as a décor and usually had several floors. This wall was richly decorated with marble covering slabs, columns, semi-columns, niches and statues. In the wings (*paraskenia*) of the stage were changing and storage rooms.
On the outside of the stage building in Aspendus, square blocks can be seen along the upper edge. Wooden poles were stuck into these squares to fasten a canvas (*velum*), protecting the public against the sun.

▲ *Elegant dolphins embellish the seats in the theatre of the spa at Pergamum.*

On this honorary seat in the theatre of Priene one can rest ▼ *a while after the strenuous tour across the excavation site.*

From this honorary box in the theatre at Hierapolis highly-placed visitors could observe the festivities. ▼

Carefully sculptured lions' paws decorate the marble seats in the theatre of the Asklepieion at Pergamum. Entrance tickets of bone, metal, wood or stone referred the visitors to ▼ *their seats.*

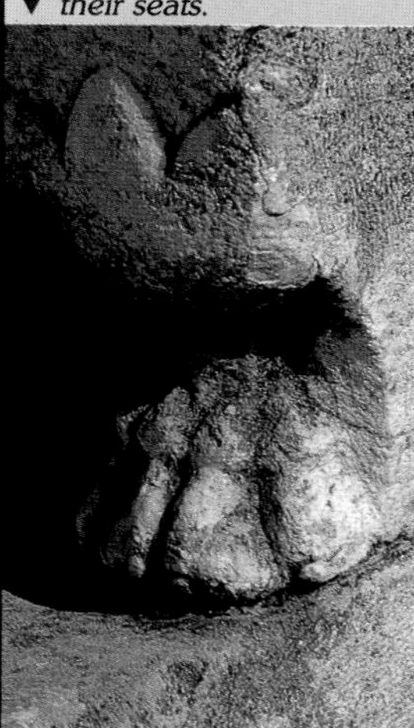

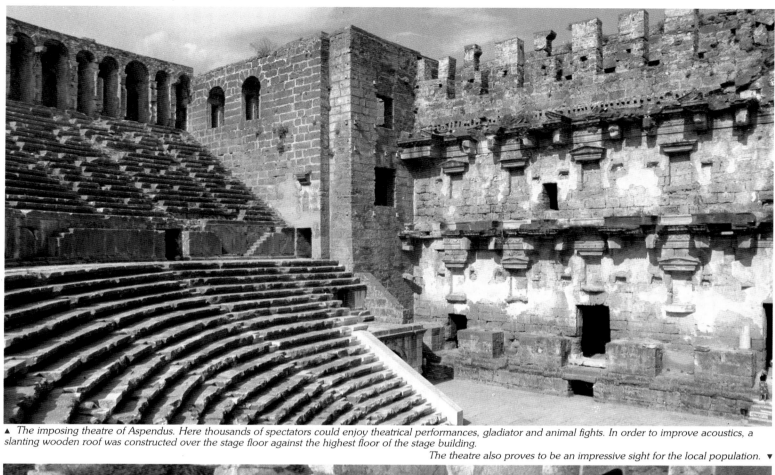

▲ The imposing theatre of Aspendus. Here thousands of spectators could enjoy theatrical performances, gladiator and animal fights. In order to improve acoustics, a slanting wooden roof was constructed over the stage floor against the highest floor of the stage building.

The theatre also proves to be an impressive sight for the local population. ▼

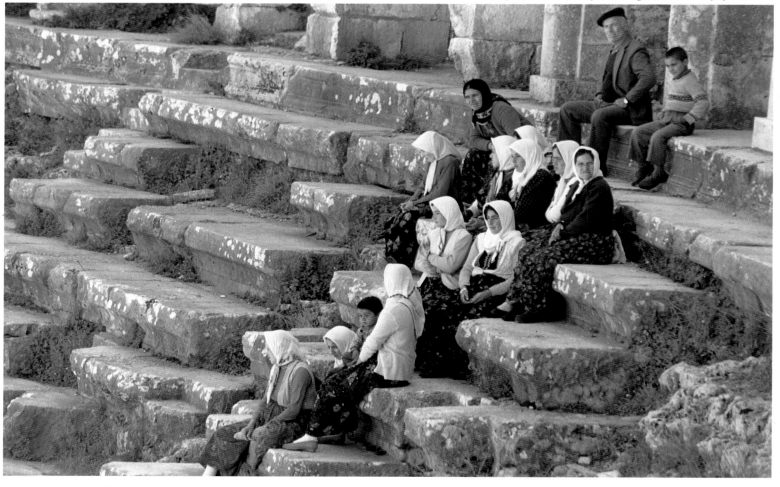

There are countless ► means of accommodation in the popular seaside resort of Side. Hotels, camping-sites and apartment blocks attempt to cope with the tide of tourists. A beach-holiday can here be alternated with a visit to one of the many ancient ruined cities along the south coast.

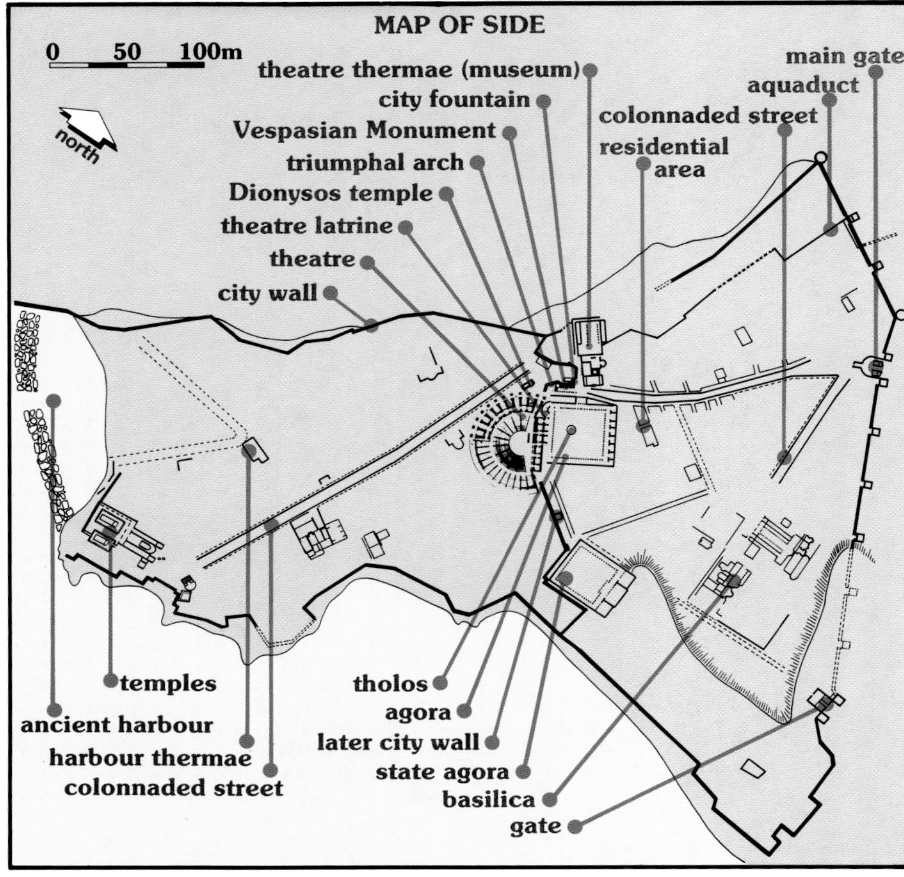

The building remnants of ancient Side lie in neat rows on the agora. In the middle of the market ▼ square are the foundations of a round temple which was dedicated to Tyche or Fortuna.

Modern tourism among antiquities

Side, 76 kilometres east of Antalya, was the most important harbour town of Pamphilia in ancient days. Side is located in a fertile plain, making it an attractive settlement site for colonists. Nowadays the place is inhabited by a small community living from fishing, and increasingly from the tourist industry. The thriving town is surrounded by orange-trees, cotton shrubs and banana-plantations.

The ancient city is situated on an 800 metres long peninsula. Lacking a natural port, two artificial harbours were constructed in Side at the end of the peninsula by means of two piers.

According to a legend, the city was a colony of the north-Aeolian city of Kyme. The shape and the decoration of a basalt column-base show Hittite characteristics. It was presumably made in the eighth or seventh century B.C. and proves that Side was already inhabited at that date. Moreover, the name Side is not Greek, but old Anatolian; this also proves that the settlement dates from before the Greek colonization. In the second century B.C. Side was a cultural and scholarly centre. The Pergamene king, ally of Rome, occupied Pamphilia up to the Akşu river, but did not manage to conquer Side. The *Nike* on coins from the second century B.C. and reliefs with weapons at the eastern city gate of Side refer to a victory over Pergamum.

Pirates from Cilicia were attracted by the various shipyards and started to use the city as a sortie-base. Not until 66 B.C. did the Romans succeed in definitely clearing the region from pirates. In the second century and the first half of the third century Side reached its heyday. From 268 until 270 the city was besieged by mountain tribes, albeit unsuccessfully. The fourth century marked a period of decay. Socles from statues in the colonnade from the times of Diocletian, Julian and Gratian were re-used, a sign of poverty. The region was harrased by piracy once more. In order to maintain the defensive system of the city, a second wall was constructed on the narrowest part of the peninsula.

In the fifth and sixth centuries the city flourished again and Side became the centre and the bishop's see. The importance of agriculture and trade in Pamphilia contributed to the expansion of Side, which outgrew its Hellenistic city walls.

In the seventh century the city had to endure Arab attacks and was destroyed by fire a number of times. The Byzantine emperor Constantine Porphyrogenetes (913-959) called Side a pirates' haunt. Around 1150 the population left the city. For a long time Side remained deserted, until Turkish immigrants from Crete founded the village of Selimiye here about 1900.

The walls and towers of the ancient city are in fair condition. Cities lying in flat regions, such as Side, needed solid defence walls. Originally, the city walls had been ten metres high. Outside the walls runs a partly preserved aquaduct, constructed in the second century and restored in the third. Side itself has no natural springs, therefore all the water had to be supplied via a 30 kilometres long system of channels, tunnels and aquaducts.

Opposite the city gate, outside the city walls, the aquaduct ended in an elegant fountain. This *nymphaeum* also dates from the second century. The façade on the side of the city gate originally had two floors. The water spouted from pipes and was collected

in basins constructed in three large niches. The walls of the *nymphaeum* were decorated with marble reliefs depicting amorous scenes.
In front of the *nymphaeum* lies the city gate. Although it has not been preserved very well, it is a good example of a gate with an inner court. The gate was flanked by square towers on the outside, making it possible to harrass a potential enemy from several sides. Behind the court lies an oblong hall, forming the final defence line of the gate. As a result of the Pax Romana the city gate lost its defensive purpose in the second century and acquired a decorative function.
Near the city gate two ancient streets begin their course. One to the south, which has not yet been completely excavated and one to the west, the main street. The latter leads to the theatre, the bathing building, the *agora* and further on to the harbours.
On both sides of the main street were colonnades and shops with houses behind them. North-east of the *agora* some of these houses have been excavated. The houses had two floors and consisted of a central court surrounded by rooms of various sizes. The houses in the rear could be reached through narrow alleys.
The ancient *thermae* nowadays house the Archaeological Museum. Here sculptures and sarcophagi, primarily from the Roman period, found in Side and its surroundings are on display. Opposite the baths lies the *agora*, constructed in the second century. This large market square is enclosed by columns, which once supported the wooden roof of the shopping arcades. In the square was a *tholos*, a round small temple, on a high dais surrounded by twelve Corinthian columns. South of this market square lies the so-called state *agora*. It was not only meant for commercial purposes, but also for meetings of city governors. The rectangular hall on the east side was the library. The façade was decorated with statues, of which now only *Nemesis*, the goddess of vindictive justice, remains in place. In the middle of the state *agora* is a high platform, presumably used for the slave-trade.
Just past the bathing building the colonnaded street passes the second city wall. At this spot one can find a fountain with three basins from the third century. The floors of the basins are covered with marble slabs.
Opposite the fountain is a partly restored monument, which, as appeared from an inscription, was erected for emperor Vespasian and his son Titus in the year 74. The middle niche was filled with a statue of Vespasian, flanked by statues of his wife and his son. The monument used to have a different location in the city and was placed against the city wall in the fourth century.
In the shade of the theatre lie the foundations of a small temple, built in the Hellenistic period in honour of *Dionysos*. The location alongside a theatre is very appropriate for a temple dedicated to the frivolous *Dionysos*.
The outer wall of the stage house of the Roman theatre forms a part of the later Byzantine city walls. This theatre, with a seating capacity of 17,000 spectators, is the largest in Pamphılia. Under the Roman construction the remains of a smaller Hellenistic theatre have been discovered. Around the *orchestra* lies a channel with a stone wall, which had been made water-proof with pink mortar. Via this channel the *orchestra* could be filled with water providing the possibility to re-enact sea-fights. Through a pipe system the water was drained off, making the theatre also suitable for gladiator games.
The circa 20 metres high façade of the *scaenae* building was provided with a *frieze* showing scenes from the life of *Dionysos*. In front of the façade were two floors with repeatedly four columns on one socle. The lower row of columns was of granite with white composite capitals. The upper row was of coloured marble with Corinthian capitals. The

◂ *Marble sarcophagus in the museum in Side. This group of children passes, merrily making music. On the lid of the coffin rests a statue of a well-fed man.*

The thermae-museum of Side. In one of the ancient baths amphorae, anchors and other objects are on display, which have been retrieved by means of underwater archaeology. In the background a water-channel and a gutter in the shape of a lion's head are visible. ▾

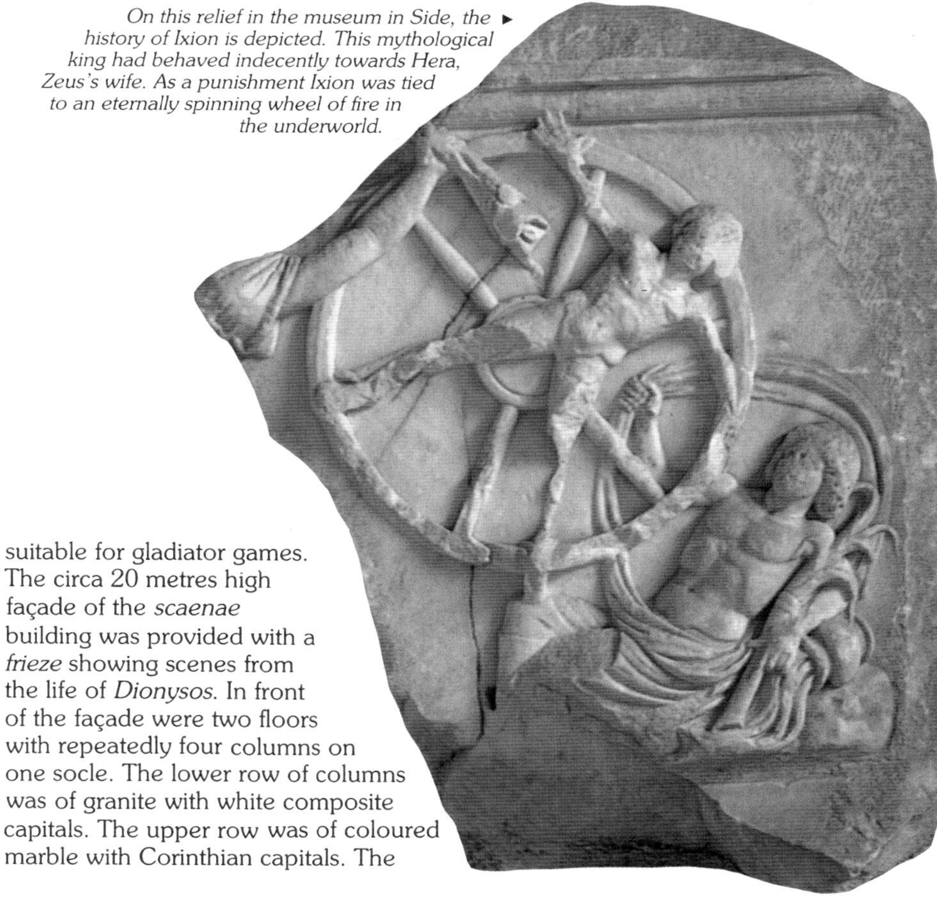

On this relief in the museum in Side, the history of Ixion is depicted. This mythological king had behaved indecently towards Hera, Zeus's wife. As a punishment Ixion was tied to an eternally spinning wheel of fire in the underworld. ▸

▲ In the garden of the thermae-museum of Side this beautiful stylized theatre-mask can be found among the sculpture fragments, statues, sarcophagi and reliefs.

▲ Bananas are harvested unripe. The bunches or separate hands are packed in boxes and shipped.

Bananas

Along the subtropical south coast of Turkey the climatological conditions are so favourable that a fruit like the banana (Musaceae), of tropical origin, can be cultivated on a large scale. As is the case for many Third World countries, bananas are mainly an export product for Turkey. The price of this kind of cash crops on the world market is liable to heavy fluctuations. The tropical-like banana plantations along the coastal road therefore provide an uncertain existence.

The female flowers of the banana-tree can form fruit without pollination. This fertilization is even undesirable, for the hard seeds then make the bananas unsaleable. ▼

▲ Flowering Aloe (Aloe arborescens). The Roman historian Plinius already recorded that the fresh leaves of the Aloe had a therapeutic effect.
Massaging the scalp with the juice of this plant mixed with dry wine was supposed to prevent loss of hair. ▼

façade decorations of the upper part nowadays lie in the *orchestra*. On the fragments *Apollo*, *Artemis*, *Athena*, *Demeter* and *Kore* are depicted. During the persecutions of the Christians under emperor Diocletian executions took place in the theatre. During the fifth and sixth centuries the theatre served as an open-air church. The *parodoi* functioned as chapels in those days. In the western *parodos* frescos from the early Christian period are still visible. Inscriptions starting with a cross have been scratched in the seats, denoting these were meant for monks.

From the theatre a busy shopping street leads to the beach, where delicious smells lure the numerous tourists to the small fish-restaurants. The southern colonnaded street used to run from this site to the harbours of Side. The west wind caused the harbours to silt up, therefore the inhabitants of the city constantly had to keep them in repair. This has led to an old saying: ‘As difficult as keeping the harbours of Side clean’.

Near the harbour are *thermae*, with three large halls, connected by narrow doors. Some of the rooms have a *hypocaust* system; the floor was laid out on small pillars, allowing for hot air to circulate under the bathing space.

South of the harbours, in the most western part of the city, were two Corinthian temples close to the sea. They were presumably dedicated to *Athena* and *Apollo*, who were also often depicted on the coins of Side. The inhabitants of the city worshipped both gods as guardians of the harbour and its ships. In the Byzantine period the temples were demolished and replaced by the *atrium* (open forecourt) of a large three-nave *basilica*.

Mighty fortresses

From Side a road fringed with flowering verges runs through the fertile coastal plain in the direction of Alanya. After three kilometres the busy town of Manavgat is passed. The nearby waterfalls in the river of the same name are frequently visited by mainly Turkish tourists.

The old city of Alanya is situated on a steep and rocky peninsula and was therefore called Kalonoros (Beautiful Mountain) in the Byzantine period. Nowadays the town is a popular tourist resort extending over both sides of the peninsula. Along the sandy beaches of the two bays hotels and apartment blocks pop up like mushrooms.

The settlement was founded in the fourth century B.C. and was a notorious pirates’ haunt in Roman days. In the thirteenth century Kalonoros was annexed by the Seljuk sultan Alaeddin Keykubad. He had his winter residence here and also a naval base. The fortress dating from that period is still the most impressive building in Alanya.

The precious cedarwood from the woody hinterland was used for shipbuilding and was also an important export product. Near the harbour lies a unique mediaeval shipyard with five vaulted workshops. An inscription above the entrance mentions the foundation year 1227. The access to the yard is at the Red Tower (Kızıl Kule), named after the colour of its stones. The tower was part of Alaeddin’s fortress and served to protect the harbour and the shipyards. Another tower south of the shipyard, the Arsenal, also had a defensive purpose.

A winding road with beautiful panoramas leads to the citadel and passes picturesque houses of the old city with gardens full of exotic flowers. In the busy seaside-resort the holidaymakers can spend a cloudy day visiting old mosques, a Byzantine church, a *bedesten*, a *karavanserai* and *cisterns*. 150 towers of the double-walled citadel still stand. The most important part of the fortifications is the inner castle, the so-called Ehmedek. Such an inner castle is characteristic of Seljuk fortress architecture. The base of the walls dates from the Hellenistic period, when the city was called Korakesion. South of Ehmedek lies the Süleymaniye Camii. The main part of this rectangular mosque is covered by an imposing dome. As is common use, the mosque has a separate section for women, partitioned off by a wooden screen. South of this mosque is a building dating from the seventeenth century with 26 rooms and a warehouse. The rooms are grouped around an inner court of 13 by 35 metres. The building block is sometimes referred to as a covered market, but presumably it was an inn. The steep cliff of the inner fort is also known as Adam atacağı, meaning 'place where people are thrown down'. The wall at this point is 235 metres above sea level. Some sources recount how people were executed at this site.
The Cılvarda is a cape of about 400 metres' length on the south-west side of the peninsula. This tongue of land cannot be reached from the fortress, but only across the sea. A 60 metres long wall does reach from the fortress in the direction of the cape, as a means of defence. At the very end are the remains of a monastery and of a building referred to as 'mint'.

▲ *In the courtyard of the massive fortress in Anamur the Seljuks built a small mosque.*

The mighty defence fortress was founded at the end of the twelfth century by king Leo II of Armenia Minor. A walk over the battlemented walls gives a good impression of ▼ *the enormous size of this sea-fortress.*

Along red rocks and rustic ruins

The most beautiful coastal route of Southern Turkey starts at Gazipasa, almost halfway between Alanya-Anamur. The road winds along slopes overgrown with pine-trees, which descend steeply towards the turquoise water of the Mediterranean. The present-day Anamur is located some kilometres inland. Just outside the town are the ruins of the ancient Anemurium with a double city wall, a theatre, an *odeion* and a *necropolis*. On the coast, hemmed in by two sandy bays, lies the impressive crusaders' castle Mamure Kalesı. In the inner court of this twelfth century castle stands a small restored mosque. From the fortress one has a splendid view across the surrounding area.

▲ *A Greek land tortoise (Testudo hermanni) enjoys a sunbath on one of the sarcophagi in Hierapolis. If a tortoise is left undisturbed by tourists and animal traders it can reach an exceptionally high age.*

Tortoises, terrapins and turtles

Tortoises (order of Testudines) belong to a very ancient group of reptiles, which have existed on earth since the Trias. Their remarkable appearance has not been subject to many changes during all those years. Tortoises have managed to survive any kind of danger for a period of 180 million years, but nowadays they are classified as an endangered species due to the fact that man has seriously affected their environment. In Turkey several species of tortoises and terrapins occur, leading a fairly undisturbed existence on the demarcated excavation sites. The situation of the sea turtles (Cheloniidae) however is alarming. Hotels and apartment blocks mushroom up along the beaches, the places where the females lay their eggs. The Caret turtle (Eretmochelys imbricata) and the two metres long Leather turtle (Dermochelys coracea), which have swum around in the warm water of the Mediterranean since time immemorial, are now threatened with extinction.

The European pond tortoise (Emys orbicularis) lives in the neighbourhood of brooks, swamps and mudpools. ▶

Near Silifke, 140 kilometres east of Anamur, are the remnants of the old Seleukia. This city was founded by Seleukos I on the south bank of the river Calycadmus (the present-day Göksu), at the beginning of the third century. During the Third Crusade the German emperor Frederick Barbarossa drowned in this river. The modern bridge across the river is situated on the same spot as the bridge of the years 77/78. That bridge was constructed by authority of governor Octavius Memor in honour of emperor Vespasian and his two sons Titus and Domitian. Among the humble remains from the Roman period are a theatre, a temple and a considerably large cemetery. After the First Crusade, a huge castle was built on the top of a hill west of the city, dominating the entire area.

North of Silifke a magnificent mountain route leads to the sparcely inhabited interior. Alongside the road are remarkable tombs in the shape of small temples. After 30 kilometres the excavations of Uzunzaburç (the ancient Olba/Diocaesarea) are reached, during the Roman era an important city. In Uzuncaburç the columns of the temple of *Zeus* Olbios with their fine capitals have been partly re-erected. This temple dating from the third century B.C. is, as far as is known, the oldest Corinthian temple of Asia Minor. The later rebuilding into a church can be detected from the arch-shaped doorcase between the columns. Somewhat further on are the less well-preserved remains of a *Tyche* temple and of a triumphal arch, spanning the ancient colonnaded street. Near the huge access gate of the main street lie the poor remnants of a small Roman theatre. The present-day Turkish village owes its name to the more than 22 metres high Hellenistic tower (Uzuncaburç = high tower) in the city walls.

One kilometre south of Silifke lies the shrine of Mereyemlik. In memory of the Christian citizen Thekla a church was founded at this site in the fifth century. The lower church, with in the middle nave a row of columns with Byzantine cushion capitals, has been almost completely preserved. ▸

Two grave houses near the village of Demircili. The grave on the left has a large chamber with a shallow entrance hall. The temple-like building has been provided with Corinthian columns. Next to it is a double-grave with two floors. The columns of the lower chamber are of the Ionian order, those of the upper chamber have Corinthian capitals. ▾

From Silifke a deserted minor road leads to Olba. Impressive grave monuments lie scattered in the rugged mountain scenery. In this grave house are several sarcophagi. The lid with the lions originally belonged to another coffin. ▸

The middle opening of this triumphal arch in Olba spans a side-street of the ancient main street. There used to be statues on the consoles against the façade. ▾

The damaged early Corinthian columns of the Zeus temple in Olba. After some alterations, such as the construction of a door opening between two columns and the addition of an apsis, the temple was brought into use as a church. ▾

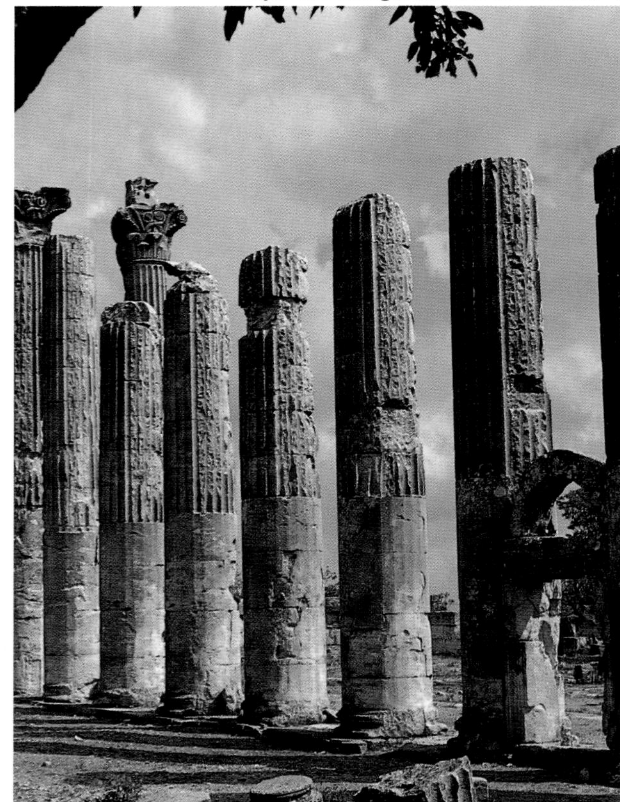

Some twenty kilometres north-east of Silifke a turning leads to two crevices. An underground river has worn them away through an age-old process of erosion. The inhabitants from the surrounding area associated the crevices with heaven and hell, names they also donated to them: Cennet and Cehennem. At the bottom of the largest crevice (Cennet) is a church dating from the fifth century, dedicated to the Virgin Mary. The *apsis* and walls bear traces of paintings, probably of Christ flanked by saints. Cehennem lies 200 metres more to the north. As the walls are very steep, the bottom can only be reached by using special equipment. This crevice is called Hell due to its awe-inspiring depth; whoever fell down, never got out. According to legends, the cave of the fire-spitting monster *Typhon* was to be found somewhere in the surroundings of Corycus. The two crevices Heaven and Hell could be related to these legends.

Corycus is a town 25 kilometres north-east of Silifke. The winding coastal road leads through the picturesque wall remains of one of a double castle. These castles were built by Armenian kings at the beginning of the twelfth century. The second castle, Kiz Kalesı (girls' fortress), is situated on an island about 200 metres off the coast. The castles were constructed simultaneously and were connected by a wall in the sea.

Just outside Corycus the ruins of the old city Elaiussa-Sebas are hidden behind knotty olive-trees. Among the fragments are temple-like burial monuments, sarcophagi and two aquaducts. The theatre has been plundered of most of its seats. The stones on a protruding tor are the scanty remains of a temple, which had been consecrated as a church in the early Christian period.

Almost ten kilometres past Corycus, a yellow sign indicates the turning to the seldom visited monuments of Kanlıdıvane (the old Kanytelis). Around a deep gorge a palace, a church and a block of monasterial buildings have been preserved. The weed grown path between the ruins is flanked by sarcophagi and temple-like tombs. In the wall of the red-coloured gorge a grave has been hewn out decorated with Roman citizens in relief. The rock reliefs in the adjacent valley bear witness, despite their provincial simplicity, of a fine craftsmanship. The decoration consists of soldiers and individuals on reclining beds.

◂ *In Korykos lie the ruins of a Roman city and a mediaeval double-castle. The second fortress, Kiz Kalesı, lies on a small island just off the coast.*

The Church of Mary at the bottom of Cennet. To facilitate the descent, stairs have been hewn out in the rocks. ▾

◂ *In the wall of the crevice at Kanytelis graves have been hewn out. A path leads into the ravine to a small plateau, from where the reliefs with representations of Roman citizens are clearly visible.*

In the rock wall of a valley near Kanytelis a group of remarkable graves has been hewn out. Presumably the local ▾ *rulers are depicted on the reliefs.*

On the edge of a deep crevice are the remains of the city of Kanytelis. The caves in the limestone formations form an ideal accommodation for bats. ▾

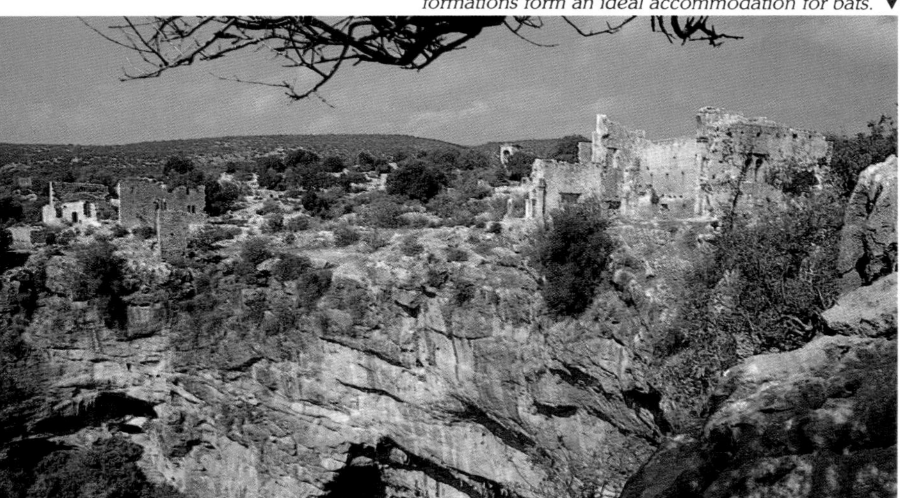

The modern city of Viranşehir, an attractive port for seaside visitors, is located eleven kilometres west of Mersin. Around the year 700 B.C. colonists from Rhodes founded the ancient Soloi at this spot. Pompeius, the famous Roman general and statesman, subjugated the local pirates in the middle of the first century, and changed the name of the city into Pompeiopolis. The remaining ruins are insignificant. Only an ancient colonnaded street overgrown with reed-panicles, dating from 150-250, cuts through the modern residential district. Corinthian capitals crown the 28 remaining columns.

The port-town of Mersin has a long history. Excavations, three kilometres west of the city near Yümük Tepe, have resulted in the discovery of an important prehistoric and Hittite centre.

The finds from Yümük Tepe are nowadays on display in the regional museum in Adana, the capital of Cilicia. The old bridge (Taş Köprü), across the Seyhan in the centre of Adana, was presumably built by Auxentius. This might be the same Auxentius who lived around the year 384 in Rome and was a bridge constructor in his day. Adana is a fast growing agricultural and industrial centre, also accommodating a sizeable NATO-base.

In Sirkeli near Adana a relief of the Hittite king Muwatalli (1306-1282 B.C.) has been hewn out in a rock along the bank of the Ceyhan. Till now this is the oldest known large-scale sculpture dating from the Hittite period.

Beyond Mersin the main route leaves the coast, Adana is situated 50 kilometres inland in the delta of the Seyhan. More to the east, just before the castle of Toprakkale, the road branches off. The crowded mainroad from Toprakkale via Gaziantep and Urfa leads eastward to the countries of the Middle East. The Turkish lorries are all overloaded and underpowered. The warning 'Dikkat! Tehlikeli Madde' (caution, dangerous substances) on the rear of the tankers crawling along, does not seem superfluous. Among this mechanized pandemonium, drivers of trucks full of luxury goods from the west (TIR) try to find their way across the crowded mountain passes. The southern route leads to the Syrian border via İskenderun and Antakya. Here Alexander the Great defeated the Persian king Darius III at the river Issus in 333 B.C.

In the first century Antakya (the renowned Antiochia) was the largest city of the ancient world after Rome and Alexandria. The apostle Paul also stopped at Antiochia on his travels. The city is attractively located on the river Orontes and breathes an oriental atmosphere. The Hatay Museum in Antakya offers a unique collection of Roman mosaics.

▲ *The tobacco of these farmers from Antakya lies ready to be transported to the processing factories in Adana.*

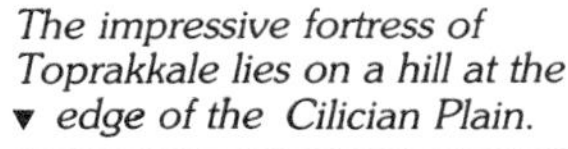

The impressive fortress of Toprakkale lies on a hill at the ▼ *edge of the Cilician Plain.*

▲ *A mosaic in the Hatay Museum at Antakya. On this representation the Evil Eye can be seen that is attacked by a picking raven, a trident, a sword, a scorpion, a snake, a barking dog, a centipede and a panther. The dwarf has a huge phallus as an evil-repelling symbol.*

Döşemealtı

Yorüks are semi-nomadic tribes, encamping on the plains near the south coast with their flocks of sheep both summer and winter. From the sheep's wool, dyed with natural colours, the Yorüks make their Döşemealtı carpets. The villages around Antalya are also production centres of this type of carpet. The influence of the shepherds can be recognized from the characteristic dark-green, blue and red natural colours and the geometrical patterns. The central motive symbolizes a nomadic tribe with tents. In the corner a stylized Kybele can be seen with a scorpion next to it, the symbol of pride. Knotting a Döşemealtı takes about three months. One square metre contains as many as 90,000 to 120,000 knots.

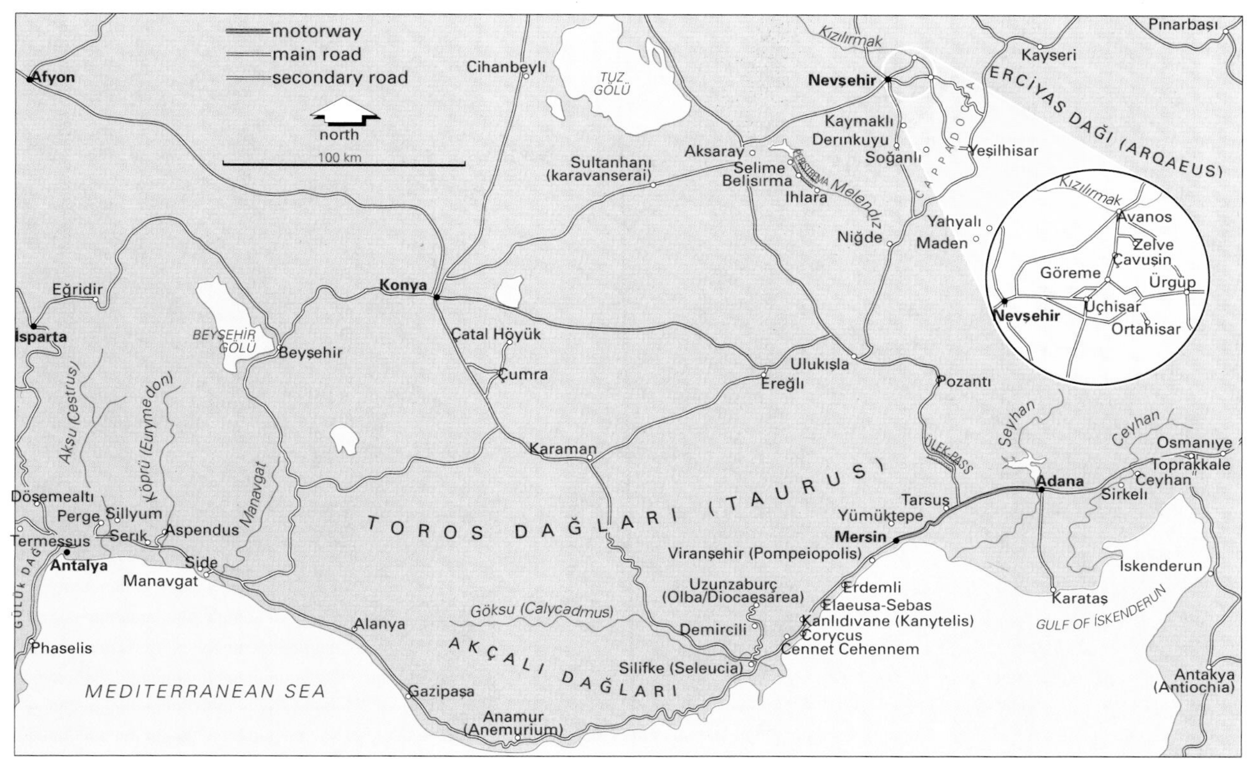

Cult places in Cappadocia

Halfway between Mersin and Adana lies Tarsus, Paul's birthplace. From Tarsus a wide asphalted road leads to Cappadocia across the spectacular Bülek-pass. As early as antiquity, this narrow crevice in the Taurus Mountains formed an important passage-way in the north-south connection and was known as the Cilician Gate. The famous 100,000 men of the Persian king Xerxes marched through this crevice in the fifth century B.C. Alexander the Great's troops and later the Crusaders also travelled through the Cilician Gate.
Cappadocia is the region in Central Anatolia between the cities of Nevşehir, Kayseri and Niğde. Here a completely different world unfolds before the eyes of the visitor. The region is renowned for its lunar landscape and the fascinating rock architecture dating from the ninth until the thirteenth centuries. The soft rock has beautiful pastel hues: white, cream, grey, pink and yellow. This delicate colour gamut contributes to the unearthly appearance of Cappadocia.
More than 30 million years ago the Erciyas Dağı (Arqaeus Vulcano), about twenty kilometres south of Kayseri, deposited large quantities of volcanic rock. In the eighteenth century stories about mysterious fires circulated. Apparently, the volcano was still active at that time. The layers of tuff vary in solidity. For millennia wind and rain have eroded the softer rock, leaving a remarkable landscape with hundreds of intersecting valleys and undulating rocks. Erosion is also the main cause of the most striking characteristic of the scenery: high conical tuff-formations, which have been preserved owing to a chunk of harder rock lying on top of them.
At first sight the countryside seems barren and dry, only a single tree and some shrubs grow in scattered places. Yet, water flows abundantly in the underground rivers, emerging to the surface in some places in the shape of springs. The water comes from the mountains and, until late in the hot summer, brooks flow through the strange valleys.

At the end of the fourth century Cappadocia was part of the Byzantine Empire. The most important connecting roads from Constantinople to the east and the south led along this province and crossed in Kayseri. In the seventh century Arab attacks commenced. The border of the Byzantine Empire was moved to the west and until well into the ninth century Cappadocia was an unsafe region. Although in the second half of the same century Byzantine power was restored, the eastern border remained disputed.
In the eleventh century another danger threatened, this time concerning Seljuk attacks. The most critical fight took place at Mantzikert in 1071. The battle was lost by the Byzantines and the Seljuks set out on their march into Anatolia. Around 1085 the greater part of Cappadocia was in the hands of the sultan of Konya.
Since there was hardly any wood or building material in the region, the inhabitants hewed out their houses in the tuff, which could be easily tooled. Such shelters offer an excellent protection against the hot summers and the icy winters. These days many caves serve as dovecotes and form an important link in local agriculture. Until the introduction of fertilizer, the droppings were used as manure for the arid soil and even today pigeon manure is sometimes strewn out across the fields. The dovecotes consist of rough chambers, often in rows on top of each other, with a myriad of small holes in the walls.
Cappadocia has always been sparcely inhabited with farmers who mainly provided their own livelihood. The small number of inhabitants seems contradictory to the enormous amount of rock dwellings. Yet, obsolete houses were never restored. It cost hardly any effort to hew a new dwelling-place out of the soft tuff. The rooms hewn out of stone served as farmers' cottages, as stables and as shelters near the fields. They were simple rectangular rooms with flat ceilings, usually on several levels.
Besides cave dwellings Cappadocia has underground cities, such as Derınkuyu and Kaymaklı. These are

Bizarre tuff formations are characteristic of the scenery in Cappadocia. ▼

▲ *Panoramic view across the valley extending between Üçhisar and Göreme. Between the pointed rock formations lie arid fields.*

CROSS-SECTION OF KAYMAKLI

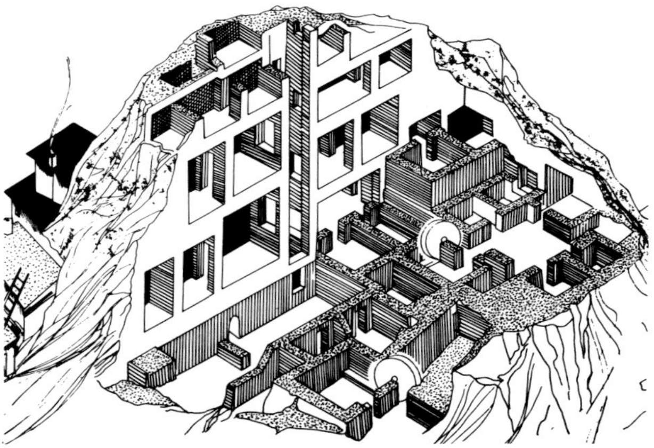

Kaymaklı has seven ▶ underground levels. The heavy boulder served to close off the entrance and was provided with a mechanism, which allowed the boulder to be rolled in front of the opening only from the inside.

labyrinths, sometimes up to seven levels under the ground, with very roughly executed connecting rooms. Some passage-ways can be closed off with a large boulder. The rooms are small and completely dark, only in some places vertical air-shafts have been constructed. It is difficult to imagine that such cities were permanently inhabited. In the torchlit rooms the air would soon become stale. It is assumed for that reason, that the underground cities mainly served as places of refuge. In some rooms submerged storage pots have been discovered. The lack of graffiti, except that applied by tourists, is further proof that the underground cities never accommodated humans. Most of the rock churches were hewn out of the rock in the early Christian period of bloom, before the Arab attacks. Under Byzantine rule, Cappadocia knew a period of comparative peace and quiet from the end of the ninth until the second half of the eleventh century. The rock churches and rock monasteries of Cappadocia play an important role in Byzantine cultural history. The province was a monastic centre, probably comparable to Athos and Meteora in Greece. Unfortunately no archives have been preserved substantiating this. On the other hand, the churches often have elaborate and colourful murals, providing information about the religious thoughts of those days. The 'building' process using tuff is quite different to the one using wood and stone, for the material is not added but removed. Therefore none of the elementary building principles is applicable to rock architecture; a hewn-out dome is weightless, thus needs no columns to carry it. It is striking that all these churches are replicas of conventional architecture in their shape. Building in tuff mountains seems simple, but mistakes

7 Sultan Cities

The smells and sounds of a bazar mingle with the stench and noise of buses, taxis and lorries. In dusty streets pedestrians swarm along shops of coppersmiths, leather-workers, silver- and goldsmiths, carpet traders and spice vendors. From the minaret high above the flow of city-traffic, the electronically amplified voice of a muezzin spurs the faithful to prayer. The sultan cities of Turkey seem like a fairy-tale from 1001-Nights in a twentieth century setting.

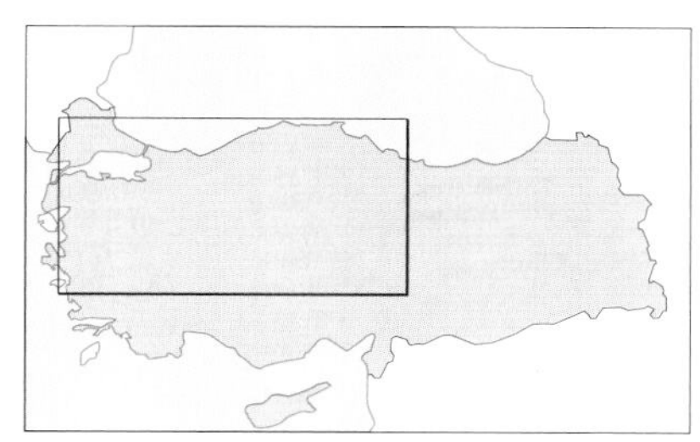

Driving past cities which were mainly subject to Islamic influences, the journey continues. The skyline of these cities is determined by mosques, minarets and *medresses*. Tile mosaics from İznik adorn the many Seljuk and Ottoman buildings. Naturally, İstanbul will receive most attention in this chapter. From this metropolis the journey leads right through Thrace to Edirne on the Bulgarian border. The southern route brings the visitor via Iznik to Bursa with its green hills and 'green' monuments. The religious centre of Konya, the city of the dancing *Dervishes*, has a central location on the Anatolian Plateau. Along old *karavanserais* the road goes eastward in the direction of Urfa and Diyarbakır. The tour is rounded off with a visit to the Christian places of interest in Ahtamar, Sumela and Trabzon.

Link between Europe and Asia

The street scene of İstanbul is dominated by monumental remains, giving evidence of a turbulent history. According to tradition, the city was founded around the middle of the seventh century B.C. by colonists from the Greek city of Megara. They named the new settlement Byzantion, after their leader Byzas. The city is favourably located along the Bosporus and on both sides of the Golden Horn (Haliç). The Bosporus is the narrow passage-way between the Sea of Marmara and the Black Sea. The location on this strait was of strategical significance, for many Greek cities imported their corn from the Black Sea region. Toll collections caused Byzantion to flourish.
The first settlement was probably situated on the same hill that is now the site of the world-famous Topkapı Palace and the imposing Hagia Sophia. Historical sources mention that the inhabitants of Byzantion had all the usual facilities of a Greek city at their disposal: a

◄ The Great Bazar of İstanbul numbers more than 300 jewelleries. The attractively illuminated shop-windows create a fairy-tale-like atmosphere. The gold content of the jewels on display varies from 14 to 22 carats.

◄ The enormous amount of traffic is a daily recurring problem for the inhabitants of İstanbul.

theatre, temples, sports buildings and water reservoirs. Archaeologically however, little is known about the buildings of the classical and Hellenistic periods, as the city has remained permanently inhabited from that period and was destroyed several times.

From the first half of the second century B.C. Byzantion was part of the Roman Empire. During a civil war under emperor Septimius Severus (193-211), the city was once again destroyed. Septimius Severus built the city up again and enlarged it by erecting a new defence wall, about 500 metres west of the old city wall. The Hippodrome, the oldest monument of İstanbul, also dates from this time.

In 324, Byzantion was proclaimed capital of the East-Roman Empire and re-named Constantinople by Constantine the Great. The succeeding period can be characterized by its immense building activity. Constantinople had to become a second Rome and was therefore built on seven hills too. All over the city palaces, *fora*, aquaducts and baths arose, which were embellished with marble statues and columns gathered from all over the empire. Theodosius II (408-450) doubled the surface-area of the Constantine city, by constructing a new city wall one-and-a-half kilometres further to the west.

During the Nika Rising in 532, in an attempt to depose emperor Justinian from the throne, a large part of Constantinople was destroyed. Justinian rebuilt the city in a more splendid fashion than before, with as its showpiece the Hagia Sophia. Broad streets, some with roofed-over, two-floor colonnades, ran through Constantinople. The inhabitants could make use of underground water pipes and reservoirs for their watersupply. In the palaces the emperor, 'God's substitute on earth', lived in indescribable affluence. He owed his wealth to the function of the city as a transit port between Asia and Europe.

An all-time low in the history of Constantinople was the occupation by the Crusaders between 1204 and 1261. The city was wealthier and possessed more Christian relics than any other city in the world and was consequently thoroughly looted.

As a result of repeated attacks by Slavs, Arabs and Turks, the Byzantine Empire crumbled away and gradually disintegrated. In the fourteenth century nothing more remained of this, once so grand empire, than a region around Constantinople and some enclaves on the Black Sea and in Greece. On 29 May 1453 Constantinople also fell into the hands of the continuously advancing Turks, who were led by Mohammed the Conqueror. The name of the city was changed into İstanbul, a corruption of the Greek words 'is tin polin', meaning 'to the city'. İstanbul became the nerve centre of the Ottoman Empire, which, at its height, extended from Hungary down to Egypt and from Algeria up to Persia.

In 1923 İstanbul lost its political function when Atatürk Kemal Pasja proclaimed Ankara capital of the Turkish Republic.

However, due to its location on the border of Europe and Asia, İstanbul has remained a cosmopolitan city, not just geographically, but also culturally and economically.

Nothing is left of the fortifications from the Greek, Hellenistic and Roman periods. The city wall, built on the assignment of the Byzantine emperor Theodosius at the start of the fifth century, is still visible however. This defence line consists of three elements: the landwall in the west, the seawall in the south and the wall along the Golden Horn in the north-east. Theodosius' wall comprised an extensive system of defence works with a main wall, a front wall, a parapet and, in some places, a moat. The main wall was almost five metres thick, eleven metres high and provided with 96 towers each of about twenty metres high. The towers lay 70 to 75 metres apart. Seven large and four smaller gates had been constructed in the wall. The front wall lay more than fourteen metres ahead of the main wall and was eight metres high. This front wall also had 96 towers, which had been placed alternatingly in relation to the towers of the main wall.

In several places, about ten metres before the front wall, a dry moat had been dug to which a low battlemented parapet had been added. Due to frequent earthquakes and attacks the wall had to be regularly maintained and fortified. These repairworks can be easily recognized from the different kinds of brickwork and elements of demolished buildings which were used in the reconstruction of the wall, such as columns and ornamental frames.

During the siege in April 1453 Turkish artillery caused considerable damage to the city walls. Initially, the walls were repaired, but after the government of Mehmed II, also known as Mohammed the Conqueror (1451-1481), the defence system fell into decay. In the twentieth century the walls were broken through in some places, in favour of road and railway constructions. Plans to demolish the entire city wall have fortunately never been executed. Even at this moment, a part of the landwall between the Belgradkapı and the Silivrikapı is being restored to its former splendour. A walk along and upon the city walls is certainly worthwhile, despite the poor condition of the wall in places.

About 600 metres north of the Sea of Marmara lay the main entrance to the city, the Porta Aurea (Golden Gate). This city gate had gilded doors or fences and was only used on the occasion of triumphal entries by the emperor. The Porta Aurea was erected as a triumphal arch around the year 390 and was at that time situated outside the city. When, twenty years later, Theodosius' walls were built, the Porta Aurea was included into them and a strong front gate was added to the inadequately defensible triumphal arch. In the Byzantine period the northern entrance was completely

A colourful street market at the foot of the restored city gate near the Topkapı bus-terminal. Thousands of people daily pass this traffic junction on the western ▼ exit road of İstanbul.

walled up and the middle entrance partially so. The southern passage-way has still been preserved. Behind the Golden Gate the pentagonal fortress Yediküle (Seven Towers) was constructed by Mehmed II in 1457. The fortress was used as a prison, a place of execution and a treasury.

Emperor Manuel Komnenos (1143-1180) had the northern part of the landwall demolished and replaced by a more westernly situated wall. Hemmed-in between this wall and the Golden Horn used to be the Palace of Blachernae. Between 1261 and 1453 this was the palace where the emperor resided in fabulous wealth. Due to the bombardments during the siege of 1453 the building was so heavily damaged, that it was never used again and completely fell into decay. The only part that has remained is Tekfur Saray, the Palace of the Ruler. Tekfur Saray was built in the thirteenth or fourteenth century using the decoration of geometrical patterns in red brick and white limestone, characteristic for those days. After the conquest of the city in 1453 the palace was restored to serve respectively as a zoo, a brothel, a tile pottery, a paupers' home and a bottle factory.

The walls along the Golden Horn and the Sea of Marmara have only been partially preserved. The seawall is hardly visible anymore, as several fragments were assimilated into buildings of later periods.

In addition to the defensive works, water supply received ample attention. As springs within the city walls were scarce, water had to be supplied via pipes from the surrounding area. It was stored in large *cisterns*, open or roofed-over reservoirs. After Constantinople had been proclaimed capital of the East-Roman Empire, the number of inhabitants strongly increased. The water supply system was extended with aquaducts and reservoirs, of which the Aquaduct of Valens dating from 375 is the most eye-catching. This building, 971 metres long and 29 metres high, bridges a valley between two hills. These days the Atatürk Bulvarı, an important arterial road of modern İstanbul, runs through the valley.

Of the innumerable large and small *cisterns* the city once possessed, only a few have remained. The best-known is Yerebatan Saray (Underground Palace) opposite the Hagia Sophia. This huge underground reservoir, built in 532, had to supply the imperial palace and its surrounding buildings with water. The ceiling of the large room (140 by 70 metres) is supported by 336

The renovated Aquaduct ▲ of Valens crosses the crowded Atatürk Bulvarı. An endless stream of cars roars between the wide arches day and night.

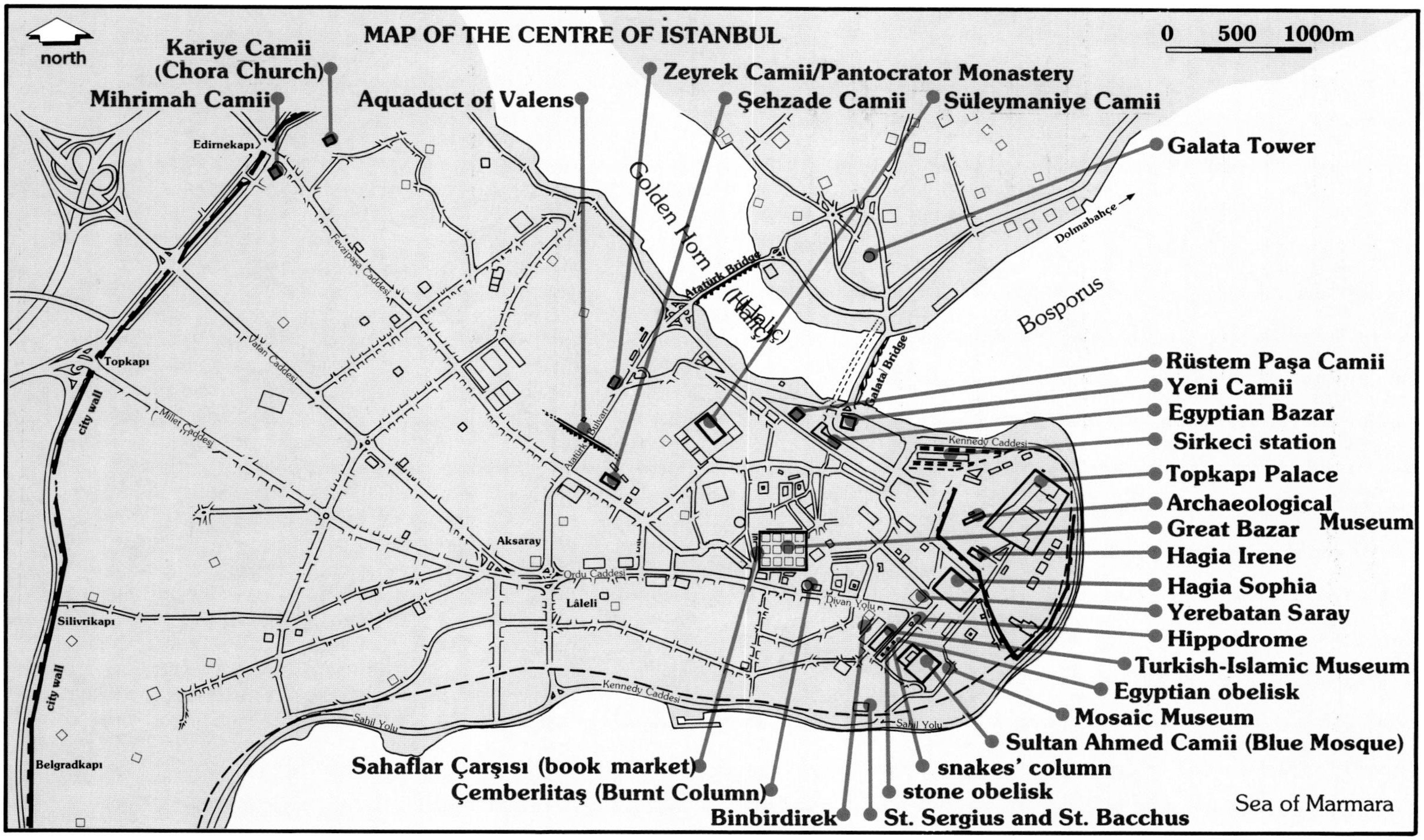

MAP OF THE CENTRE OF İSTANBUL

north
0 500 1000m
Kariye Camii (Chora Church)
Mihrimah Camii
Aquaduct of Valens
Zeyrek Camii/Pantocrator Monastery
Şehzade Camii
Süleymaniye Camii
Galata Tower
Edirnekapı
Golden Horn (Haliç)
Atatürk Bridge
Dolmabahçe
Bosporus
Galata Bridge
Fevzipaşa Caddesi
Vatan Caddesi
Millet Caddesi
Atatürk Bulvarı
Topkapı
city wall
Aksaray
Ordu Caddesi
Lâleli
Divan Yolu
Kennedy Caddesi
Sahil Yolu
Silivrikapı
Belgradkapı
Rüstem Paşa Camii
Yeni Camii
Egyptian Bazar
Sirkeci station
Topkapı Palace
Archaeological Museum
Great Bazar
Hagia Irene
Hagia Sophia
Yerebatan Saray
Hippodrome
Turkish-Islamic Museum
Egyptian obelisk
Mosaic Museum
Sultan Ahmed Camii (Blue Mosque)
snakes' column
stone obelisk
St. Sergius and St. Bacchus
Binbirdirek
Çemberlitaş (Burnt Column)
Sahaflar Çarşısı (book market)
Sea of Marmara

▲ *The Binbirdirek Cistern has not got 1001 columns but 280, in contrast to what the name might imply (bin=thousand). The entrance is in a small building, of which the key is available at one of the shops in the neighbourhood.*

▲ *On the former spina of the Hippodrome stands an Egyptian obelisk of red porphyry. This memorial needle originally had a place in the temple at Karnak. The austere hieroglyphs glorify the god Horus and pharao Tuthmosis III.*

▲ *Remnant of the bronze Snakes' Column at the Hippodrome. Once this three-headed column adorned the oracle sanctuary of Apollo at Delphi. Nowadays the street level is considerably higher than at the time of Theodosius.*

different columns from older buildings. Nowadays the visitor can walk through the cool vaults of Yerebatan Saray to the reverberating sounds of classical music.
An unknown, yet not less impressive reservoir is the Binbirdirek, the Cistern of the 1001-Columns. It is located west of the Hippodrome under a square on the Isik Sokak. The reservoir dates from the time of Constantine and was rebuilt in the fifth or sixth century. The *cistern* was originally nineteen metres deep, but during the course of time a more than four metres thick layer of mud and rubble has accumulated. The 224 columns of the Binbirdirek are remarkable, because each column consists of two smaller columns on top of each other with a broad boulder between them.
The park opposite the Blue Mosque, At Meydanı, has the elongated shape of the horse-racing track, which once lay at this spot. This Hippodrome was built on assignment of emperor Septimius Severus around the year 200. The racetrack was not only a centre of sports and entertainment, but was also used for important state ceremonies such as triumphal processions and inaugurations of emperors. Here, Constantinople was solemnly consecrated as the capital of the East-Roman Empire on 11 May 330. During the government of Constantine the Great the Hippodrome was enlarged and decorated with objects of art from all over the empire. Political disputes were often settled here too. During the Nika Rising, causing enormous damage to the city in 532, 30,000 rebels were executed in the Hippodrome. At the time of the occupation of Constantinople by the Crusaders the racetrack was used for tournaments.
The rectangular building was 420 to 440 metres long and 117 to 125 metres wide. The short side in the south-west was semi-circular. The stands could seat an estimated 30,000 spectators. Nowadays only the structure of the semi-circular end (*sphendone*) can be observed in the narrow streets behind the Hippodrome. Against the large brick arches houses were built at a later period.
The original level of the racetrack was more than seven metres below the present street-level. In the longitudinal axis of the Hippodrome there once stood a long wall, the *spina*, on which memorials were placed. In the middle of the park three of these monuments can still be seen: an Egyptian obelisk, a fragment of a snakes' column and a stone obelisk.
The Egyptian obelisk, dating from the time of pharaoh Tuthmosis III (1490-1436 B.C.), had been transported to Constantinople by emperor Theodosius in the fourth century. Only the upper part could be put up, as the obelisk had been damaged in transit. On the pedestal reliefs have been applied, depicting Theodosius I and his family in the imperial box of the racetrack. This box was situated in the middle on the east side of the Hippodrome. On the west side of the pedestal the emperor is depicted watching prisoners-of-war, who kneel in front of him, paying tribute. On the south side Theodosius is a spectator at the chariot races. The east side shows the public and the imperial family observing a performance of dancers and musicians. The north side of the pedestal depicts among other things the transport and the raising of the obelisk.
The second monument of the former *spina* that has been preserved, is the bronze column in the shape of three entangled snakes. This column once stood in the sanctuary of *Apollo* in the Greek city of Delphi. The Snakes' Column had been erected in 479 B.C. after the

▲ *A relief on the socle of the obelisk. Emperor Theodosius and his family watch the chariot races in the Hippodrome from the honorary stand.*

victory of the Greeks over the Persians. By order of emperor Constantine the column was taken to Constantinople and initially placed in the court of the Hagia Sophia. According to the seventeenth-century author Evliya Çelebi the heads of the snakes possessed the magical power to keep vermin out of the city. A fragment of one of those heads is now on display in the Archaeological Museum of Istanbul.
On the south-west side of the Hippodrome is a large limestone obelisk, dating from the fourth century A.D. In the tenth or eleventh century this obelisk was covered with gilded bronze slabs. The slabs were robbed by crusaders in the thirteenth century. The remaining fastening holes give the obelisk a pockmarked appearance.
The most famous monument of İstanbul is undoubtedly the Hagia Sophia (Church of the Holy Wisdom). In 532 the predecessor of this church was destroyed during the Nika Rising. In order to rebuild the church, the architects Anthemios of Tralleis and Isodoros of Miletos were employed, in their time scholars of fame. During the festive inauguration-ceremony in 537 emperor Justinian exclaimed: 'Praise God, who has considered me worthy of finishing this work; I have surpassed you, o Salomo!'. Not only the giant size of the dome, but also the speed in which it had been built, caused the construction to have a poor resistance against earthquakes. As a result, the dome collapsed three times. During the occupation of the city by the crusaders the Hagia Sophia was mercilessly looted. Many objects of art and famous relics ended up in Western Europe. That is how, for instance, the treasury of the San Marco in Venice has come to house a large number of precious objects from İstanbul. The bronze horses of emperor Nero, which used to stand on the Hippodrome, were also moved to Venice in those days.

The majestic Hagia Sophia dominates the old centre of İstanbul. The building has been painted in its original brick colour. The colossal buttresses on the outside contrast sharply with the staggering three-dimensional effect of the interior. ▶

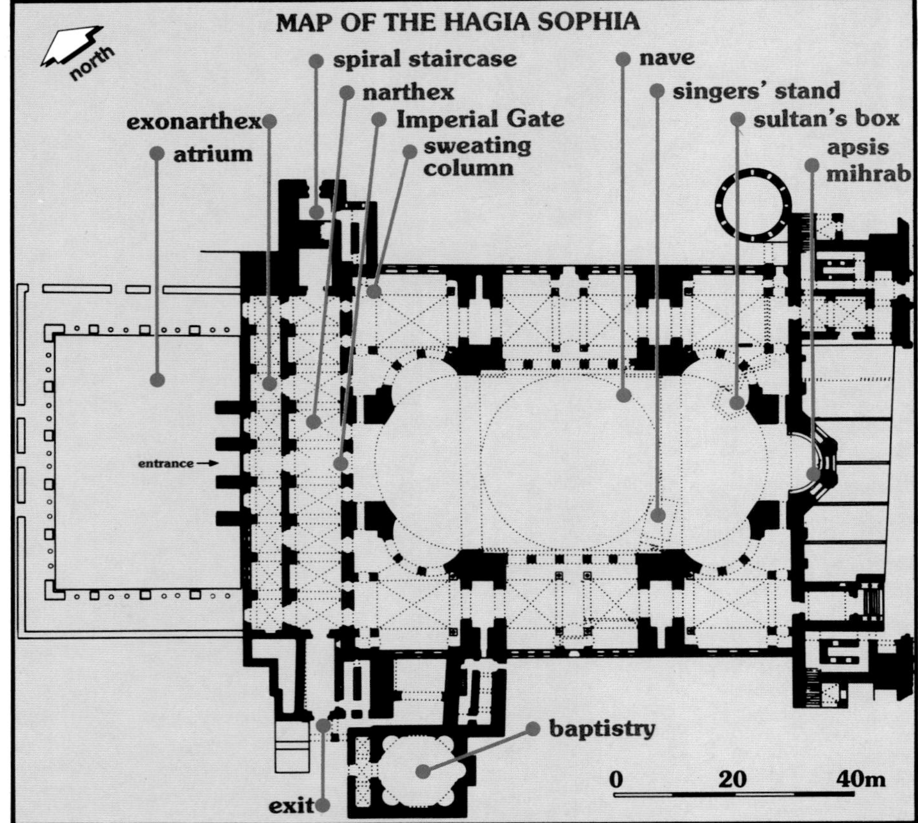

The interior reveals ► a mixture of Christian and Islamic influences. Giant shields on which the names of the first caliphs have been applied, decorate the four corners of the central hall. These calligraphic masterpieces date from the seventeenth century.

The Hagia Sophia was in a deplorable condition when sultan Mehmed II decided to change the church into a mosque immediately after the conquest of the city. The building was more or less completely left in its original state. On behalf of Islamic services minarets, a *minbar* and a *mihrab* were added. The name was altered into Ayasofya Camii, Mosque of the Hagia Sophia. After the proclamation of the Turkish Republic the building became a museum. The present-day visitor will notice a mixture of Islamic and Christian traditions.

The contrast between the interior and exterior of the Hagia Sophia is striking. From the outside the building makes a massive and bulky impression. However, once inside the enormous space, the visitor is overwhelmed by gold-coloured mosaics, green and dark-purple columns, richly veined marble slabs and the famous dome.

The Hagia Sophia can be entered through respectively an *atrium* (forecourt), an *exonarthex* (outer entrance hall) and a *narthex* (entrance hall). The scanty remains of the *atrium* enclosed by columns and of the older church are situated in front of the entrance. As was common with early Christian churches, there is an *exonarthex* in front of the *narthex*. This outer entrance hall has not been decorated. The walls of the *narthex* are covered with slabs of marble in various colours. The slabs have been sawn out of one piece and have then been applied reflectively next to each other against the wall, causing the veins to form symmetrical patterns. The mosaics in the vault show geometrical motives. From the *narthex* nine doors give access to the nave of the church. In the Byzantine period the three doors in the middle were exclusively used by the emperor and his court. Over the central door, the Imperial Gate, a mosaic has been applied with Leo VI (886-912) kneeling in front of Christ on a throne. On both sides of Christ Mary and the archangel Gabriel are depicted. The central room of the Hagia Sophia consists of a square space of about 31 by 31 metres with above it the dome, resting on four colossal pillars. Large triangular surfaces (*pendentives*) form the connection from the pillars to the dome. The diameter of the dome has been indicated in the floor by means of small crosses. The top is situated about 56 metres above the surface of the floor. During favourable weather conditions a dazzling wreath of light penetrates through the 40 windows along the bottom of the central dome. Already in antiquity Procopius, Justinian's biographer, uttered praise about this 'hovering' dome. The huge dome strongly emphasizes the middle of the church. Yet, the Hagia Sophia makes an oblong impression, as the aisles are separated from the middle nave by a screen of columns.

On the east and west sides the central room is supported by two semi-domes. The four corners of the middle nave are buttressed by four smaller domes. This construction is not only impressive, but also has an architectural purpose; the immense lateral forces exerted by the central dome on the walls are absorbed by the two semi-domes and conducted to the foundation. As the central dome is only supported on two sides in this way, the forces are not sufficiently conducted. This was one of the reasons why the vault collapsed repeatedly. An attempt was made to solve the problem by building sturdy buttresses against the north and south side of the building in order to brace the four corner pillars supporting the central dome. However the opposite effect was achieved. The lateral forces are insufficiently absorbed due to the bad foundations and the enormous weight of the buttresses. The side walls of the building are pressed apart, as it were, by the central dome and the heavy buttresses. To prevent collapse a metal bracing band was fastened around the dome.

In the north-west corner of the Hagia Sophia there is a column covered with copper slabs. Magic forces are ascribed to this 'sweating' column. By kissing or rubbing it the faithful believed their ailments would be cured. These age-long touches have worn a hole in both the copper covering and the column itself.

The interior of the Hagia Sophia is particularly imposing. The capitals and ornamental frames have been provided with lace-like sculpture and marble slabs. Mosaics and paintings have been applied on the walls. At the time of Justinian the church was not decorated with figurative mosaics, but with stylized plant motives and crosses on a gold background. These mosaics have been preserved in the central dome, the aisles and the galleries. After the reign of Justinian figurative mosaics became fashionable, however during *iconoclasm* (726-843) they were practically all destroyed. The dome of the *apsis* is covered with a mosaic dating from the period immediately after this iconoclastic fury. It depicts the Virgin Mary with Christ in her lap, seated on a jewel-encrusted throne. A representation of 'Christ Pantocrator' (Christ as Ruler of the World) on the central dome was replaced by a proverb from the Koran.

At the north of the *narthex* a spiral-staircase leads to the upper gallery where one has a view on the nave of the church. The renowned mosaic with Christ, Mary and John the Baptist can be admired in the north-west corner of the gallery. In the south-west corner is a mosaic of Mary with Christ as a child, flanked by emperor John II Comenius and empress Irene. The adjacent mosaic shows Christ with empress Zoe and Constantine Monomachus, her third husband.

In the walls of the gallery are small niches with glass rods, an invention of the Ottoman architect Sinan in order to check the building for damage caused by light earthquakes.

◄ *The diffuse incidence of light emphasizes the 'hovering' effect of the huge dome of the Hagia Sophia. In the dome a Koran text has been applied on top of a painting of Christ as Ruler of the World. The pendentives, which form the transition from the circular dome to the square central room, have been painted with cherubs.*

The room south of the *narthex*, nowadays the exit of the Hagia Sophia, originally formed the connection with the nearby imperial palace. The visitor looking back, will see a fine mosaic over the door, dating from the final quarter of the tenth century. This is also a representation of the Holy Virgin with Christ in her lap. On her right is emperor Constantine who offers the city of Constantinople, symbolized by a small replica. On the left of Mary is emperor Justinian who hands her a scale-model of the Hagia Sophia.

In Byzantine architecture the Hagia Sophia did not have many successors, but it did have a lot in the Ottoman period. The Süleyman Mosque and the Sultan Ahmed Mosque have been strongly influenced in their ground plans and structures by Justinian's church, although the architects have assimilated the Byzantine style characteristics in an entirely personal way. On the premises of the Hagia Sophia are some *türbes* (burial tombs) from the Ottoman period, among others those of Selim II (1577), Murat III (1599) and Mehmed III (1603). The graves of Mustafa I and his cousin Ibrahim have been housed in the former baptistry of the Hagia Sophia. The buildings are decorated with tableaus of beautiful İznik tiles. Among the *türbes* traces of kitchens and a hospital have been discovered.

▲ *Diagonally placed glass rods in small niches along the walls registrate light earthquakes and possible subsidences. The fact that most of these rods are broken gives food for thought!*

◄ *This picture of Christ can be found in the southern gallery and forms a climax of Byzantine mosaic art. The pattern in the gold-coloured halo and the expression of empathy on the face bear witness to an extraordinary craftsmanship.*

The nearby Hagia Irene is the sister church of the Hagia Sophia. The two churches are dedicated to important aspects of Christ, respectively Holy Peace and Holy Wisdom. The Hagia Irene is located on the site once belonging to the oldest Christian sanctuaries of the city. The original church was founded in order of Constantine the Great. Until the construction of the Hagia Sophia, the Hagia Irene was the patriarch's see. The present-day church was completed simultaneously with its sister church, after the predecessors of both churches had been devastated during the Nika Rising. Apart from small damage due to earthquakes, the Hagia Irene was spared great disasters, such as were afflicted on the Hagia Sophia. The building still has almost the same appearance as it had at the time of Justinian. Only the *atrium* was lost in a fire in 564, but in the Turkish period this forecourt was rebuilt. Since 1464 the Hagia Irene is situated within the walls of the Topkapı Palace. The church served as a house of God for the Christians working at the court. Later the building served respectively as an arsenal, a warehouse and a museum. Nowadays this splendid Byzantine church is used as a concert and exposition hall.
The Hagia Irene is divided into a wide middle nave and two narrow aisles. The *apsis* is semi-circular on the outside and pentagonal on the inside. The central section of the nave has a dome, resting on a *drum* (elevated ring) with windows. The diameter is more than fifteen metres; *drum* and dome are supported by four large arches. Above the *narthex* and the aisles are galleries. The church is of the usual rectangular type. Deviating however are the roofings of the galleries. These are covered with barrel vaults set at right angles to the middle nave. Moreover, the galleries are not screened from the nave by rows of columns. This has led to more spatial effect on the middle instead of on the axis between entrance and *apsis*.

The old church buildings in İstanbul form an ideal accommodation for the ▾ numerous pigeons.

In the *apsis* the only Byzantine *synthronon* of İstanbul has been preserved. This is a semi-circular dais of six steps, intended for the priests of the church.
Little is left of the original decoration of the church, yet the bare brick walls are impressive. The mosaics in the *narthex* presumably date from the time of Justinian. The wooden balcony and the graceful steps on the west side of the nave were added in the Ottoman period.
South-west of the Hippodrome, on the Sea of Marmara, lies a remarkable Byzantine church, dedicated to the saints Sergius and Bacchus. This is one of the many smaller churches dating from the reign of emperor Justinian. The church was probably finished in 532. The building consists of an octagonal central room within an irregular square. The dome is supported by eight pillars. The central room is separated from the aisles by rows of columns. Up to this point the Saint Sergius and Saint Bacchus is somewhat comparable to the Hagia Sophia. In Turkish the church is called Küçük Ayasofya, the Small Hagia Sophia. Important differences are that the east and west sides of the central room are not supported by semi-domes. The semi-circular niches of the Saint Sergius and Saint Bacchus have been built right against the central room. In that way, more than in the Hagia Sophia, attention is drawn to the middle of the church. The transition from square to dome has been solved in an unusual way. The dome has been divided into sixteen segments, eight flat and eight round ones, joining each other at the highest point. This causes the undulating shape of the dome, which is also clearly visible on the outside of the church.
High on a terrace, on the west side of the Atatürk Bulvarı, used to lie the Pantocrator Monastery. All that has remained of the buildings, are two churches and a burial chapel built between 1118 and 1136. The Pantocrator Monastery was largely devastated during the recapture of the city by the Byzantines in 1261. Apart from churches, the buildings comprised an old peoples' home, a hospital, a mental home, a medical school and a bathhouse.
The churches are in very bad condition, yet certainly worth a visit. The southern church, the oldest, is nowadays used as a mosque (Zeyrek Camii). The northern church was constructed after 1134. Both churches have a so-called four-column ground plan, typical of late Byzantine architecture. Characteristic is the high central dome, resting on four columns. In this case the columns dating from the twelfth century, which had undoubtedly been made of beautifully coloured stone, were replaced by rather bulky, square pillars of brick in the eighteenth century. In the southern church a part of the original decoration can still be seen; the floor has been laid with coloured kinds of stone and the walls of the *apsis* have been covered with marble slabs. Noteworthy is the *minbar*, built from fragments of Byzantine sculpture. Nothing of the original decoration has remained in the northern church, with the exception of a sculptured ornamental frame.
After the completion of the second church in 1136, a burial chapel for the dynasties of the Komnenes (1081-1185) and the Palaeologes (1261-1448) was erected between the two buildings.
Afterwards the walls between the churches and the burial chapel were broken through. Unfortunately the beautiful spatial effect thus arising, is nowadays nullified by wooden and plastic screens, separating the mosque from the rest of the building.

Pastane

Confectionery shops (pastane) can be found in every city in Turkey. The different kinds of confectionery, like baklava (puff-pastry) and tel kadayıf (string pastry) are saturated with honey and rosewater. Other delicacies are Mustafa Kemalpaşa (honey balls) and helva, a substance of butter and sugar to which cinnamon, sesame or pistachio can be added. In the shop windows all kinds of chocolate, toffees, lokum, bonbons, almonds in syrup and brightly coloured acid drops are temptingly displayed. A climax in Turkish sweet culture is the Islamic Sugar Feast for children at the end of the ramadan.

◂ *Every self-respecting city has alluring confectionery shops. Various kinds of pastry like baklava and tel kadayıf, but also icecream (dondurma) are in great demand.*

The skillfully arranged dishes with delicacies are richly ▾ *strewn with pistachio.*

Besides confectionery chocolate pudding, coconut cookies, peanut rocks, honey and liquor cake, almond pie, helva, hazelnut biscuits and vanilla flan belong to the repertoire ▾ *of the Turkish confectioners.*

All over Turkey, but especially in the district around Afyon, one can enjoy the taste of lokum. This soft sugar jelly in various tastes is often filled with nuts and ▾ *thereafter rolled through grated coconut.*

This vendor of simit, the popular circular sesame rolls, sits with his cart in front of a shop with dairy products. ▾

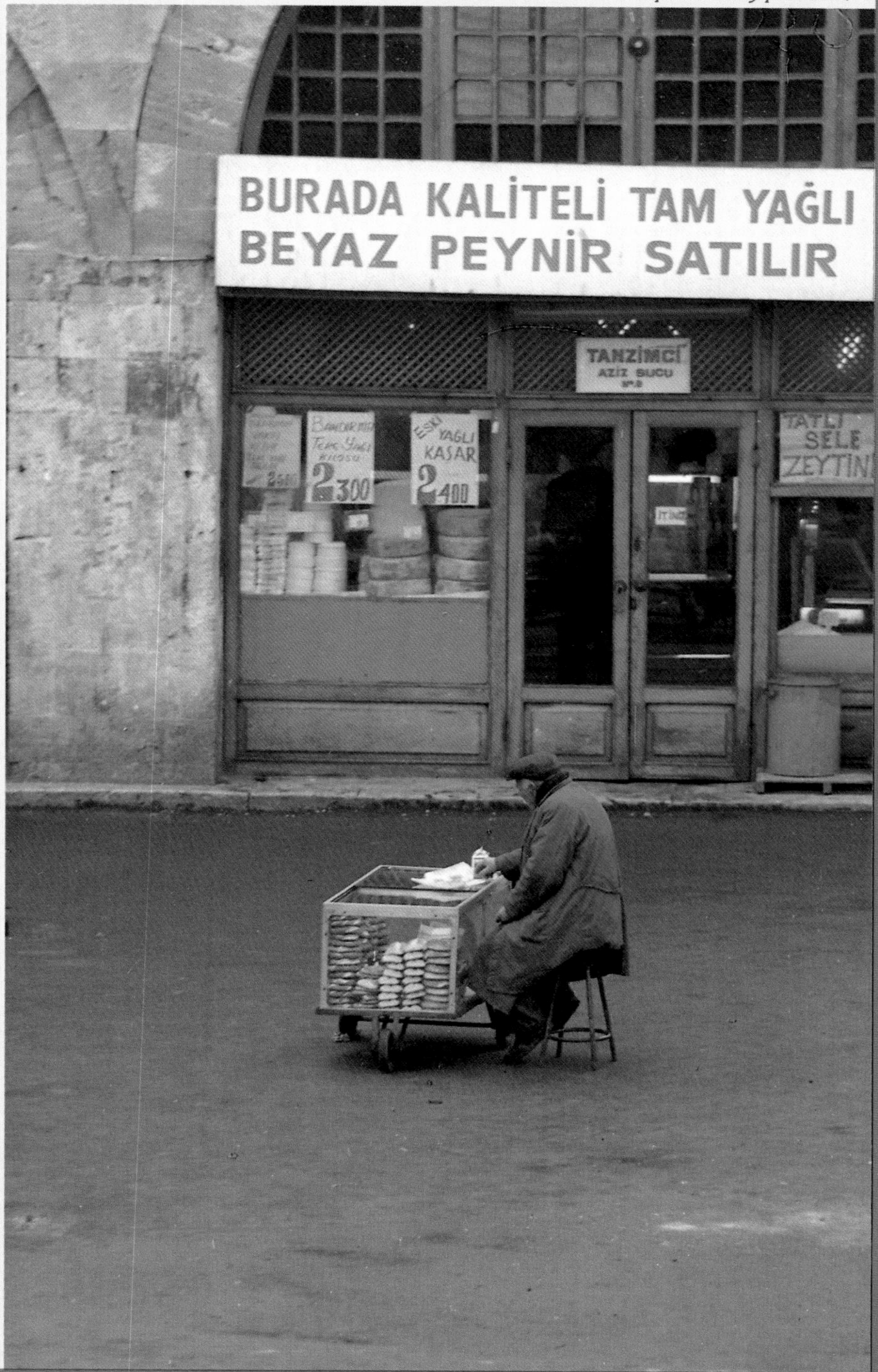

BURADA KALİTELİ TAM YAĞLI
BEYAZ PEYNİR SATILIR

▲ *At the outskirts of the old city lies the small Chora Church (Kariye Camii), which is packed daily by masses of tourists. In 1510, after the change into mosque, a minaret was added to this Byzantine monastic church.*

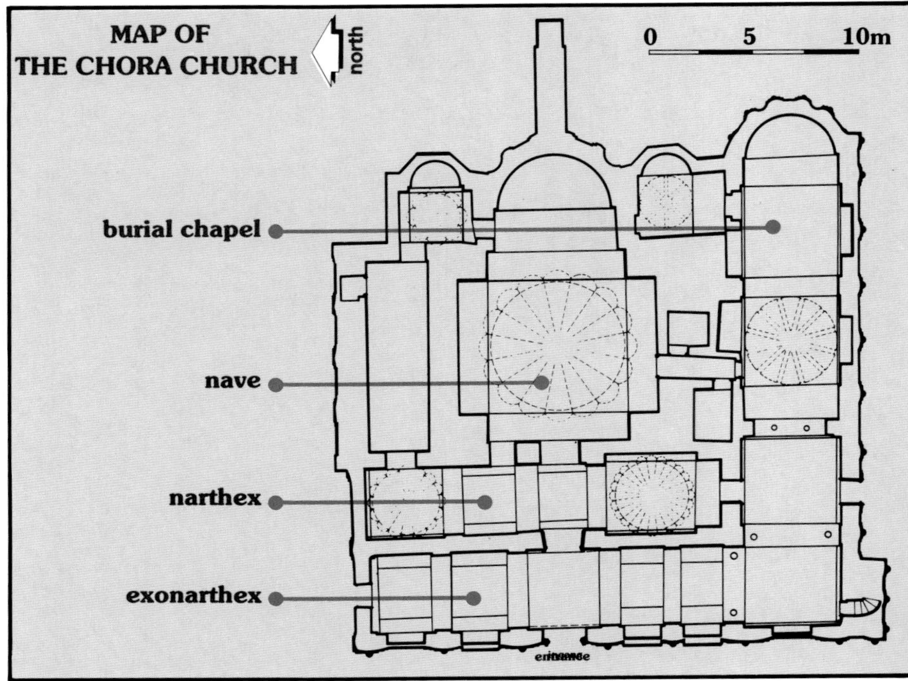

The Chora Church (Kariye Camii) is undoubtedly a unique monument. The small church is world-famous owing to its Byzantine mosaics and paintings adorning the walls. The representations in the Chora Church form a milestone in Byzantine art together with those of the churches of Ravenna and Monreale (Italy).
The monastery to which the church originally belonged, had been built outside the city walls in the third century and was therefore dedicated to Christ in Chora (Christ in the Fields). Due to the construction of Theodosius's wall, the Chora Monastery came to lie within the city. The church was built between 1077 and 1081 and received its present shape during a thorough rebuilding early in the twelfth century.
The Chora Church has a ground-plan in the shape of a Greek cross with a dome in the middle and three *apses* on the east side. In front of the nave are a *narthex* with two smaller domes and an *exonarthex*. This *exonarthex* is L-shaped and divided into seven *bays* (vault surfaces). Five of these *bays* are situated in front of the *narthex* and two serve as an entrance porch of a burial chapel on the south side. This chapel consists of two rectangular sections and an *apsis*. In the walls four niches have been left open for sarcophagi. The founder of the monastery, Theodoros Metochites, is interred here among others.
Between 1315 and 1321 the *narthex* and the side *apses* were rebuilt and the burial chapel was added to the side of the church. At that time the mosaics and the paintings were applied as well. After the monastery had been converted into a mosque at the beginning of the sixteenth century, the representations on the walls and the vaults were hidden from view by a thick layer of plaster and dirt. It was not until 1860 that the decorations were rediscovered and they were restored between 1947 and 1958.
The mosaics and the paintings of the Chora Church are among the best-preserved dating from the late Byzantine period. The scenes form a coherent whole and can best be studied consecutively. The mosaics in the church depict themes from the life of Christ and Mary. The paintings in the burial chapel represent, among others, The Resurrection and The Last Judgement. The characteristic wooden houses around the Chora Church have been restored to their former lustre and the entire city district is nowadays a protected area. The nearby city walls and the beautifully restored city gate Edirnekapı are also part of the area.

Judas tree

Although the Judas tree (Cercis siliquastrum) belongs to the family of the crown of thorns it does not bear any thorns itself. In early spring the Judas tree flowers exuberantly. Clusters of purple-pink flowers appear on the old and new branches. The petals are about two centimetres in size and resemble butterflies. The Judas tree grows on rocky hills and is also often planted as a decorative tree.

◄ *Around the Chora Church a small park has been laid out. This Judas tree is in full blossom and enhances the snug atmosphere of the church and its surroundings.*

▲ *Sixth bay of the exonarthex. At the top the Healing of the Paralyzed. Beneath that the Massacre of the Innocents. The soldiers receive their orders from Herod. On the right the slaughter is depicted, the mother makes a desperate gesture.*

Mosaic in the third bay of the exonarthex. The Miracle at ▼ *Cana, with Christ turning water into wine.*

◀ *Second bay of the exonarthex with tableaus about the birth of Christ. A bright beam of light illuminates the manger with the child. As a symbol of her virginity the feet of Mary have been tied together. At the top right the shepherds with their animals can be seen, at the bottom left the baby is bathed for the first time and a pondering Joseph sits in the foreground.*

Chora Church

The representations on the mosaics in the Chora Church can be divided into seven groups:

group 1 – The panels over the doors of the *narthex* and the *exonarthex* show scenes from the life of Christ and Mary. Over the door to the nave of the church Theodoros Metochites presents Christ with a replica of the church he built.

group 2 – In the two domes of the *narthex* the ancestors of Christ have been depicted, such as Adam, Noah, Abraham, Salomo and other Old Testament figures.

group 3 – In the intermediary *bays* of the *narthex* the life of Mary is represented in twenty scenes.

group 4 – In the arches of the *exonarthex*, beginning on the north side, thirteen scenes from the life of Christ can be seen.

group 5 – On the vaults of the *exonarthex* and in the southern part of the *narthex* the Charitable Works of Christ are portrayed.

group 6 – The arches of the *exonarthex* bear portraits of saints.

group 7 – In the nave of the church, over the door to the *narthex*, one can find a scene with Mary on her deathbed. Christ holds on to her soul, symbolized by a baby.

The side chapel of the Chora Church was painted in the years 1320-1321. In the chapel four series can be distinguished:

1 – In the semi-dome of the *apsis* the famous picture of the Resurrection can be seen. Christ pulls Adam and Eve out of their graves. He has just broken down the gates of hell, the fragments lie in front of his feet.

2 – On the vault before the *apsis* the Last Judgement has been painted. On the right of Christ are the saved souls and on the left the doomed.

3 – In the first compartment behind the *exonarthex* there are scenes from the Old Testament, such as Moses at the burning bramble-bush.

4 – Under the cornice a row of saints and martyrs has been depicted on the walls of the chapel.

In the apsis of the burial chapel a scene has been applied of Christ pulling Adam and Eve out of their graves. The mural depicts Christ as conqueror of death with at his feet the broken gates of hell and a bound Satan. ▼

▲ *The slender minarets of the Süleyman Mosque have been provided with balustrades with lace-like sculpture.*

Not only the Byzantine period is well represented in İstanbul, the Ottoman monuments are also very impressive and of a high quality. Near the Edirnekapı lies the Mihrimah Camii, built by the famous architect Sinan around the year 1550. The building order had been given by Mihrimah, the daughter of Süleyman the Great and his favourite wife Roxelane. The interior of the mosque shows beautiful deep-red paintings, accentuated by a remarkably clear incidence of light.
The Süleymaniye Camii comprises a large number of buildings. It was common use for sultans to found *külliyes*, building blocks which did not only serve a religious but also a social function. One of these *külliyes* is situated around the Süleyman Mosque and was constructed by order of sultan Süleyman the Great, halfway through the sixteenth century. The mosque in the old centre of İstanbul is one of Sinan's masterpieces. Apart from a mosque, the *külliye* encompassed four Koran schools, a medical school, a hospital, a soup kitchen, an inn and a bath-house.
The Süleymaniye Camii has been built in the middle of an artificial terrace, overlooking the Golden Horn. The other buildings have been grouped around this terrace. The court of the mosque is enclosed by a domed gallery with columns of porphyry, granite and marble.
The basic shape of a mosque consists of a square on which a round dome has been placed. The four corners and the circle in this construction symbolize both the finiteness and the boundlessness of the universe. The Süleymaniye Camii has a similar basic shape. As in the Hagia Sophia, the central dome is merely supported by semi-domes on the east and west sides. The aisles are covered with a row of smaller domes. In contrast to the Hagia Sophia the aisles are not screened off from the central section by columns. In this way the mosque is not divided into smaller rooms, which has resulted in a remarkable spatial and light effect. The decorations, like the marble of the *mihrab*, the İznik tiles, the wood carving inlaid with ivory and mother-of-pearl and the calligraphic Koran texts have been executed with great care.
Behind the mosque is a rustic cemetery with hundreds of tombstones close together. Islamic graves are usually orientated in the direction of Mecca, with a stone at both the head and foot. Some tombstones have been provided with a sculptured head covering, such as a turban or a fez, symbolizing the social status of the deceased. The graves of the women have been decorated with flower motives. In the middle of the cemetery lies the tomb of Süleyman the Great in an octagonal *türbe*. The building has been decorated with colourful tiles, just like the small round *türbe* of his wife Roxelane.

The floor of the Süleyman Mosque is covered with dark-red carpets. The prayer niche with columns and a stalactite vault indicates the direction of Mecca. A prominent place is always taken by a clock in mosques, for the prayer exercises have to ▼ *be executed at regular times.*

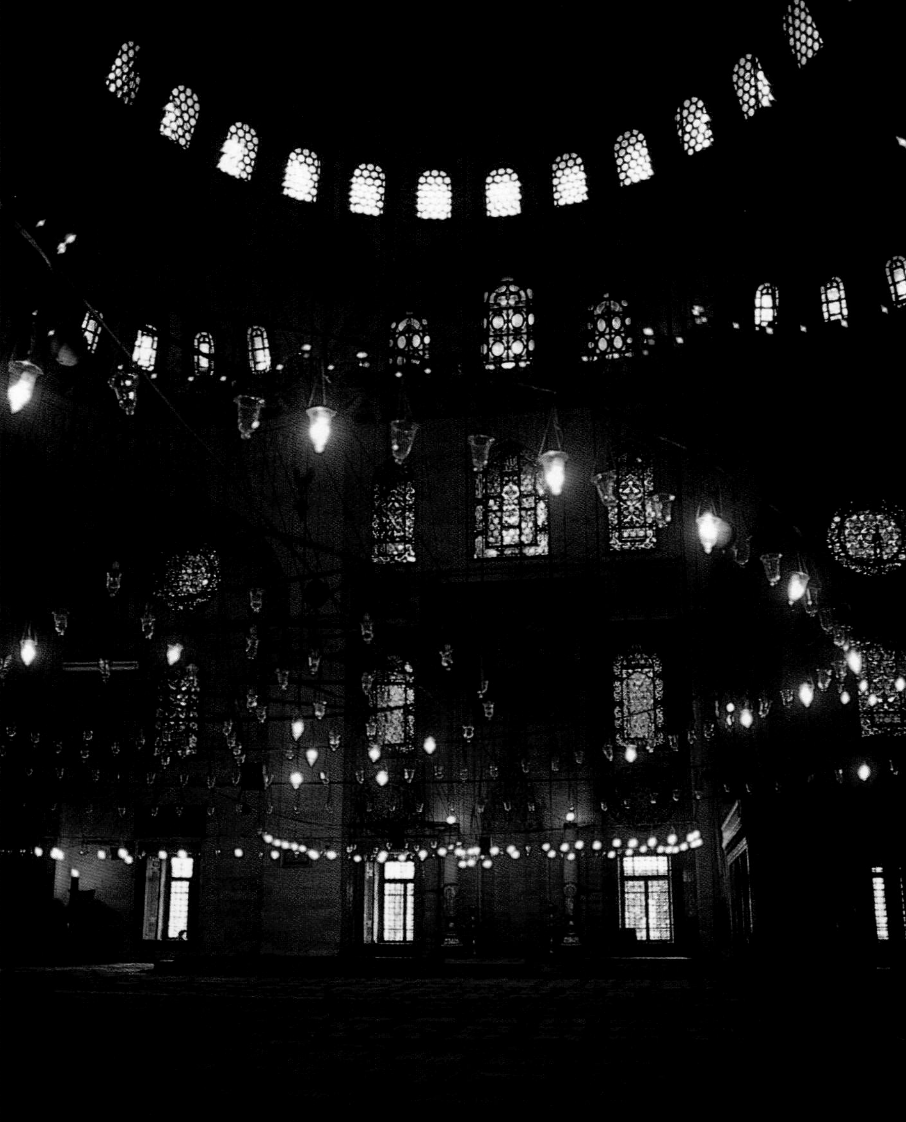

▼ *The türbe of Süleyman the Great next to his mosque.*

An impressive collection of signboards of accountants, lawyers, doctors and pharmacists in one of the streets of Konya.

▲ *In the courtyard of the karavanserai in Sultanhanı, more than 100 kilometres east of Konya, are the remains of a small mosque.*

Stopping places

Like beads on a necklace the *karavanserais* lie along the old trade routes of Anatolia. The stopping places are situated about 30 kilometres from each other, the distance a trade caravan could cover in one day. The Seljuks developed a fixed ground-plan for the *karavanserai* : a rectangular central court with a smaller rectangle for the stables behind it. On the long axis of the building lies a monumental entrance gate with a stalactite vault. The entrance to the stables pointed in the same direction and was generally also designed with a decorated porch. A large *karavanserai* was not merely an inn with stables and warehouses, guests also had a mosque, workshops, kitchens, baths, a library and a doctor's practice at their disposal. Everything was arranged to secure a pleasant stay for the travellers, while at the same time shelter against possible attackers was provided.

Along the road from Konya to Aksaray lies Sultanhanı with on its courtyard a charming *mescit* (small mosque). Within the walled-in settlement one can clearly imagine how the camel-drivers spent the night.

Ağzikarahan and Örsin Hanı near Aksaray also offer a good impression of a thirteenth century stopping place. North-east of Kayseri lies another *karavanserai* named Sultanhanı. The towers of the heavily walled-in settlement all have a different ground-plan. In the middle of the courtyard is a small prayer hall.

Kayseri, the ancient Caesarea, is the capital of Cappadocia and especially worth visiting for its monuments dating from the time of the Seljuks. The heavy wall around the citadel was built in the sixth century out of black chunks of basalt, a kind of stone found in the neighbourhood of the nearby volcano Erciyas Dağı. The small bazar of Kayseri is the centre of a brisk trade in carpets. Besides the multi-coloured woollen carpets, this region also produces high quality silk carpets. While the *karavanserai* served as a stopping place for caravans transporting merchandise from the orient to the west, nowadays an infinite stream of lorries roars past in the opposite direction along the Turkish roads. The trucks transport luxury articles destined for countries in the Near East.

Urfa, the former Edessa, on the edge of the Anatolian Plateau, has been an important intermediate station for this stream of goods since time immemorial. The city is situated on the spur of the Nemrut Dağ, near the heavily guarded border with Syria. Urfa has always been the plaything of local rulers and passing armies, due to its location in the fertile valley of the Euphrates and its situation along the route to the east.

The city was successively ruled by the kingdom of *Mitanni*, the Hittites, the kings of Antiochia, the Romans, the Byzantines, the Persians, the Arabs, the Seljuks, once again the Byzantines, the Crusaders, the Mongols, the Mameluks and the Ottomans. Urfa might have been the birthplace of Abraham (Arabic: Ibrahim). In the turbulent region the city was a refuge for Jews and Christians. Nowadays Urfa is a centre of Islamic fundamentalism.

As a result of its tempestuous past Urfa has few remains worth visiting. Apart from the fortifications on the citadel and the small archaeological museum the colourful bazar is also worth seeing. The mediaeval streets and the tobacco market are pervaded with the aroma of the orient.

At the bottom of the citadel lies the spring that feeds the large pond around the seventeenth century mosque and *medresse* of Abd ar-Rahman. The huge carps swimming in this 'pond of Abraham' are considered holy by the local population.

▲ *In Urfa one can find mosques and medresses with ramified water basins. Shady parks and ponds full of fish create an idyllic atmosphere in this 'city of Abraham'.*

Around Urfa a lot of tobacco is cultivated. In the authentic bazar the merchants are awaiting buyers for their ▼ *aromatic varieties of tobacco.*

Harran is a dusty village 45 kilometres south of Urfa. The village with its biblical origin (Charan, Genesis XI, 31, 32 and XII, 4, 5) is much frequented because it has characteristic loam beehive-houses. A building tradition actually more typical of the north of Syria and stemming from a lack of wood as building material. The Arab population in this border region make a living out of agriculture and cattle breeding, a burdensome existence in this desert area scorched by the sun.

◄ Among the beehive-houses in Harran manure turfs meant for the ovens are drying.

Strategic bulwarks

Diyarbakır (the former Amida) lies 150 kilometres north-east of Urfa and not far from the Tigris. The imposing city wall made of large basalt chunks was constructed during the reign of the Byzantine emperor Constantius II (337-361). The wall is more than five kilometres long and has 72 defence towers. The fortification system has been strengthened by two bastions: Evli Beden Burç and Yedi Kardes Burç. In addition to the citadel four monumental gates have been incorporated into the city walls in the direction of the points of the compass. Inscriptions, ornamental decorations and stone reliefs in the shape of eagles, lions and *sphinxes* embellish the dark basalt chunks. As early as 636 Diyarbakır fell into the hands of the Arabs and since that time it has been governed by a series of local dynasties. The city has a great number of mosques, of which the Ulu Camii dating from 1115 is the most interesting to visit. The large court with two cleansing fountains is surrounded by re-used Byzantine columns. The mosque was built on the site of the former Thomas Church. The resemblance to the Omayyaden Mosque in Damascus is striking.
Due to its central location between the Black Sea, Anatolia and Iran, the charming trade city of Erzurum has since time immemorial occupied a strategic place among the neighbouring cultural regions. The name Erzurum is derived from the Arabic 'Ard ar-Rum' (country of the Romans) and was introduced after the Turkish victory at the battle of Mantzikert in 1071.
The main sights in Erzurum date from the Seljuk and Ottoman periods. The austere Ulu Camii dates from 1179 and still reveals the characteristics of the original pillar-hall mosque despite numerous alterations. The Çifte Minare Medresse dates from 1253. The building has recently been restored and gives a good impression of an old Islamic Koran school. The Yakutiye Medresse was built in 1308 and is especially known for the beautifully tiled minaret and the porch, decorated with classical Seljuk motives. Erzurum is still of strategic significance, which appears from, among other things, the large NATO base just outside the city.

In the picturesque Hasan Paşa Hanı of Diyarbakır leatherware, carpets and antiquities are for sale. ▼

In the east of Turkey travelling troubadours perform ballads and poems. ►

Christian centres

The Byzantine churches and monasteries in Turkey are part of a long Christian tradition. Spread over the whole of Anatolia, from İstanbul to Cappadocia and from the west coast to Antakya (Antiochia), the traces of Christian communities are discernible. In the middle and in the south of Turkey Paul's journeys have also left their mark.
Within present Turkish society the Christian groups are a minority. Small groups of Syrian-orthodox Christians live in İstanbul and in the south-eastern province of Mardin. In Diyarbakır worship services are still held

◄ The spacious court of the Ulu Camii in Diyarbakır is surrounded by galleries into which ancient Byzantine columns have been incorporated.

The monastic church of Ahtamar lies on a minuscule island and is considered to be the pearl of Lake Van. The church of the Holy Cross among the almond trees has been embellished with remarkable Armenian reliefs. The porches, walls and cornices on the outside of the church have been decorated with motives derived from the Old Testament. The reliefs on the east side show Christ in the pediment and beneath it scenes from Paradise. ►

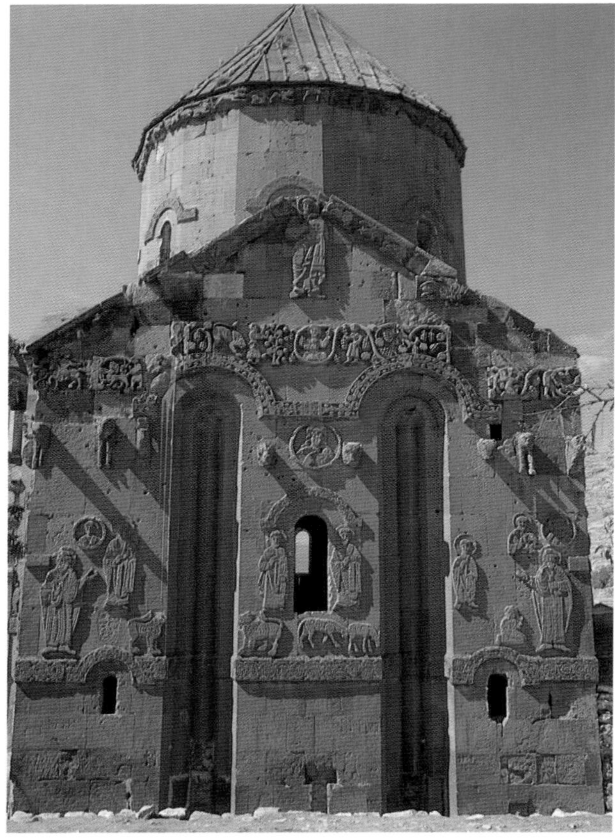

in Aramaic, Christ's language. In Western Europe members of the Syrian-orthodox community are erroneously referred to as Christian Turks.

Near the border with the former Soviet Union lie the cities of Kars and Ani, famous for their relics of Christian architecture. The many deserted churches bear witness to the once flourishing art and culture in this region. A short boat-trip takes the visitor to the splendid Church of Ahtamar, dating from the tenth century, on a small island in Lake Van. The exterior in particular deserves extra attention. Several biblical scenes have been applied in relief over the porches and along the walls. The dominating theme is Adam and Eve in paradise. The style reveals a fascinating mixture of eastern and western influences.

From Lake Van in the direction of the Black Sea coast the country is transected by the Pontic Mountains. The monastery of Sumela is situated in a very inhospitable region on the top of a steep mountain ridge, 48 kilometres south of Trabzon. The location against the wooded slope is breathtaking. After a stiff climb along a path hewn out in the rocks the remains of this Byzantine monastery and the church can be visited. The monument has been completely neglected and is in an advanced state of decrepitude. The interior used to have murals, but they have been severely damaged and daubed with graffiti.

On the left of the south porch reliefs with Jonah and the Whale can be seen. ▼

The monks of Sumela built their monastery against a steep mountain wall. The building block was destroyed by fire during the Greek-Turkish war and since that time the outside has a ▼ *much better appearance than the inside.*

On the right of the south porch the saints are surrounded by medallions with angels. ►

Hestia Boulaia [with the Romans: Vesta] symbolizes the tie between the mother city and the colony by means of the eternally burning hearth fire of a city
hypocaust heating system of a room under the floor and along the walls by means of hot air

Iconoclasm controversy over images and statues (726-843) in the Byzantine period
imam Islamic spiritual leader, usually the person who leads the prayers in a mosque
imaret soup kitchen belonging to the building block around a mosque
Ishtar Mesopotamian goddess of war and love
Isis Egyptian fertility goddess
iwan room closed-up on three sides, of which the open front faces an inner courtyard

Kaplıca bath with mineral springs
karavanserai place providing night accommodation for travelling tradesmen
karum Assyrian trade settlement
karyatides columns in the shape of young women
Kestros river god in Pamphilia
Kore statue of a young woman standing up
külliye block of buildings around a mosque
Kybele Phrygian mother goddess, goddess of fertility and ruler of animals

This mosaic in the floor of the eastern temple of the Letoon shows the symbols of Artemis and ▾ Apollo, the bow and the lyre.

Leto mistress of *Zeus*, mother of the twins *Apollo* and *Artemis*
logeion roof of the *proskenion* serving as a stage floor
lunette semi-circular space over a door or window

Maenads ecstatically dancing women in the retinue of *Dionysos*
Marsyas *satyr* who challenged *Apollo* to a musical contest and lost, was tied to a tree as a punishment and skinned alive
medresse Islamic theological school
Medusa one of the three Gorgon sisters [monstrous women with wings and snake's hair at whose glance people turned into stone]
megaron rectangular building consisting of a shallow forecourt with two columns and beyond that a room with a central fire place
Men moon god from Asia Minor
mescit small mosque
metope part of the Dorian *frieze*, panel between two *triglyphs*, closing the opening between the roof-beams
mihrab prayer niche in the direction of Mecca
minbar pulpit in a mosque
Minotaur monster on the isle of Crete, half human, half bull
Mitanni empire in the north of Mesopotamia (fifteenth and fourteenth centuries B.C.)
monolith monument out of one massive chunk of stone
muezzin prayer caller of the mosque
Muses the nine daughters of *Zeus* and Mnemosyne (Memory), sources of inspiration for poets and singers

Narthex closed forecourt right across the width of a church
necropolis city of the dead
Nemesis personification of divine and vindictive justice
Nereids sea goddesses, daughters of the sea god Nereus, guardians of sailors and of the deceased on their journey to the hereafter
Nike goddess of victory
Niobides the seven daughters and seven sons of Niobe, killed by *Apollo* and *Artemis*
nymphaeum richly decorated well-building
nymphs goddesses of free nature, inhabitants of the seas, rivers, wells, mountains and forests

Odeion small covered theatre, generally used for musical performances
Odysseus Greek hero from the Trojan War
orchestra circular dancing site in a theatre where the performance took place

Palaestra open colonnaded court covered with sand at a sports school or bathing building
paraskenion side wings of a stage house
Paris Trojan prince, referee at the beauty contest between *Hera*, *Athena* and *Aphrodite*
parodos side entrance of a theatre between the seats and the stage house
pasha Ottoman title for highly-placed civil servants and military men
pediment gable
pendentive triangular transition constituting the connection between a rectangular space and a round dome

▴ *Pendentive in the Karatay Medresse at Konya.*

peristasis row of columns around a temple
peristylium roofed-over colonnade around a courtyard
pinax (pinakes) painted panels hanging between the door opening of a stage house
pithos large earthenware barrel for the conservation of food and fluids
Pluto Roman god of the underworld [with the Greeks: Hades]
polis Greek city state
Polyphemos one-eyed giant, one of the Cyclopses
potern sortie tunnel in a fortress
pronaos forecourt of a Greek temple
propylon monumental access gate
proskenion porticus in front of the stage house carrying the stage floor (*logeion*)
protome the front side (head and forelegs) of an animal
prytaneion building where the executive government of a Greek city state gathered

Qibla wall in a mosque, facing in the direction of Mecca

Ramadan month of fasting, ninth month of the Islamic calendar
refectorium diningroom in a monastery

Satrap Persian governor with extensive political and military power
satrapy district of the Persian Empire
satyr natural demon, half human, half animal with donkey's ears, beard and a tail
scaenae frons front of a stage house/building
Semele mother of *Dionysos*
Serapeum sanctuary where *Serapis* was worshipped

Serapis a deity originating from Egypt, with the Greeks and the Romans he represented heaven (*Zeus*) and the underworld (*Hades*), he was also worshipped as god of recovery
Sharumma Hittite god, son of *Hepat* and *Teshub*
Shulinkatte Hittite god of war
Silenos *satyr*, in particular a bald old man who was always drunk and was one of the tutors of *Dionysos*
sirens mythical animals with human head and birds' body
sphendone semi-circular end of a stadium
sphinx mythical animal with human head and winged lion's body
spina middle axis of a race track
spolia ancient remains which are re-used
stele tombstone
stoa covered colonnade
strigilis object used to scrape sand and oil from the body
Sufism ascetic and mystical sect within the Islam
synthronon public stand for the clergymen in the main *apsis* of a Byzantine church

T

Tekke Islamic monastery for *Dervishes*
temenos holy area around a temple
tepidarium room for luke-warm baths in a Roman bathing building
Teshub Hittite storm god
tetrapylon monumental gate with four times four columns on a junction of two important streets
thermae Roman bathing building with cold, luke-warm and hot baths, a changing room and a sports room
Theseus Greek hero in Athens, accomplished numerous legendary feats
tholos round temple
triglyph part of a Dorian *frieze*, the very end of the roof-beam, a rectangular stone with two vertical grooves and three slanting raised ledges
troglodite cave dweller
tugra the monogram of a sultan
tumulus round burial mound
türbe Islamic grave monument
Tyche Greek goddess of luck with a crown in the shape of city walls
tympanum rear wall of a triangular façade area
Typhon one of the *Giants*, fire-breathing monster with snakes' heads (opponent of *Zeus*)

V

Velum canvas with which a theatre was spanned in order to protect the audience against the sun
vomitorium wide vaulted corridor, through which the seats of a theatre can be reached

W

Wabartum small Assyrian trade settlement

Y

Yalı villa with wooden bay on the Bosporus

Z

Zeus Greek god of the heavens, ruler of the Greek world of gods [with the Romans: Jupiter]

On national feastdays many children, like these girls ▼ *in Yozgat, wear colourful traditional costume.*

Index

Besides the geographical denotations, historical periods, personal names and names of population groups, the key-words on top of the pages have also been incorporated into this index.